Key W

& the Lower Keys

by Karuna Eberl & Steve Alberts

Great white heron, near Key West

QUIXOTIC
TRAVEL GUIDES

We want your opinion (especially about how much you love this book)... and also we'd like to know what we bungled up and what would be helpful to add to the next one.

Also, if you own a local business and you think you should be in an upcoming edition, we are happy to meet you and see what you're all about.

Please email comments and suggestions to editorial@quixotictravelguides.com.

Thank you. May your days be filled with adventurous exploration, random wanderings, peace, love, laughter and the most amazing views.

Thank you to all who helped:
Jo Harper, Genevra & Charles Alberts,
Dennis Eberl, Fritz Dillingham, Arlene Schaffer,
Adam Wintermyer, Bill Keogh, Ron Ieva, Luna,
Mike Perna, Teala Krapfl, Kibber & Tom Buschman,
David Greenbury, and everyone else.

Dragonfly, Sawyer Key, Lower Keys Backcountry

Key West & the Lower Keys Travel Guide
First Edition

by Karuna Eberl & Steve Alberts

Copyright 2017 by Quixotic Travel Guides

All rights reserved. Printed in the United States of America. No part of this book
may be printed, scanned or reproduced in any form whatsoever without prior
written permission from the author and publisher, except in the case of brief
quotations used in critical articles and reviews. For information contact: editorial@
quixotictravelguides.com.

ISBN: 978-0-9988589-0-6 (trade paper)

Library of Congress Catalog-in Publications data:
Eberl, Karuna S. and Alberts, Louis S.
Key West & the Lower Keys Travel Guide
Cover design and artwork by: Karuna & Steve
Photography mostly by Karuna & Steve

Illustrations and some photos thanks to
the creatives at Pixabay and Deposit Photos.
All maps courtesy Stamen Design.

www.quixotictravelguides.com
www.wanderingdogcreations.com

Printed in the United States of America by
American Web printers, Denver, Colorado.

Printed on recycled paper with soy ink and other critical
environmental considerations.

Table of Contents: continued on next page

Dedicated to the Florida Keys:
to the people and creatures
large and small, and to the
grace and magic here,
where anything is possible
if you let it be.

RAINBOW, LOWER KEYS

Table of Contents: continued from previous page

The Florida Keys

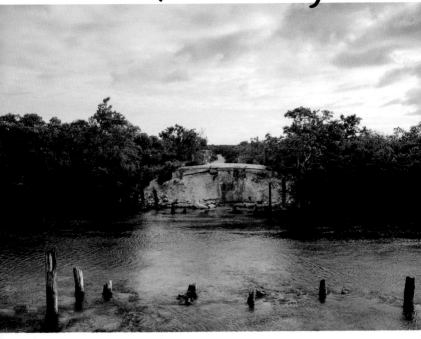

Some are born here. Some retire here. Some end up here like we did...

*H*ere is where people go when they wake up one morning and their soul can suddenly take no more of insincere smiles, collared shirts, and frozen roads. When they wake up and instead of brewing a cup of coffee and watching the morning newscast, they start driving. Driving until the car breaks down or they run out of gas, and then they hitchhike, and walk, and crawl if necessary. Losing possessions along the way. Possessions once so dear, now just baggage. Winter coats, lost relationships, forgotten dreams, and underwear scattered in their wake. With each mile, the weight in their hearts growing slightly lighter. With each step, more conviction. With each breath, more warmth, more hope. An awakened, rejuvenated spirit.

Until they finally reach the end of the road.

Here.

The Florida Keys...

...The great box of misfit toys.

And so people pile up here, for better... and sometimes for worse. The flotsam and jetsam of a society, the tiny string hanging off of the toe of the great sock that is Florida. Some break under the new low-pressure lifestyle, burnt-out on sauce while their underused minds slowly rust back into the earth like an abandoned automobile. Others shine, savoring every moment of their new perspective and warm life. They are the ex-rocket scientists pouring drafts behind the bar, or the once-insurance agents painting sunsets at the beach, unrecognizable to those who knew their former selves, because they have discovered their path to happiness.

Welcome to Key West and the Lower Keys. We hope you enjoy your stay. And should you decide to actually return home, we hope you do so with a healthy dose of sunshine, great memories, peace, happiness, and global hope.

1
The Basics

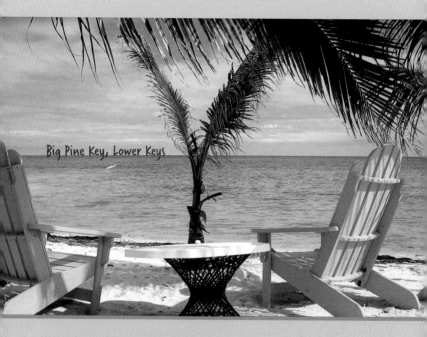

Big Pine Key, Lower Keys

IN THIS CHAPTER

Why visit Key West & the Lower Keys
About the Keys
One Human Family
Where and when to stay
Getting here and navigation
Local transportation
Drinking laws & customs
Other indulgences
& things you might not know
                    you need to know

Why Visit the Keys

Palm trees. Barrier reef. Warm water. Island breezes. Partying. Snorkeling. Kayaking. Scuba diving. Rum bars. Sandbars. Mojitos. Mangroves. Bikinis. Flip-flops. Shirtless men. Shirtless women. Fish. Fishing. Fresh seafood. Spanish treasure. Art. Writing. Solace. Hammocks. Rest. Nature. Birds. Boats. Relaxation. The shorter question is, "Why not the Keys?" Surfing. There is no surfing here.

Why Visit the Lower Keys & Key West

After the Overseas Highway departs from mainland Florida, it winds over 126 miles of islands and bridges before ending up in Key West. The last 40 or so of those miles are the Lower Keys. The Middle and Upper Keys are nice too, but we feel a particular affinity with the Lower ones, as they are farther from the mainland, and therefore further from reality.

Location

The Keys are easy to find on a map. Just run your finger 1,400 miles due south of Cleveland, Ohio and 8,429 miles east of Mount Kailash, Tibet. Those two lines intersect in the Keys. The Keys are also geographically south of Nassau, Bahamas.

Keys Stats

NO. OF ISLANDS: 1,700. 43 of them are joined by Overseas Highway
LENGTH: 200 mi (322 km), road 126 mi (203 km), 42 bridges
LAND MASS OF ALL KEYS: 137.3 mi^2 (356 km)
POPULATION: 73,000 Keys, 25,000 Key West
SIZE OF KEY WEST: approx. 2 x 4 miles (3x6 km) **AKA:** Conch Republic
DISTANCE: 160 mi from Miami (257km); 90 mi from Cuba (145km)
AVERAGE TEMP: winter 76/66, (24/19 C) summer 89/80 (32/27C)
FUN FACT: Temp in Key West has never dropped below 41 F (5C)
COUNTY: Monroe   **AREA CODE:** 305   **ZIP CODE KW:** 33040
HIGHEST ELEVATION: 18 feet (5.5 m), Solares Hill, Key West
FIRST NEW WORLD VISIT: 1521, Ponce de León lands Dry Tortugas
DATE U.S. TERRITORY: 1821, Key West was largest Florida city 'til 1990
LONGEST BRIDGE: Seven Mile Bridge (11 km)
GREAT FLORIDA REEF: third largest barrier reef in the world
GEOGRAPHY: Southernmost point in the continental U.S.
LANGUAGE: English, plus some Cuban Spanish and Haitian
CURRENCY: U.S. dollar   **EMERGENCIES:** 911
TIME: Eastern Time Zone (GMT -4 summer GMT -5 winter)

What are the Keys

The Keys are an island chain stretching nearly 200 miles from the tip of mainland Florida southwest to the Dry Tortugas, splitting the Atlantic Ocean and Gulf of Mexico. A road takes you the first 126 miles or so, all the way to Key West. The Keys are the only tropics you can drive to in the United States, and they feel like a different country, a world away from the stresses, politics and prejudices of mainland life. We even fly our own flag here, for the self-proclaimed Conch Republic. Here people seem to follow a set of life rules that are relaxed, free-flowing and inclusive, while making sure not to take themselves too seriously.

One Human Family

To understand the human equation of Key West, look to the city's official philosophy. In 2000, the city unanimously adopted "One Human Family," proclaiming the equality and interconnectedness of mankind. This phrase came from local artist J.T. Thompson, who had set out just 10 months earlier, on the first day of the millennium, to distribute a handful of bumper stickers bearing that phrase. His goal was to raise awareness that "like fingers on a hand, we appear separate but each of us are in fact an integral part of each other." Many people agreed with him, and today he has given away more than 2 million stickers and 300,000 wristbands, some of which can be found on cars and bicycles from Key West all the way to Tibet and Antarctica.

Things You Know You Need to Know

1

Where to Stay

Key West has a very distinctive community atmosphere and historic presence that is conducive to inquisitive travelers. The majority of visitors to the Lower Keys stay in Key West, which is the partying, eating and shopping epicenter. Those looking for intimate island time, relaxation and seclusion might like it a little further outside of town. You will find both options in this book.

Key West has two sections, Old Town and New Town. If town is your thing, staying in historic "Old Town" is absolutely the most desirable. It is packed full of historic architecture, lush foliage, secret alleys and, of course, Duval Street. On a map, Old Town is the farthest part of the island as you drive into Key West, and it's where most of the restaurants, tourist attractions and bars reside. If you are west of White Street, you are within a 15-minute walk or a few-minute bicycle ride to virtually everywhere you might want to go.

Duval is the epicenter of bars and shops. The south half is quieter and closer to the prominent beaches. The north is the nightlife action. Scattered all through Old Town are marvelous shops and restaurants.

Most of the lodging in "New Town" consists of resort hotels and chains, some of which were either rebuilt or renovated in 2016. These are great for a typical vacation, but with a little less local flavor and the added necessity of having to hire a cab or bicycle to get to attractions and dining outside of the hotel's restaurant.

If the country is your thing, there are scattered hotels, B&Bs, vacation rentals and campgrounds in the Lower Keys, which are glorious, secluded hideaways so long as you have a car for grocery and rum runs, or are patient enough to take public transportation. These options are in this book as well.

When to Visit

The absolute best time to visit Key West depends on what kind of weather you enjoy, how social you want to be and how much spending cash you are willing to part with. The second best time is — well, now. Any time is a great moment to end up in paradise.

CROWDS & COST

The prime tourist season, and therefore the biggest social scene, happens January to April. It peaks in March when Spring Break is in full swing and the rest of the country is most desperate to escape the cold. Seasonal residents depart in April and May, and tourism tapers off, but remains steady through summer. August and September are the slowest months, and a few local restaurants even close down at this time. But come the end of October, the tourists and part-time residents both start rolling back in, building up steadily for the new season. The cost of lodging is directly proportionate to the number of visitors in town. The more expensive season runs from late December through March, with another smaller season when school is out in June and July. The town also fills up for certain events, listed below. If you are planning travel during these dates, or over the winter months, book your room early. May, August, September and October are the best times to come for affordability and tranquility. But if you want a guaranteed party every night of the week, New Year's Eve through March should be your target.

FESTIVALS

There are a lot of festivals in Key West, but the big ones to take into consideration for planning travel dates are Fantasy Fest, which is the last 10 days of October, New Year's Eve, and the week surrounding Lobster Mini-Season, which is the last Wednesday and Thursday in July. Rooms for these dates are generally jacked up in price and booked far in advance.

WEATHER

The Keys have the only tropical climate in the continental U.S., which means it never freezes here. Even Miami, San Diego, and Houston have frozen, but not the Keys. However, unlike tropical places closer to the equator, such as Hawaii and Puerto Rico, the Keys have clearer temperature differences between seasons. So, choosing the best time to visit comes down to your personal needs. Most visitors, regardless of where they hail from, find the weather delightful year round. December through February are the coolest months, when you might like jeans and a hoodie sweatshirt on some nights, but probably still bikinis and swim trunks during most days. June through September are hot and humid, with zero chance of wanting long clothing, except in an air-conditioned restaurant. But summer has some grand benefits, such as affordability, water in the 80s (mid to upper 20s C) and calmer winds for boating. It rarely gets into the 90s (32+ C) during the hottest days, and rarely drops below the mid 60s (18 C), on coldest winter nights – though with the humidity, temperatures feel more extreme than they do elsewhere.

WIND & WATER

The water temperature mimics the air temperature. It's generally above 80 degrees from May through October, and in the 70s for the winter. For wind, the slower it's blowing, the lower the waves, the better the boating (at least for boats without sails). Winter has fewer calm days, and if getting out on the water for diving or snorkeling is the major purpose of your visit, consider alternate months. There are certainly nice days in the winter, but a couple of weeks can go by with seas uncomfortable for boating. The most consistently good weather for boating, especially offshore, is from May through November. In nature's big joke, hurricane season is June through November.

HURRICANES & WIND

Hurricanes are nothing to panic about. While the danger of a hurricane should not be taken lightly, the chances of being injured in a hurricane while visiting Key West are almost non-existent. Weather forecasting combined with an award-winning hurricane safety and evacuation plan provides ample time to get visitors out of the Keys if a hurricane comes close — which in itself is a rare occurrence. If you actually are worried about them, then avoid mid-September to mid-October, as that's historically the highest potential for landing one. The upside of hurricane season is that unless a storm is underway, it is the best season for enjoying the water. Winds are down, seas are calm, water temperature is up, and hotel rates down — a great combination for scuba diving, fishing, snorkeling, wave running and all other adventures on the water.

A NOTE ON CRIME

The Keys have a low crime rate, especially violent crime. Most locals feel very safe, many don't even lock their doors. Bike theft, bar scuffles and DUI are the most common. However, there are neighborhoods, such as parts of Stock Island, that are rougher around the edges. As with any tourist town, there is the potential for foul play anywhere. Always use caution, be aware of your surroundings, and don't wander around drunk and alone in the middle of the night.

How to Get Here

AIR TO KEY WEST

If you have some frequent flyer miles or a little extra to spend on a ticket, flying directly to Key West (airport code EYW) is amazing, partly because it has the best airport in the world. The ocean is just a block away. We once drove our skiff to the seawall by the airport to pick up a guest. There are virtually no security lines and TSA are all nice people with good senses of humor. It has almost as many bars as gates. There's a bar in the terminal, one in the concourse, and in season there's a bar in baggage claim. There is an open-air, sunny smoking lounge by the gates with a sand floor, colorful shade umbrellas, and a waterfall. It's very hard to miss a flight there as they will track you down in security or the bar if you neglect to board on time.

TIP: GET A WINDOW SEAT. THE VIEW OF THE KEYS FROM THE AIR IS SPECTACULAR.

AND FLY IN AT SUNSET. OR DAYLIGHT, AT LEAST.

HOW TO SPOT A LOCAL AT EYW: THEY SHOW UP 30 MINUTES BEFORE THEIR FLIGHT, AND STILL HAVE TIME FOR A DRINK AT THE BAR.

How else to spot a local

You can easily spot them in the winter. On land, they wear coats and jeans once the temp drops below 75 degrees. In the water, they are... not in the water. No way. The water is in the 70s. Most locals get in when it breaks 80, though everyone else thinks it is plenty warm for a dip year round.

1

On the down side, currently only four airlines provide flights: Delta, American, United and Silver (a regional Florida/Caribbean carrier), so ticket prices can be really high. We miss the days when Southwest flew here, as they kept the prices reasonable. Come back, Southwest!

AIR TO MIAMI & FORT LAUDERDALE

A more affordable option can be flying to Miami (MIA) or Fort Lauderdale (FLL) and renting a car or taking a shuttle to the end of the road. The drive from Miami is a little more than 3 hours, a little under 4 from Fort Lauderdale. Shuttles by Keys Shuttle www.keysshuttle.com, 888-765-9997, and by CRT, 786-831-0156, marathoncrt.com, run around $100 each way. Otherwise a rental car is a nice way to explore on the drive down. U.S. 1 (or the Overseas Highway) is scenic and gives ample time to decompress into island vacation mode. See "the Drive Down," chapter 12 for more info.

BY CAR: To get to the Keys from either airport, follow signs for Florida's Turnpike toward Key West, Homestead or Florida City. It is a toll road, but by far the fastest and least congested way to get to the end of the mainland. Don't be tempted to take U.S. 1 all the way through Miami. It sounds romantic to traverse the old highway, but in reality it adds several hours of uninteresting strip malls and traffic lights to the drive. Save the exploring for the Keys. The tolls are all electronic, with "bill-by-plate" or pre-purchased SunPass passes. This means you don't have to stop to pay them, but find out from your rental car company how they handle the fees. They will probably just add them to your final bill. Because of the Turnpike, it can be difficult to figure out where to get food and basic provisions for a little bit, so plan accordingly at the airport (i.e. use the restroom there, and arrive with a few extra cigarettes and a bottle of water). There is a Turnpike service station at mile marker 19, about a half hour from MIA without traffic, with gas, a convenience store and a Dunkin Donuts. Or if you can wait until the turnpike ends, at U.S. 1 in Florida City/Homestead, you'll have your pick of fast food chains and gas stations before fleeing the mainland. From there, continue along the Overseas Highway until the road ends. It's pretty easy to figure out.

PUBLIC TRANSPORTATION: It is possible, and quite affordable to take public transportation from the airport, but it requires some shuffling around. First, see the Metrobus website for schedules from the airport to Florida City, miamidade.gov/transit/routes.asp. Then catch the Dade-Monroe Express bus service, which runs from Florida City to Marathon. The bus line to take is the #301, which comes several times a day, see miamidade.gov/transit, for rates and schedules. Check to make sure the one you're on goes as far as Marathon (mile marker 50 on U.S. 1), as most of them only go to Islamorada (mile marker 74). They are pretty reliable, clean and affordable, if you don't mind the wait. To continue to Key West, get on the Lower Keys Shuttle at Marathon. They run every 1 to 3 hours; seecityofkeywest-fl. gov, for rates, schedules and a live map of each bus' location. Once you reach Key West, four city bus lines loop through Key West at 1 to 2 hour intervals, and their schedules are also at cityofkeywest-fl.gov.

BUS: Greyhound and Go Buses offer $15 routes from Miami to Key West, but from Miami proper and South Beach, not the airport; greyhound.com, 800-231-2222; gobuses.com. 855-888-7160.

FERRY: Key West Express runs daily ferries from Fort Myers Beach and Marco Island to Key West, and they are a real treat to ride. The trip takes around 3.5 hours, and the fast-moving catamarans are between 140 and 170 feet long. We love riding up top in the sunshine with the breeze and ocean views. Others prefer the cozy indoor seating with air conditioning, galley (food), and bar. Board early to score reclining seats and booths. Dogs allowed in crates. Around $150 round trip. keywestexpress.net, 888-539-2628.

CRUISE SHIP: Several cruise ships stop in Key West. The hurried people aboard those only get to see town for a few hours. We recommend a longer stay.

BOAT: If you are fortunate enough to have your own boat, there are plenty of marina slips around for transitory docking. See chapter 9, "marinas" for details.

Mile Markers & Navigation

Like many things in the Keys, navigation is done differently here. Street addresses are mostly insignificant. With one main road for 126 miles, locations get translated into mile markers. Key Largo starts at mile marker 107, and the numbers diminish to zero by the time U.S. 1 ends in Key West. The Lower Keys begin at mile marker 40. There's a small green sign with the number every mile, so it's difficult to get lost for long. Similarly, right and left are replaced with gulfside (or bayside) and oceanside. If you are headed from the mainland to Key West, everything on your right is gulfside, everything on your left is oceanside. North, south, east and west are also replaced with up or down. If you are going toward Key West, you are going down the Keys (southwest). If you are going to Miami, you are going up the Keys (northeast).

Local Transportation

See chapter 16 "Resources," for transpo, taxi & rental phone numbers.

WALKING & BICYCLING

By foot and atop bicycles are marvelous ways to experience the rich architecture, foliage and culture of Key West. Since you are on island time, getting to your destination can be as relaxing and interesting as wherever it is you intend to go. Lush landscaping, footloose chickens and quaint alleyways offer plenty of exploring. Many guest houses offer bicycles, plus there are numerous places to rent them affordably.

SCOOTERS: Scooters, golf carts and electric vehicles are other popular methods for getting around the island. There are many rental locations in town, with everything from a basic one-person scooter, to 8-seater carts with custom Humvee and other sporty designs.

TROLLEYS: Trolley vendors combine rides around town with an entertaining history lesson. The Conch Tour Train snakes through Old Town with three hop-on hop-off stops to take a break from the ride and explore whatever catches your fancy. The Old Town Trolley, more of a San Francisco throwback, drives around the whole island, with 13 stops. Either one is a great activity, recommended to take early in the vacation to give you a feel for the town's history, layout, and activities. Both cost around $30 with a second-day option for an extra $10. Save by booking online. Conch Tour Train 305-294-5161, 303 Front Street, conchtourtrain.com. Old Town Trolley, 305-296-6688, 1 Whitehead Street, trolleytours.com/key-west.

RIDE SHARING: As of printing, Uber is banned in Key West, but CRT offers a web-based app for local ride service, marathoncrt.com.

TAXIS: Key West's distinctive pink "Maxi Taxi" is one of a few running in the Lower Keys. Since the island is small, fares don't get too outrageous, but they do feel high for the short distance. If you leave the Key West vicinity, check on costs beforehand as they quickly get expensive. Taxis can be found near most attractions and on Duval Street. When going car-less, taxis are highly convenient for a run to the supermarket, Kmart and other provision providers not readily available in Old Town.

RENTAL CARS

A car is a bit of a hindrance in Old Town, as finding parking can be frustrating at certain times of day, especially if your lodging doesn't provide space or when the nightlife starts hopping. One is necessary to explore anything outside of town. Several national chains offer rentals on the island, and a couple of local businesses also rent custom-decaled "theme" Jeeps and sand rails (dune buggies). We still don't know where the off-roading is, but at least you'd be ready for it.

PEDICAB: Pedicabs can be easily hailed as they cruise up and down Duval. Some find them perfect for a romantic ride or a welcomed break for the feet. However, their steep rates always surprise visitors, so make sure you understand the fare prior to departure.

PUBLIC TRANSPORTATION

Four city bus lines loop through Key West at 1-2 hour intervals, depending on the time of day and Lower Keys Shuttle Buses run from Key West to Marathon and back every 1-3 hours. They are clean and affordable, if you don't mind a wait. See www.cityofkeywest-fl.gov, for rates, schedules and a live map of each bus' location.

HOTEL SHUTTLE

A few hotels have airport and around-town shuttles. Check with your hotel for their particular offerings.

Gypsy Chickens

A large number of free-roaming chickens and roosters live in Key West. These handsomely colorful gentlemen, their ladies, and adorable chicks can be spotted in parking lots, parks, restaurants and yards throughout town. Yes, they sometimes cross the road, but we usually don't ask why. They've been here nearly as long as the town. Immigrants brought them from Cuba and elsewhere for their eggs and cockfighting. Today, some people love them, while others get angry about their willy-nilly lifestyle. For a while the town had a chicken catcher, until pro-chicken factions discovered they were being shipped up north and executed. Now any nuisance chickens are adopted to people outside of the Keys who must sign an agreement not to eat them. In return, they receive a Key West gypsy chicken authenticity certificate signed by the mayor.

Resist the Urge to Overpack

1

The Keys are about simplifying life, being comfortable and getting rid of baggage, both physically and metaphorically. For the most part, it's a quick pack: flip-flops or shoes that can get sand and seawater on them, shorts, t-shirts, sunglasses (very important, the sun is really bright), sunscreen (a reef-safe brand please), a brimmed hat for the sun, a swimming suit or trunks, and a long-sleeved shirt or sweatshirt.

Light colors are best as they help deflect the intensity of the sun, and if you're going boating, consider a windbreaker, sun cover-up or rash guard. If you can't bear to leave your snazzy evening attire at home, there are a few places you will enjoy wearing it. Some visitors wear a light raincoat, but most locals just get wet, and eventually dry off. From December through February, keep the shorts and swimsuit, but also add a pair or two of long pants and a sweatshirt or jacket. Though 65 degrees doesn't sound cold, the humidity makes that kind of cold snap feel a lot chillier. If you forget any of these items, don't worry, there are a lot of places that are happy to sell them to you.

There is one really important thing to leave behind — anything that doesn't make you smile. If a few negatives, insecurities or other silly fears happen to stow away with you, just let the island breeze blow them away.

"What day is it?" Pooh asked.

"It's today," squeaked Piglet.

"My favorite day," said Pooh.

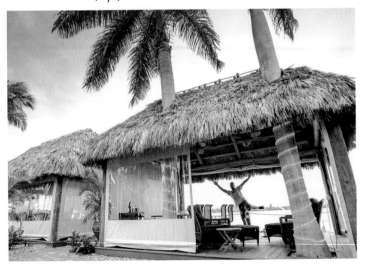

Things you Might not Know you Need to Know

Drinking Laws & Customs

Bars close at 4 a.m. Duval really kicks off after 10 p.m. Key West loves its come-as-you-are, drink-up and enjoy atmosphere.

If you want to be mobile with your festivities, request your drink in a plastic to-go cup. Most bars don't mind if you leave with your cup, and a lot won't turn you away when you show up with one. Especially on Duval Street, it's generally acceptable to walk around with an open container, as long as it's not glass. It might be acceptable, but it is not legal. However, the open-container law is rarely enforced. Maintaining a party-friendly culture is central to Key West's tourism draw, and also reflects the ideologies of the natives. Basically, if you don't act like a lavvy-heided numpty, you are free to drink at your convenience. If you can't help acting like one, then may we recommend a vacation in Daytona. Sorry, Daytona.

Liquor stores are plentiful in town, but can be remarkably expensive the closer you get to Duval. With a little planning, drinking affordably is possible. If you're driving into the Keys, there's a great liquor store at mile marker 25 to stock up. If you are in Key West, in New Town the Walgreens, Publix by Kmart, and Winn-Dixie grocery stores have reasonably priced, predictable selections. Beer and wine can also be found in most grocery and convenience stores.

Upon requesting the song "Margaritaville," be kind and tip the musician at least $20, because he or she is really sick of playing it.

SMOKING: Cigarette smoking is not allowed in restaurants by Florida law, except in places that open to the outside or are partially outside. In the Keys, that includes most bars and restaurants, thus many allow smoking. Cigarettes are neither embraced nor shunned here, but courtesy in crowded areas and around children is expected.

MARIJUANA: Key West may be just a few feet above sea level, but it has a long tradition as a high culture. We hear that finding a little green for your vacation should not be too difficult. Much of it is decent quality. Key West recently decriminalized the possession of up to 20 grams, and by the time you read this, Monroe County might have done the same. Florida also voted in legal medicinal use in late 2016. Despite that, keep in mind that just like walking around with an open container of alcohol, marijuana is illegal and there are inherent risks of partaking in any illegal activity.

NUDITY: Like open containers and marijuana, public nudity is also illegal in Key West — meaning that there is a decent chance you will see some exposed boobies or a wiener during your stay here — maybe even your own! There are no nude beaches in town, but it isn't terribly uncommon to see a topless sunbather. Just keep the naked away from the children. That is frowned upon. Some boutique hotels and B&Bs allow topless sunbathing and others have clothing-optional sun decks and swimming pools. Duval has a clothing-optional bar. There are even naked stand-up paddleboard tours, for a real au naturel experience avec la nature. But if it's exuberant knockers and flapping phalluses you're seeking, then the last week of October changes everything. Fantasy Fest is the height of nudie season, where all shapes, sizes, ages, and colors strut their parts up and down Duval, decorated with costumes and body paint. During the festival, there's a Fantasy Zone, where naked painted bodies are officially allowed, along with open containers. But... let's just say that there are a lot of non-painted, non-clothed body parts to be found as well. Authorities seem to be mostly fine with it, unless you're acting like an imbecile or being lewd. Lewd acts are not tolerated.

Conversely, if you are offended by the unclothed human body, this is not the week to visit Key West.

HANKY PANKY:

As a city unencumbered by cold air, alcohol enforcement, clothing and modesty, Key West is an excellent place for a single person to hook up for a meaningless night of fun. Curvy, hairy, sexy, hefty, there's someone for everyone in Key West, at least for one night. Around Duval is a good place to start searching the old-fashioned way for the perfect fellow tourist or a horny local. One thing to keep in mind: there are a few bars that are clearly gay and some that lean toward straight, but most just cater to people of all sorts. This mix can be uncomfortable for those not used to it, so if someone

who doesn't share your sexual orientation tries to pick you up, decline and take it as a compliment. It's not something to be angry about. If you're more of a technology-driven or shy person, try any number of proximity-based hook-up apps like Tinder. There are a lot of people using them around town. However, if it's a long-term relationship you're seeking, you are now forewarned that Key West is not the best place to start looking for one of those.

OVERINDULGENCE:

Sun, sex, smoke and spirits is a good day, unless it's followed by a crippling sunburn, a dose of puking, and waking up under a tree in a parking lot at dawn with an infectious virus. We know it goes without saying that what seems like a good idea at the time can ruin a vacation early, but even the best and brightest fall to such folly on occasion. Luckily all are preventable with a slight bit of planning: sunscreen, a wide-brimmed hat, a hearty dinner, ample hydration, and condoms.

This photo is honest. It was not staged. It's okay, though, he made a full recovery.

STAYING OUT OF JAIL: As you may be learning, if you've read the rest of the chapter thus far, in Key West passing a law and caring to enforce it can be two completely different things. Keys law officers generally follow the same principles as the population — live and let live. Most of them don't want to enforce the liquor laws, the nudity laws, the noise ordinances, the leash laws, or any of the other nit-picky rules of mainland civilization. Those laws are simply in place so they have a legal right to dispose of people acting like buffoons. However, there are a few tourist-prone actions that are strictly not tolerated:

FIGHTING: Many people come to Key West to get drunk and laid, and sometimes that combination ends poorly. As a general rule in life, avoid hitting on someone else's significant other. Another good rule is, don't hit on someone if you have a significant other. Finally, if either of these two things happen, physically hitting someone will not solve the problem.

SPEEDING & DUI: Speed limits change frequently through the Keys, and travel, like life here, is slower than most places north. Police and locals have a low tolerance for speeding, illegal passing and driving under the influence. There is a reason for this intolerance. Despite our road being straight and flat with a mostly 45-mile-per-hour speed limit, too many of our friends and neighbors die in traffic collisions. For those who have a tendency to race from place to place, we hope you consider slowing down, soaking in the view, and changing your perspective — enjoy where you are in the present moment, rather than focusing so hard on trying to get where you think you want to be. Also, Florida does have a seatbelt law, and texting while driving is illegal.

POACHING: Catching and eating fresh fish and spiny lobster are a joy. Unfortunately, some feel the daily limits and seasons don't apply to them. Keeping undersize lobster, exceeding daily bag limits, taking endangered conch, and killing far more fish than can be eaten before they get freezer burn are some of the most common offenses. Locals don't hesitate to report violators. Most of the rules are laid down not out of government tyranny, but to protect the youth of the species so they can reach breeding age to sustain populations for recreational and commercial fishing. Enjoy your legal catch and keep the rest in the ocean for next vacation — and also so you don't get a fine, which can be as high as $10,000 per offense plus jail time.

IMPORTANT WEBSITE: Every day mug shots and arrest reports are posted on the Monroe County Sheriff's office website. If you are missing a member of your party, check the Arrest Reports section of www.keysso.net. It is also great entertainment to see what trouble everyone got into the night before. The MCSO Facebook site and phone app are also invaluable to learn about traffic, accidents, and DUI checkpoints.

HOMELESS POPULATION: The Keys have to be one of the most desirable places to be homeless, thanks to the climate and ocean views. There are a lot of homeless, or those who have a home but appear homeless because of their scraggly hair, dirty clothes and sun-weathered complexions. Most are friendly, if a little over-talkative at times, and very few ever harass a tourist.

DOGS: All public spaces in Monroe County have a leash law. Well-behaved dogs view it as more of a suggestion than a rule. Despite the climate being a bit hot and humid for fur-bearing beasts, there are a lot of dogs in the Keys, who are both visitors and residents. Most restaurant and bar patios welcome dogs and many have water bowls waiting. Some charter boats, hotels and attractions love them too. There's a dog section in chapter 11 discussing this more. Whether to bring the best friend is more a decision on how well they can tolerate the heat, keeping in mind that on outings where they can't come, the car will be too hot of a place to leave them.

THIS BOOK: We put together this book because we want to give visitors, locals and armchair travelers a great experience, broaden horizons through travel and knowledge, and generally try to make the world a happier place. We try to spread the words "be nice," nice to each other and to all of the Earth's creatures. Reviews and opinions in here are based on our personal experiences and those of our friends and guests, independent from any compensation or publishing mandates. We hope you enjoy it, and your vacation!

Lower Keys backcountry

JAYWALKING: Some say the "Keys disease" is overindulgence in partying, but the more prevalent one is forgetting a principle every first grader knows — look both ways before crossing the street. There are scores of visitors here who suddenly forget what the red hand means at the stoplight. We try diligently not to hit you, but hope that you will also practice some basic self-preservation instincts.

LGBTQ: Key West enjoys a large gay population, along with its straight one. We are only stating this because we realize some places are less fortunate and still use sexual orientation to define one another. Here, One Human Family works, with one exception — there is little tolerance for the intolerant.

ENVIRONMENT & NATURE: The Keys are a highly sensitive area, with the delicate barrier reef, mangrove nurseries and salty wetlands. All of it is under designation as a National Marine Sanctuary. Here are a few ways to be kind to the wilderness and wildlife here:

DE-BEAUTIFY: We are just starting to realize the harm chemicals in skin-care and hygienic products do to the reefs and oceans. Bug sprays, deodorants, makeup and sunscreens all have negative impacts on the health of our oceans. Fourteen tons of sunscreen end up in reefs worldwide, and most of those contain ingredients that, even in tiny amounts, kill coral. Covering up versus slathering on is one solution, along with reef-safe sunscreen. Unfortunately, big-box stores don't carry it, but most dive shops, marinas and health-food stores do.

PLASTICS: So convenient. So trashy. More than 10 million plastic bags get doled out in the Lower Keys every year, where inevitably some end up in the bellies of endangered sea turtles, pelicans, fish and other wildlife. It's heartbreaking to see a turtle with a plastic straw stuffed up his nose, or strangled with six-pack rings. The Keys are trying to ban plastic bags, as soon as Florida will let them. Please avoid plastic bags, straws and to-go cups as much as you can stand.

BROWN ANGELFISH, LOOE KEY REEF, LOWER KEYS

GRATUITY: It is customary to tip restaurant servers at least 20 percent, or 10-15 if service is not satisfactory. Tips are most of their income, and a typical studio apartment in New Town starts around $1,800 a month. Sure, the trade-off is living in paradise, but an extra buck goes a long way toward brightening someone's day.

HOLIDAYS: Most restaurants, bars and tourist services are open on holidays, though banks and such will be closed. Usually holidays mean higher hotel occupancy rates. For those coming from outside the U.S., those include: New Year's, Martin Luther King Day (Jan.), President's Day (Feb.), Easter, Memorial Day (May), Fourth of July, Labor Day (Sept.), Columbus Day (Oct.), Veteran's Day (Nov.), Thanksgiving (Nov.), and Christmas.

TOURISTS VS. LOCALS

Tourism is the main industry here, with 3 million or so coming in every year. Unlike other tourist towns that sell T-shirts asking, "If it's tourist season, why can't we shoot them?" most locals here welcome our visitors, happily mingle with them, and often try to impart a little bit of Keys philosophy in the hopes it may travel northward and make the world a happier place. This philosophy will probably be some version of:

• Everything unfolds at its own pace.
• Enjoy each moment as it comes.
• Trust in the universe.
• Avoid negatives, like evening news and television.
• Spread happiness. Love freely. Laugh often. Be honest. Be nice.
• Work were you can wear comfortable shoes, or better yet, no shoes.

It doesn't take too many days of simple living and sunshine to forget what it was that was so important about the rat race on the mainland.

STEVE, LOWER KEYS

2

Lodging: B&Bs, Hotels, Resorts

IN THIS CHAPTER

Tricks for finding affordable lodging
Lodging highlights Key West
Lodging highlights in the Lower Keys
Houseboat rentals

Not all those who wander are lost...
but sometimes they are.

2

The roosters have already been crowing for awhile when the sun's first rays spill down Duval. As the air warms, the town begins to unfold peacefully. First a jogger. Efficient and tidy strides. Focused and driven. He looks like a well-rested fellow who enjoyed a comfortable bed last night.

Next, a homeless man pushes his bicycle. Einstein hair, a clutter of chaotic belongings dangling from the seat and handlebars. He is engrossed in self conversation. He looks like he slept decently, albeit outside under the mangroves.

A deafening roar temporarily interrupts the tranquility as a city worker pilots his street-sweeper. The truck lumbers by, indifferently consuming the evidence from last night's festivities. Plastic cups, Mardi Gras beads and pizza crusts all gobbled up in its wake, leaving the gutters, and inhabitants, with a fresh start for a new day.

MORNING ON DUVAL STREET, KEY WEST

Soon, a few hungover-looking hotel guests begin to emerge, seeking breakfast and coffee. A trim woman bicycling in yoga shorts turns heads. One too many heads. An exhausted-looking man lugging multiple suitcases receives a vigorous verbal retribution from his girlfriend.

Other folks dock their dinghies after a night sleeping on their boats on the hook. A few shop owners unlock their front doors. A dog stops to check messages on the fire hydrant. And a clean-cut young man, barefoot with disheveled hair, staggers by.

He stops.

"Excuse me," he asks in very broken English. "Do you know where is my hotel?"

> "What is the name of your hotel?" We ask.

> "Can remember, no. My hotel is. On a street."

> "Hmm, which street?"

> "Street with... hotels." He looks down at his feet, searching for a memory and realizing the pointlessness of the conversation.

> Or maybe he was just wondering where his shoes had disappeared to. At least it was warm out.

> This was not a surprising situation — the fact that it was warm out, and that there was a shoeless man who couldn't find his hotel. A number of people, like this fellow, pay good money for a perfectly nice hotel room only to wake up under a tree or in an alley. In their defense, through inebriated eyes these places can look like splendid spots to curl up for the night.

 The young fellow looks up from his grimy, liberated feet, cracks an embarrassed half smile as if to say thanks for having this conversation, turns and shuffles off, slowly, to enjoy his day.

Lodging Resources

Lodging options in Key West are truly alluring because the majority are charming independent boutique inns, cottages and bed and breakfasts where secret garden paths meander by secluded tropical swimming pools surrounded by historic architecture. There are guest houses for every taste. Some are made for families, others cater toward gay travelers, some are exclusively over 21, and many have naked sunbathing decks. Some are very social with community barbecue areas, some have a younger club vibe, others offer more formal and proper elegance. Some do not allow spring breakers and may turn you away if they learn you have been dishonest about it. Nearly all of them are in Old Town and have or rent bicycles. See the "kids and dogs" chapter 11 for a larger list of lodging that specializes in those.

Key West has its chain hotels and resorts as well, which cater to those who like the predictability of amenities and services. Some have private beaches. Many have been recently renovated, and the ones in New Town tend to offer slightly more affordability. Whatever you book, make sure to check its location on the map. Some larger hotel chains are misleading with their description of their proximity to Old Town and the beaches. For more information, see "Where to Stay" and "When to Visit" in chapter 1.

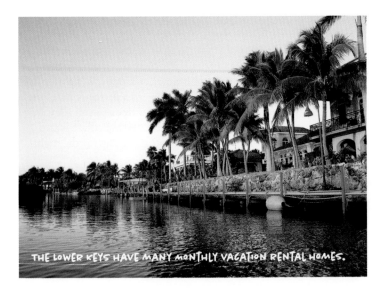

THE LOWER KEYS HAVE MANY MONTHLY VACATION RENTAL HOMES.

BOOK EARLY

Finding the property of your dreams will be easy. If you are visiting in the winter, finding a vacancy and paying for it won't. When you decide to come to the Keys, if you're coming in the high season, book your lodging as early as possible. This level of pre-planning goes against our primal travel nature, which centers around driving until we find an interesting place to stop. But in the Keys during season, unless you don't mind chancing $500 a night or more for a room, pre-booking is a pretty good idea. Same goes for camping, as sites are reserved far in advance, sometimes 11 months or more, and outside of formal campgrounds there are few places to legally or even illegally pitch a tent or park an RV. (For campgrounds, see chapter 9.) It all changes from May through September, though, when some great deals abound, except for several weeks in July when there is a string of festivals and events.

PRICING

When my mom visited for the first time, she commented how the Keys didn't look like she imagined. She had read some Carl Hiaasen books and pictured a little ramshackle house out in the mangrove and palm-treed woods with some old, sun-weathered man tying fishing flies on the porch, smoking a joint, a hound dog sleeping by his side, maybe a Budweiser on the table. From many stories we've heard, those Keys did exist. Their heyday was back in the '60s and '70s. Today developers have overloaded the system with luxury vacation properties, driving up rents and real estate to near the breaking point. There are upsides to this — those opulent properties are magnificent, for those who can afford them. For the rest of us, we need to use a little bit of initiative and ingenuity to find an affordable room in a good location.

This chapter contains a few of our recommendations, but there are so many wonderful places to stay that we suggest you do some independent hunting. Many of the gems won't show up in a search on major travel sites, so below are good places explore.

KEYWESTINNS.COM: A visually appealing website for independently owned and operated bed and breakfasts and boutique hotels. Good photos and descriptions. Great for checking pricing, availability and giving up the credit card. Listings here are partnered with booking.com, 800-492-1911.

VACATIONKW.COM
Search hotels by budget, and inns by categories including: family-friendly, luxury, pet-friendly, quaint, and exclusively gay. It's a good place to start looking at options, but booking is not offered on this site.

FLA-KEYS.COM/KEYWEST/PLACESTOSTAY.CFM
Once you succeed in correctly typing in this concise url, you'll be inside Monroe County's Tourist Development Council site, where you can happily search lodging according to the main categories of: hotels, motels, resorts; guest houses, inns, bed and breakfasts; homes, cottages and condo rentals; gay accommodations; and RV and campgrounds. There's also a subcategory amenities search, which includes pets, swimming pool, hot tub, green lodging, waterfront, clothing optional, Old Town, boat dockage, parking and more.

VRBO.COM, VACATIONRENTALS.COM
In a town where real estate is at a premium, more unconventional lodging options flourish, too. These two sites are great for finding privately owned houses, apartments and even houseboats, not just in Key West but all around the world. See cautionary note under Air B&B below.

AIRBNB.COM
Air B&B is widely known as the gathering place where people offer up their houses, spare rooms or couches for a fee. It's also a great way to get to know some locals. We love the site, but a word of caution: Monroe County and the City of Key West are so irked at this concept that they have recently hired a police officer and committee to covertly locate and shut down unlicensed rentals, which is most of them because licenses aren't often granted in residential areas. Despite the offensive against the nefarious airbnb landlords, many have chosen to ignore the fun police and continue on renting. But it does mean there is a chance the owner may be forced to close it down before you arrive. Generally speaking, rentals that are a month or longer are legal without a permit.

COUCHSURFING.COM
This site is where people offer up couches on which to surf (sleep). The nature of the site, and the term "couch surfing" means it is free to crash, though sometimes donations are in order for the host.

Alternatively, you can try to stay for free the old fashioned way. Head to the bar, pick someone up, and suggest you go back to his or her place for the evening... or the whole week.

Houseboat Rental Tips

Sleeping on the water is relaxation and adventure all rolled into one. Watching seabirds and manatees off the front porch with a bottle of wine, then drifting off to sleep on the gentle rocking of the sea are just a few of the romantic allures. But it isn't for everyone. It can be luxurious, but generally it's more like camping than a hotel room. When deciding if and which houseboat is for you, look at pictures to make sure it's not too run down, and also consider the following.

FOR BOATS AT MARINAS:
Check the marina location on a map. "Key West" can also mean Stock Island, which is fine, but further from town, with a few areas that are not safe for night exploration. Consider boat amenities, such as a head (toilet), shower, and air conditioning. If there isn't a toilet, decide if you are okay with hoofing it across a marina at night to pee. Also consider marina amenities, such as laundry and parking. Decide what level of cramped-ness you're comfortable with for sleeping quarters and if you desire outside hang-out space that is protected from sun and rain.

FOR BOATS THAT ARE MOORED:
For boats anchored offshore "on the hook" consider: Transportation to and from land. Most have a dinghy, but some require paddling. Think about your comfort with crossing the water in dark or rough seas and how far it is from land, both in distance and time. Is there electricity and what is it capable of running, such as air conditioning and kitchen facilities? Ask if you'll have access to a marina or facilities on land, and if there's a safe place to park your car, if you have one.

HOUSEBOATS AT KEY WEST BIGHT

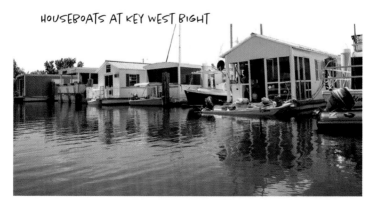

B&B and Inn Highlights - Key West

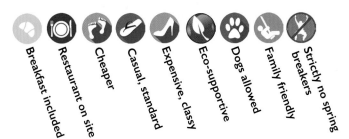

Breakfast included

Restaurant on site

Cheaper

Casual, standard

Expensive, classy

Eco-supportive

Dogs allowed

Family friendly

Strictly no spring breakers

Note: Numbers correspond to map on page 30.

1 EDEN HOUSE

From cheapo to swanky, this collection of Conch houses and art deco space blends cost, convenience, funk and style. The exuberant social scene starts with a free check-in beer and continues in the tropical courtyard with guest barbecues, hammocks, a sun deck, jacuzzi, and happy hour at the heated pool. For seclusion, book a tranquil apartment suite with a private porch swing and outdoor bamboo shower. Those on a budget, or just in need of a place for sleep, can book a tiny single or a Euro-house-style space with shared bathrooms. Rooms have Wi-Fi and air conditioning, but intentionally lack alarm clocks and phones. edenhouse.com, 1015 Fleming Street, Old Town, Key West, 33040, 800-533-5397, 305-296-6868.

2 ISLAND CITY HOUSE

Walking onto the grounds of the Island City House feels like stepping back in time to a simple elegance, accented by white sheer curtains waving in the tropical breeze, while mint juleps sweat on a wrought-iron table. Touted as the island's oldest operating guest house, circa 1889, today the historic compound has spacious rooms with full kitchens, Keurig coffee makers, hardwood floors, tropical gardens, and an outdoor pool. Some have separate living spaces, great for families or friends traveling together. Not to be confused with the Island House, a famous gay resort here. islandcityhouse.com, 411 William Street, Old Town, Key West. 305-294-5702.

3 MARQUESA HOTEL

When it's time to masquerade as a classy grown-up, unpack your silk bathrobe at Marquesa Hotel and revel in repose amidst a chamber replete with a marble bathroom and a nightly turn-down. Four 1884 Conch houses comprise the high-quality boutique hotel, which dons an impressive list of "world's best" awards. Ditch the flip-flops and play dress-up, lounge at the bar with a martini, then eat on-site at the Café Marquesa, which has also won a ridiculously long list of awards. One block from Duval. Children 14 and older only. marquesa.com. 600 Fleming Street, Old Town, Key West. 305-292-1919.

4 THE BANYAN RESORT

A perfect blend of history and modern convenience just two blocks from Mallory Square. Swimming pools, hot tub, lush gardens, full kitchens. No spring breakers allowed. thebanyanresort.com, 323 Whitehead Street, Old Town, Key West, 33040, 305-296-7786.

5 GARDENS HOTEL

Chic boutique guesthouse. gardens, aviary, ponds, self-serve wine bar, pool, LGBT friendly, pets with daily fee in cottages only. gardenshotel.com, 526 Angela Street, Old Town, 305-294-2661.

6 HERON HOUSE

Relaxing, romantic, adult-only getaway, stylish, sundeck, rare plants in exotic gardens, pools, hot tubs. 21 and over. heronhouse.com, 512 Simonton Street, Old Town, Key West, 305-294-9227.

7 THE ARTIST HOUSE

Historic Victorian guesthouse, stately rooms, elegantly refurbished, jacuzzi, circa 1890, kids over age 5 okay, artisthousekeywest.com, 534 Eaton Street, Old Town, Key West, 33040, 305-296-3977.

8 OLD TOWN MANOR

Steps from Duval, 14 unique rooms, wedding popular, tropical gardens, organic vegetarian breakfast, all-size dog friendly, smoke-free. oldtownmanor.com, 511 Eaton Street, Old Town, 305-292-2170.

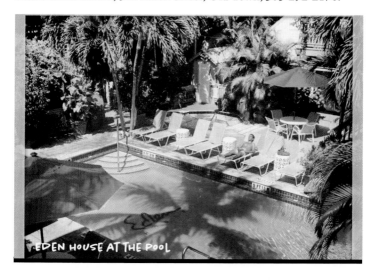

EDEN HOUSE AT THE POOL

B&B and Inn Highlights – Key West

9 SEASHELL MOTEL & KEY WEST HOSTEL

Leading the competition for the most expensive 10-bunk dorm room hostel in the world, the Key West hostel is still cheaper than tent camping anywhere in the Lower Keys. Choose from segregated or co-ed dorm rooms, or lay down the Benjamins for one of the private, modest hotel rooms. But the Wi-Fi, communal kitchen and coin-op laundry come free! Except for the price of the coins, of course. No alcohol or under 18 in dorms. keywesthostel.com. 718 South Street, Old Town, Key West, 33040, 305-296-5719.

10 ANDREWS INN & GARDEN COTTAGES

Family-run green-lodging B&B with tropical gardens, pool, cocktails, adjacent to Hemingway House. Pets and kids in cottages only. 233 Eanes Lane, Old Town, Key West 33040, andrewsinn.com.

11 THE SOUTHERNMOST HOUSE

Beachfront historic boutique house, 18 rooms, flat-screen TVs, heated waterfront pool, poolside bar, beach hammocks. 1400 Duval Street, Old Town, Key West, 33040, southernmosthouse.com, 305-296-3141.

12 ALEXANDER'S GUEST HOUSE

Upscale, world-traveler style gay, lesbian, and friends of LGBT-only. Historic guesthouse, bar, pool, hot tub, clothing-optional sundecks. alexanderskeywest.com, 1118 Fleming St., Old Town, 305-294-9919.

LA TE DA

13 CARIBBEAN HOUSE

Simple, bright and no frills in funky Bahama Village, 10-room guesthouse two blocks from Hemingway House, any-size-dog no fee. caribbeanhousekw.com, 226 Petronia St. Old Town, 305-296-0992.

14 LA TE DA:

Boutique rooms, pool, restaurant, bar, cabaret, melting pot of culture for gay, straight, and all between. lateda.com, 1125 Duval Street, Old Town, Key West, 33040, 305-296-6706.

Resort & Hotel Highlights – Key West

15 CASA MARINA

With a lobby and promenade straight out the *The Great Gatsby*, pools by the ocean and the largest private beach on the island, Casa Marina is indisputably a grand old hotel of Key West. Fish from a private pier, spa it up or nap in a beach hammock. Dare to get really classy by donning your velvet smoking jacket and heading to the outside bar for a sip of a mojito, a puff off of a hand-rolled cigar, and an unobstructed view of yoga classes. casamarinaresort.com, 1500 Reynolds Street, Old Town, Key West, 33040, 305-296-3535.

2

16 THE MARKER RESORT

Newest hotel in Old Town, along the historic seaport, 96 state-of-the-art rooms, balconies, fitness center, three pools, poolside bar. themarkerkeywest.com, 200 William St., Key West, 888-976-4594.

17 PIER HOUSE RESORT & SPA

Where the sea meets Duval, part romance, all paradise, steps from Mallory Square, private beach, pool and award-winning spa, dogs 20-pound max. pierhouse.com, 1 Duval Street, 305-296-4600.

18 MARGARITAVILLE KEY WEST (FORMERLY WESTIN)

Upscale waterfront resort, one block from Duval and Mallory Square, pool, bar, restaurant, massage studio, dog 40-pound max. margaritavillekeywestresort.com, 245 Front Street, 305-294-4000.

19 SUNSET KEY COTTAGES

Luxurious private-island resort, 7-minute boat ride from Mallory Square, exclusive beach, bougainvillea-laced cottages, fine dining. sunsetkeycottages.com, 245 Front Street, Key West, 305-292-5300.

20 REACH RESORT WALDORF ASTORIA

Boutique resort, oceanfront pool, luxury rooms and suites, private beach and balconies, quiet side of Old Town, dogs 40-pound max, one-time fee. reachresrot.com, 1435 Simonton Street, 305-296-5000.

21 LA CONCHA HOTEL & SPA

Classic Key West Hotel since 1926, renovated, on Duval, Starbucks, pool, spa. laconchakeywest.com, 430 Duval Street, 305-296-2991.

22 THE GATES HOTEL

New, chic, laid-back rooms, cigar lounge, outdoor pool, local photos, Keurig coffeemakers, mini-fridges, flat-screen TVs. gateshotelkeywest. com, 3824 N. Roosevelt Boulevard, Key West, 33040, 305-320-0930.

Lodging Highlights - Lower Keys

SUGARLOAF LODGE
Clean, scenic and affordable, Sugarloaf Lodge is our longtime go-to for housing out-of-town company. The rooms are clean and simple, with nice TVs and a mini fridge, and every room has a private porch or patio that looks out onto Sugarloaf Bay. A small marina offers complimentary boat dockage and arranges charter boat and kayak rentals. From there it's just a short paddle to meandering mangrove channels or a quick motor to prized backcountry fishing spots. The family-owned lodge has a low-key Tiki bar with live music. It was also a favorite haunt of gonzo journalist Hunter S. Thompson, which you can read more about in chapter 7 "culture." About 30 minutes to Old Town. sugarloaflodge.net, mile marker 17, gulfside, Sugarloaf Key, 33042, 305-553-6097.

BAHIA HONDA STATE PARK
A hidden secret, there are 6 duplex cabins at this beautiful state park. They are usually booked 11 months out, but if you can get one, it's one of the best deals in the whole Keys. Cabins include kitchens, central AC and heat, two bedrooms plus sofa bed. They overlook a private mangrove pond. floridastateparks.org/park/Bahia-Honda, mile marker 38.6, oceanside, 800-326-3521.

DEER RUN BED AND BREAKFAST
Nature. Water. Sand. Deer Run B&B is a one-of-a-kind paradise where owners Jen and Harry offer guests peace in every form. Peace while swinging in a hammock and kayaking off the private beach. Peace with nature, as osprey, dolphins and the ever-curious Key deer meander through their day. Peace as harmony with the earth, thanks to environmental practices and vegan and organic breakfasts. It's a bit isolated, but that's the point. It's a few miles to Bahia Honda State Park and Big Pine Key. About 45 minutes to Old Town Key West. Free use of kayaks, bikes. Guests 18 and older only. deerrunfloridabb.com, 1997 Long Beach Road, Big Pine Key, 33043, 305-872-2015.

PARMER'S RESORT
Waterfront, tranquil, heated pool, hammocks, bocce courts, boat slips, small beach, barbecues, one-to three-bedroom-cottages. 565 Barry Avenue, Little Torch Key, parmersresort.com, 305-872-2157.

THE BARNACLE BED & BREAKFAST
Eclectic family run villa rooms and cottage, private beach, free use of bikes and kayaks, tiki hut, hammock, barbecue, hot tub, Key deer, waterfall, pond, no kids under 16. thebarnacle.net, 1557 Long Beach Drive, Big Pine Key, 33043, 305-872-3298.

LOOE KEY REEF RESORT

Basic scuba-dive-centric motel. Besides dive shop and charters on site, there's a pool and tiki restaurant-bar. Rooms have free Wi-Fi, AC, flat-screen TV, minifridge, microwave, pets with daily fee. diveflakeys.com, mile marker 27.3, Ramrod Key, 305-872-2215.

LITTLE PALM ISLAND

Luxury private-island resort with award-winning restaurant, private beaches, and standard chic amenities, but no phones or television. Reach by ferry, 16 and older only. littlepalmisland.com, mile marker 28.5, oceanside, Little Torch Key, 33042, 305-872-2524.

MELODY KEY

Unique private island, three-bedroom luxury home, heated pool, jacuzzi, fishing from pier, snorkeling, jet skis, private sightseeing catamaran tours, private chef option, sleeps 8 for $1,375 a night. melodykey.com, off Summerland Key, 33042, 305-942-9197.

BIG PINE KEY FISHING LODGE

Simple, clean rooms. Keep a boat in the marina and enjoy a range of amenities and social gatherings. Rent a lodge room or a two or three-room mobile home. There's also RV and tent camping. bpkfl.com, mile marker 33, oceanside, Big Pine Key, 33043, 305- 872-2351.

OLD WOODEN BRIDGE MARINA & RESORT

Cozy, simple, affordable and friendly cottages by a great fishing bridge. Boat rentals (kayak, motor) next door. Gateway to the backcountry. oldwoodenbridge.com, 1791 Bogie Dr., Big Pine Key, 305-872-2241.

DOLPHIN MARINA COTTAGES

Simple and bright cottages, at the marina, boat rentals and store. dolphinmarina.net, mile marker 28.5, oceanside, Little Torch Key, 33042, 800-553-0308.

INQUISITIVE KEY DEER AT DEER RUN B&B

MELODY KEY

3

Food: Eating & Restaurants

IN THIS CHAPTER

Keys comfort food & local ingredients
Conchs vs. conchs
Restaurant highlights Key West
Restaurant highlights Lower Keys
Late breakfasts and brunches

Sustenance vs. Substance
An arduous spirit lurks behind Keys cuisine

Keys cuisine evokes feelings of romance, charm and comfort. It is all of those. But to appreciate today's delicious meals, served up all pretty on shaded waterfront patios with icy drinks, we need to jump back a century or two. Throughout the 1800s and the first half of the 1900s, life in Key West was the opposite of easy. From 1821 to 1870 only a couple thousand people lived on this small patch of isolated land, dependent solely on their own initiative and the mercy of the ocean, for when it would allow a delivery ship to port.

There was no air conditioning, no refrigeration, and very few trees for shade. Heat, humidity, and mosquitoes were relentless. This is where Keys cuisine was born, out of survival necessity from backyard ingredients, like fish, conch, coconuts, tamarind — and Key limes.

Some pontificate profusely about who created the first Key lime pie.

But there is little debate that it originated in the Keys shortly after Gail Borden commercialized sweetened condensed milk in 1856. Since the Keys would not have refrigeration for another 74 years, condensed milk was an exceptional product to arrive here and must have changed the level of culinary options for the better in countless ways. As for the inventor of the Key lime pie, here's what we know — millionaire ship salvager William Curry began importing Borden's milk to Key West and his cook "Aunt Sally" made him a Key lime pie. That could be how it all started...

Borden vowed to create condensed milk after seeing children die from contaminated milk on a transatlantic voyage.

Key lime pie's not-so-upper-crust origins

...However, those cans that Curry imported also made it into the hands of sponge fishermen, lending the prospect that it's more likely Aunt Sally gleaned the recipe from them. The spongers were an inventive bunch, driven by necessity, who would be out on the water for days. They adapted, combining local ingredients for sustenance — such as pelican eggs, Key limes and condensed milk. It was a dish that was well suited to their lifestyle because it required no refrigeration or baking. The acid in the lime juice reacts with the condensed milk to naturally thicken the filling.

3

Whoever put those ingredients together for the first time will probably never be known, but today eggs, sweetened condensed milk and Key limes are still the staple ingredients for any authentic Key lime pie — though most pies today also include a crust and are baked, at least for a short time, because of our fears of consuming raw eggs. There is great and unending debate about what makes for the rest of an authentic Key lime pie. A crust of graham crackers or pastry? Topped with meringue or whipped cream? This takes up a great deal of some people's time. The rest of us prefer to simply sample as many of the variations as possible and enjoy the creative adaptations.

A sponge fisherman takes his harvest to a 1900s Key West.

University of S. Florida Special Collections / Library of Congress / Hulton-Deutsch Collection.

Keys Comfort Food & Local Ingredients

The Keys have a selection of food rarely available in other parts of the country. From hogfish and grouper to authentic Cuban and conch, there is much to sample. Here are a few dishes especially paramount in Key West culture that are worth a try, at least once.

CUBAN COFFEE

Cuban coffee is strong, similar to espresso. It is commonly served with steamed milk as café con leche or as a frothy shot with sugar called bucci (a.k.a. Cuban crack). Start the day sipping one with friends, while munching on buttered Cuban bread, guava pastries, ham croquettes, or a grilled-pressed egg-and-cheese sandwich.

CONCH

Conch (pronounced konk) is the flagship, patriotic dish of the Keys. The mollusk native to the Keys and Caribbean gets served up in many forms, including chowder (red and white), fritters and ceviche. It can have a tenderness similar to a clam, or more chewy if the chef is under-skilled, hungover, or generally lacking in motivation. Though conch has been a staple food of the Keys for thousands of years, overfishing landed it on the U.S. endangered species list in the 1980s. Since then all conch meat served here is imported from the Bahamas and elsewhere in the Caribbean.

Dolphin =

≠

LOCAL FISH

Ocean and reef fish most likely to be fresh-caught and on the menu are hogfish, grouper, snapper and dolphin. Why most restaurants list their dish as dolphin instead of dolphinfish, or by its more familiar names of mahi-mahi and dorado, remains a mystery. It might have something to do with the twisted entertainment value of seeing the look of horror on newcomers' faces when they think we might actually kill and eat such an intelligent, social creature. Now you know, so you won't be the tail-end of the joke. Fish are commonly served with a choice of blackened, fried or grilled. Most restaurants will also cook your catch for you.

• Though **snappers** are a highly sought-after delicacy in many places, they are one of the more common fish caught here, so locals often snub the menu prices and just eat their catch at home. But if you don't live in the land of fresh snapper, they are well worth the dollars. Lean, delicate, firm, flaky, mild flavor. The most common are yellowtail, red and mangrove.

• **Dolphinfish** (**mahi-mahi**) are more meaty, but maintain a mild flavor that is often compared with swordfish.

• **Grouper** come in several varieties depending on the season, but all are highly coveted for their distinctive-yet-mild flavor plus higher oil and moisture content. Some compare them with halibut, but less fishy with a nicer texture.

3

• **Hogfish** are sweeter and lighter than grouper, and also a sought-after favorite. Some say they are flakier than dolphin, but rich like scallops. They are mostly caught by spearfishing, which diminishes their widespread availability.

• **Lionfish** are invasive and as such anglers are requested to kill any they catch. Rather than waste the life, some restaurants are beginning to serve them. They taste good and are white and flaky, firmer than halibut.

Sustainable Catch

With oceans in trouble worldwide, ordering fish is a trial for those with an educated conscience. While all commercial fishing has an impact, the Keys does maintain one of the most sustainable, regulated, and conservation-minded fisheries in the world. The fish mentioned above are caught with no long-lining or other intrusive by-catch methods and usually require very little fossil fuel to get from dock to table. That may or may not be the case for other fish on menus here, including swordfish and tuna. For any fish not mentioned above, ask your server if the fish is locally caught to ensure a sustainable choice.

Local crustaceans often upstage the fish. Spiny lobster, Key West pink shrimp and stone crab claws are seasonal delicacies.

Unlike their cold-water cousins, **spiny lobster** have no claws. They're best enjoyed in season, August through March. Lobster isn't often served as a tail, but rather found in sandwiches, bisques, fried bites, salads, and ceviche.

Stone crabs are considered a sustainable catch, as fishermen break off their claws and return the crab to the water, where he or she is then defenseless but will eventually grow new ones in a couple of years. Their season is mid-October to mid-May. Mostly the claws are served pre-cracked with butter or another dipping sauce.

Stone Crab
Photo by Yuri Khripin

From November through June, **Key West pink shrimp** are locally harvested, and often served as peel-and-eat due to their delicate flavor, though they are also found in pastas, soups, ceviche, sandwiches, and fried bites.

A **Cuban Mix Sandwich** or Cubano, is a delightful lunch with a long and controversial history. The traditional recipe combines Cuban bread piled with ham, slow-roasted pork marinated in citrusy Mojo sauce, swiss cheese, thinly sliced pickles and mustard, then pressed on a grill to crispy perfection. In Key West, mayo, lettuce and tomatoes are often added. Miami and Tampa (whose version includes salami) fight over the origin of the dish, but Key Westers contentedly keep quiet on the issue, knowing the truth of the matter...

How Florida got its Cuban food culture

Origins of the Cuban mix sandwich: The Spanish brought cheese and ham to Cuba in the 1500s, and eventually Cubans added their favorite roasted pork. In the early 1800s the Cubano was a common lunch food for workers in Cuban sugar mills and cigar factories.

The first Cuban cigar makers in Key West began to spring up in the 1830s. When the first Cuban independence war broke out in 1868, Cuban immigration to Key West escalated. They brought their lunch and culture with them. The cigar industry boomed for two decades, reaching a height of more than 80 factories producing more than 100 million cigars a year. More than 50,000 people traveled between Key West and Havana annually. Key West and Cuban culture were forevermore fused. But that wasn't yet true for the rest of the state.

It wasn't until 1885 when cigar magnate Vicente Martinez Ybor moved his factory from Key West to Tampa that Cuban culture and the Cubano, began to spread in earnest to other parts of the state. It would still be a decade before Miami officially became a city, with a population slightly more than 300. That city would ultimately become the clear cultural seat for Cuban immigrants and refugees... but the fusion of Cuban-American culture began in Key West.

A lector, or hired reader, entertains cigar makers. They were paid by the laborers, and would read news, literary works and even perform theatrics. Photo c. 1900, probably in Tampa.

University of S. Florida Special Collections / Library of Congress / Hulton-Deutsch Collection.

Ropa Vieja, English translation "old clothes," is shredded flank steak marinated and slow cooked to utter tenderness, then served over yellow rice and black beans. The dish originated with the Spanish in the Canary Islands, but was soon embraced and made famous by Cuba. Some say it earned its name due to its resemblance to shredded clothing. Others insist it came from a man who was too poor to feed his family, so he stewed up his clothes with all of his love, which turned it into a delicious beef stew.

Walk through an understated convenience store over to the hot food section, and you'll find a nice helping of greasy fried crispy things. In the Keys, many call it "elixir from the gods." **Dion's fried chicken** is famous throughout the Keys. It has quelled many a late-night craving and early morning hangover. It's the working-man's lunch and the picnic of choice on many boats. There are two Dion's Quick Marts in Key West, one on Stock Island, one on Big Coppitt and plenty more further up the Overseas Highway. A true family business, Dion's was founded by former WWII bomber pilot Larry Dion and his wife. Their original appliance and tire supply store soon became a service station, then Key West's first convenience store, which is still going strong nearly 70 years later.

SPINY LOBSTER: Florida's spiny lobster, or Caribbean lobster, is the largest commercial fishery in Florida with 4 to 6 million pounds

taken yearly. The crustaceans are a peculiar bunch under the water. They sport long antennae instead of claws, and are covered in spines for protection. They live in social groups that sometimes undergo mass migratory marches, where they line up one behind the next to trek to deeper water in order to avoid storms and cold water. As babes, they float great distances as planktonic larvae, possibly arriving here from as far away as the West Indies. Once near land, mature lobsters hide on shallow water reefs during the day and peruse seagrass beds at night. They can live up to 100 years, but usually get caught at a much younger age.

A tale of Conchs and men

Conch is a multi-faceted and prolific word in Key West. In nature, a queen conch is a large sea snail in the mollusk family, which can live up to 40 years. On land, a conch is a person of the Keys. The lives of both have been intertwined for thousands, perhaps tens of thousands of years.

Conchs and people go back at least as far as pre-Columbian tribes. They were essential to the sustenance of cultures in the Bahamas and Florida, including the native Calusa, or the "Shell Indians," who ate the creatures and used their shells for tools, scrapers, hammers, bowls, ornamentation, and trade. They also played an important role in communication. With slight modification, one can blow into the shell as a horn, which was used in religious ceremonies, to initiate battles, and to deliver long-distance messages. Columbus' crew wrote about eating conch near Cuba, and from there they became a staple food of early settlers.

Conchs as a term for people began after the U.S. Revolutionary War, when British sympathizers left the southern United States for the Bahamas. Soon after, the British government began taxing their food. In anger, they declared they would rather eat conch than pay those taxes. They did. Some left the Bahamas to become wreckers (ship salvage) in the Keys, bringing their Conch nickname and culinary skills with them. Today, the queen conch animal is a heavily protected endangered species in U.S. waters, so all conch served here is imported from the Caribbean. The Conch tradition, however, is alive and well in the human population.

The modern definition of a Conch is someone born in Key West, sometimes extending to those born anywhere in the Keys. It is a guarded and cherished title. Residents who have been here more than 7 years are sometimes called freshwater conchs, and occasionally someone who does great service to the community is given the title of honorary conch. In 1982 the Conch Republic was formed (see "history" chapter 14 for that story). Key West High School's mascot is the Fighting Conch. And of course, people still display their prowess at conch-blowing competitions. In short, Key West is all about the conch.

Delicious, Decadent & Dreadful

There are some truly outstanding restaurants in Key West, but many visitors here never find them. Like any destination town, there is an abundance of generic tourist-trap grub and over-fried bar fare, usually placed conveniently on the few streets most visitors roam, and heartily advertised in every hotel magazine as the best of the best of the best. But lucky for you, you have this book, so you will eat well.

3

Key West has a distinctive palate. It's overflowing with locally caught fish, lobster, stone crab, and shrimp. Cuban cuisine maintains a vigorous presence, with subtly spiced dishes of pulled pork, yellow rice and plantains. Many restaurants gasconade Caribbean infusion, which usually just means a few tasty new flavors added to otherwise staple dishes. Fusion, overall, is a popular word here, so finding something refreshingly out of the ordinary is common in many restaurants.

This chapter contains our favorite eateries, plus our friends' and neighbors' perennial picks. Many but not all of them use at least some locally sourced, fresh ingredients. Though the vegetarian, organic and gluten-free insurgency has not yet blown into the Keys, we've denoted which ones offer a selection of options greater than iceberg lettuce and grilled cheese with the "vegetarian" icon. The first listings are in Key West, further back are the rest of the Lower Keys.

Note: Numbers by restaurant name correspond to map on page 44.

Unless stated otherwise, all restaurants are in Old Town Key West.

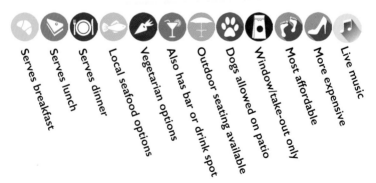

Serves breakfast — Serves lunch — Serves dinner — Local seafood options — Vegetarian options — Also has bar or drink spot — Outdoor seating available — Dogs allowed on patio — Window/take-out only — Most affordable — More expensive — Live music

Days of operation may vary with the season and motivation of the staff. It is wise to call to confirm if restaurants are open prior to disembarking on your journey there.

1 BLUE HEAVEN

FUNKY FLORIDA-CARIBBEAN

As famous for its ambiance as its food, Blue Heaven nestles patrons amidst an outside patio and bar, where they drink and dine alongside free-roaming chickens, hula-hooping locals, and upbeat live music. Play ping-pong and browse the local art mercantile while waiting for your meal. Blue Heaven's history is as colorful as its cuisine. During the last century, the property has been home to a liquor distributor, cockfighting rings, a dance house, a bordello, and boxing matches hosted by Hemingway. Today, the cocks are still there, but tend to peacefully hang out at the bar. 729 Thomas Street, Old Town, 305-296-8666, blueheavenkw.com. *Tips:* Breakfast is amazing, but can be crowded with long waits, especially on Sundays. It's worth it, but if you want to eat faster, get there early to beat the hangover crowd. *Favorites*: lobster or veggie eggs Benedict, pancakes, shrimp melt.

3

2 CUBAN COFFEE QUEEN

CUBAN SANDWICHES, COFFEE AND MORE

Locals, including us, consistently vote this place, along with Five Brothers, as the purveyors of the best Cuban coffee and sandwiches in the Lower Keys. Swing by their Margaret Street hole-in-the-wall shanty to pick up breakfast for your walk along the historic seaport, or relax in the shady outside seating of their Duval location. Affordable and fresh, with plenty of vegetarian options, also, salads, smoothies, rice and beans. 284 Margaret Street, 305-292-4747, cubancoffeequeen.com, Duval & Southard, 305-294-7787. Seating at Duval location only. *Favorites*: Café con leche, caliente Cuban mix sandwich. *Best Deal*: Half Key Wester breakfast sandwich + con leche $4.50.

3 DELUNA'S CAFE: *AUTHENTIC CUBAN DELI*

Hard workers rely on this family-run cafe on Stock Island for a hearty breakfast and lunch. There is no seating, but the kitchen

cranks out coffee, breakfast sandwiches, and a list of daily lunch specials including fresh-caught fish, Cuban-style steak, chicken, and sometimes even pigs feet and ox tail. 5790 Maloney Avenue, Stock Island, 305-453-6654.

4 SOUTHERNMOST BEACH CAFE
AMERICANA BY THE SAND

The menu offers a little of everything at this beachfront cafe, and it's all tasty. What's better is the sand just a foot away, beckoning for a post-meal siesta. 1405 Duval, 305-295-6550, southernmostbeachcafe.com.

5 GOLDMAN'S DELI -- *NEW YORK BAGEL DINER*

Goldman's is an oasis of authentic New York nestled in Key West. Their from-scratch boiled-and-baked bagels earn them acclaim as one of the 20 best bagel delis in the country. Beyond bagels, they have other New York staples, like lox, pastrami, and corned beef. They are always busy but maintain fast and friendly service, and serve breakfast late. 2796 N. Roosevelt (by Winn-Dixie), New Town, 305-294-3354, goldmansdeli.com. *Best Deal*: 2 eggs, home fries, coffee, bagel, $4.95, till 9 a.m. *Favorite*: Anything on or with a Bagel.

6 LOUIE'S BACKYARD
CLASSY DECK OVERLOOKING THE OCEAN

Locals enjoy the upscale Caribbean-American cooking and relaxing views from the giant back deck. Louie's also specializes in wine tasting. If outside isn't your style, try the elegant indoor dining room. Dogs are allowed on the deck until 5 p.m., which is nice since it's next door to the dog beach. 700 Waddell Ave., 305-294-1061, louiesbackyard.com.

7 PEPE'S CAFE
CREATIVE BREAKFASTS, STEAKHOUSE

Funky and inviting, Pepe's is cleverly disguised as a bustling breakfast eatery by morning and a steakhouse by night. The "eldest eating house in the Keys" goes back to 1909, and has one of the best ambiance porches in town. Sip mimosas on the patio while eating fresh-fruit pancakes, homemade Key lime pie, New York strip, oysters, and daily fresh fish catches. 806 Caroline St., 305-294-7192, pepeskeywest.com.

8 THE CAFÉ
VEGETARIAN AND VEGAN, PLUS A LITTLE SEAFOOD

Creative vegetarian cuisine is hard enough to find in the Keys, so it goes without saying that vegan and gluten-free options are pretty much unicorns here. For those seeking any of the above, the Café is a calming oasis of both health and flavor. Sip on a glass of wine or microbrew — gluten-free options are available, of course — and take time perusing the menu's creative, international cuisine, as well as local art displays adorning the walls. They also offer a fresh fish dish daily. Wine and beer only. 509 Southard Street, 305-296-5515 thecafekw. com. *Confession*: We tend to over-order here because everything is so good, and we're not even vegetarians. Luckily they have doggie bags. *Favorites*: Udon bowl, fig-gorgonzola-spinach pizza, mussels.

9 THE HOGFISH BAR & GRILL
LOCALS HANGOUT, SEAFOOD, AMERICAN, CARIBBEAN

We never let a friend visit without a Hogfish experience. This comfortable, open-air hangout on the working commercial fishing harbor serves seafood fresh off the docks. It is also a longtime gathering place for colorful clientele, from fishermen to food lovers and treasure hunters. Sit on the dock for fish watching and quieter dining, or at the bar for locals watching and mingling. Pool table. From the dock you might spot a big blue boat with round cylinders on the aft deck — that's a treasure boat operated by the famed Mel Fisher crew. 6810 Front Street, Stock Island, 305-293-4041, hogfishbar.com. *Favorites*: Hogfish sandwich, lobster bisque, conch chowder. *Vegetarian*: Veggie burger, yum, not many other veg options. *Tips*: The hogfish sandwich is large, and can be split by two people with modest appetites. Sunday only brunch 9:00 a.m.

3

10 MANGIA MANGIA
FRESH ITALIAN, SEAFOOD WITH AMBIANCE, GLUTEN-FREE OPTIONS

An excellent place for a romantic dinner or gathering with friends, people come to Mangia Mangia dressed in their finest attire, whether that is a suit and dress, or flip-flops and a T-shirt. The patio is the place to sit, with its tropical trees and happy lights. The pasta is all fresh-made. "Pasta to the People!" declares their motto – and they mean it. Choose from the familiar, or opt for whole-wheat, gluten-egg-free, zucchini shreds or organic quinoa. They also have an excellent wine list. 900 Southard Street, 305-294-2469, mangia-mangia.com. *Favorites*: Broccoli rabe, sea scallops with spinach fettuccine, tiramisu.

11 ONLYWOOD
WOOD-FIRED PIZZA, CREATIVE ITALIAN AND GREAT SALADS

Onlywood imports their flour and tomato sauce from Italy, the same country from which they got their 1,000-degree brick pizza oven. We have yet to have something less than delicious here, whether pasta, pizza or salad. Though on Duval, it is far from a tourist trap in terms of quality and consistency, and the back garden patio is quiet with a touch of romance. They have an extensive wine collection, and though they don't serve hard alcohol, they are allowed to make a margarita from an agave concoction that is divine. 613 ½ Duval, 305-735-4412, onlywoodkw.com. *Favorites*: the daily specials.

12 EL SIBONEY: *LEGENDARY CUBAN DINER*

Tucked away on a residential street, this family-run joint is widely considered the best Cuban sit-down restaurant in town. The daily specials are usually good and sell out early. They are progressively busy

Top Eating Picks – Key West

through dinner and service is often slow. Best to come early or sit at the bar. 900 Catherine Street, 305-296-4184, elsiboneyrestaurant. com. *History*: The Siboney were an indigenous, pre-Columbian people of Cuba who unfortunately did not survive the Spanish diseases and conquistadors, but whose legacy lives on here. *Favorites*: #1 roast pork, #26 grilled grouper, bean soup specials. *Drink favorite*: Sangria.

13 SALUTE! ON THE BEACH
ITALIAN-SEAFOOD-CARIBBEAN

Salute is the place to sip a mojito, munch on appetizers, and watch the beachfront entertainment — whether it's the ocean sunset, families making sand castles, or fit gents and ladies playing beach volleyball out front. Late afternoon and early evening are most enjoyable, when live music is often playing and the sun setting. 1000 Atlantic Boulevard, 305-292-1117, saluteonthebeach.com. *Favorites*: antipasti platter (it's large, but you can order a half-portion, even though it's not on the menu), pasta carbonara. *Nearby*: Come before 5 p.m. to stroll through the lovely (and free) West Martello Tower gardens next door.

14 THAI ISLAND
SUSHI, THAI WITH HEART

The array of standard Thai cuisine always tastes fresher here. Maybe it's because of the second-story open-air porch overlooking the marina, or maybe because the two sisters who run it put so much care into their recipes and ingredients. While they offer all of the standards, there are also many not-so-standard Asian dishes and vegetarian options. The sushi is as fresh as we've tasted anywhere. The service is remarkably attentive. This is a favorite stop for both lunch and date-night dinners. 711 Palm Avenue, 305-296-9189, thaiislandrestaurant.com. *Favorites*: playboy roll, 3 gems roll, local yellowtail sushi. *Best Deals*: Spicy tuna handroll, lunch Bento box.

15 LA TE DA - CHRISTOPHER'S
FINE DINING IN FRESH AIR

The food is astoundingly delicious here and the atmosphere always light and friendly. Nestled in a vibrant boutique hotel courtyard with additional bar seating right on Duval, La Te Da serves up international and American cuisine from a menu concocted by one of Key West's most celebrated chefs, Christopher Rounds. Many people dress up for a meal here, though T-shirts are fine too. Dinner reservations recommended during busy times. 1125 Duval, 305-296-6706, lateda.com. *Favorites*: eggs blackstone, baked crab cakes, and everything else. *Best Deal*: Wednesday prime rib special under $20.

16 & 17 HEALTH FOOD & SMOOTHIES

For superfood juice smoothies and organic to-go soups, sandwiches and salads, there are two excellent health food stores in town offering a variety of vegetarian, vegan, organic, non-GMO and gluten-free options. **Sugar Apple's** cafe fare is exclusively vegan, while **Date & Thyme** offers options with dairy. Both have markets, with Sugar Apple having the bigger of the two. Sugar Apple, 917 Simonton Street, 305-292-0043, sugarapplekeywest.com. Date & Thyme (formerly Help Yourself), 829 Fleming, 305-296-7766, dateandthyme.com *Note*: Only Date & Thyme offers seating, which is outside and limited.

18 BETTER THAN SEX
DECADENT, ROMANTIC, DESSERT-ONLY RESTAURANT

A sexy vibe permeates out of this dimly lit, mysterious space. Inside, deep, red tones and soft light set the mood for a romantic night of sweet and exotic desserts and drinks — a perfect transition for the end of an evening out, and the beginning of the evening in. Reservations recommended. 926 Simonton Street, 305-296-8102, betterthansexkeywest.com.

19 2 CENTS RESTAURANT & PUB

Colorful vibe and eclectic custom food with international flavors. Think Moroccan chicken, foie gras, ribeye, Asian calamari, and mac and cheese. 416 Applerouth Lane, 305-414-8626, 2centskw.com.

20 5 BROTHERS GROCERY & SANDWICH SHOP

Known for exceptional café con leches, cubanos and bollas, this family-owned Key West classic is always fast and friendly. Legendary local favorite, takeout only. 930 Southard Street, Key West, 305-296-5205, 5brotherskeywest.com.

21 AMIGOS TORTILLA BAR

Mexican street tacos, gluten-free options, good people watching. 425 Greene Street, 305-292-2009, amigoskeywest.com.

22 B.O.'S FISH WAGON

Funky fish shack, grilled or fried fresh-catch, good place to try conch fritters, beer, cash only. 801 Caroline Street, 305-294-9272.

23 BAD BOY BURRITO

Quality burritos, bowls, and salads, a tiny bit of outside seating. 1128 Simonton, 305-292-2697, badboyburrito.com.

24 BANANA CAFE

Vibrant French bistro, with crêpes and plenty of American options too. 1215 Duval, 305-294-7227, bananacafekw.com.

Top Eating Picks - Key West

25 CROISSANTS DE FRANCE

French bakery, bistro and coffee house. Brie, baguettes, croque monsieur. C'est magnifique! 816 Duval, 305-294-2624, croissantsdefrance.com.

26 DANTE'S KEY WEST

Everyday is a pool party at this festive tiki-clad joint, with seafood-American, a good happy hour, raw oysters. 951 Caroline Street, 305-293-5123, danteskeywest.com.

27 DOLPHIN DELI

Fresh ingredients diner style minus the grease. Creative sandwiches, burgers and mahi-mahi. 5600 Maloney Avenue, Stock Island, 305-293-0707, dolphindeli.com.

28 EL MESON DE PEPE

Cuban with upbeat atmosphere, live music and dancing, right by Mallory Square. 410 Wall Street, 305-295-2620, elmesondepepe.com.

29 HOT TIN ROOF

Upscale seaside patio restaurant with small-plate tapas and full Latin-American meals. 0 Duval Street, 305-296-7701, oceankey.com/key-west-restaurant.

30 LA CRÊPERIE

Bright and welcoming French cafe in funky Bahama Village, eco-friendly ingredients and practices plus wine. 300 Petronia Street, 305-517-6799, lacreperiekeywest.com.

31 CAFÉ MARQUESA

Très chic contemporary American cuisine and Zagat's highest-rated local restaurant. 600 Fleming Street, 305-292-1919, marquesa.com.

32 MR. Z'S

Pizza slices and authentic Philly-style subs good any time of day, but especially while on a late-night Duval crawl. Limited seating. 501 Southard, 305-296-4445, mrzskeywest.com, also New Town location.

33 PRIME STEAKHOUSE

When you need an excellent upscale steak, Prime delivers with really good family-style side dishes. 951 Caroline (above Dante's), 305-296-4000, primekeywest.com.

34 ROOSTICA

Wood-fired pizzas and entrees in an island-Italian country decor. 5620 MacDonald Avenue, Stock Island, 305-296-4999, roostica.com.

35 OLD TOWN BAKERY

Fresh-baked sweet treats, picnics to go, fancy cheese, good coffee, sandwiches, gluten-free options, a favorite. 930 Eaton St., 305-396-7450, oldtownbakerykeywest.com.

36 SANDY'S CAFE

Cuban and Mexican food, conveniently nestled into the front of a laundromat. Local legend. Open late. Very limited seating. 1026 White Street, 305-295-0159, kwsandyscafe.com.

37 SANTIAGO'S BODEGA

Worldly tapas bar in Bahama Village, adored by many for its warm atmosphere and house sangria. 207 Petronia Street, 305-296-7691, santiagosbodega.com.

38 SCHOONER WHARF BAR

Possibly the most beloved local hangout, serving bar fare and live music on the waterfront. 202 William Street, 305-292-3302, schoonerwharf.com.

39 SIX-TOED CAT

Artistic cafe next to the Hemingway House. Light and creative. 823 Whitehead Street, 305-294-3318, sixtoedcatkeywest.com.

40 SUNSET PIER OCEAN KEY

Quintessential location on a picturesque pier by Mallory Square. American tropical food theme, popular with tourists. 0 Duval Street, 305-296-7701, oceankey.com/key-west-sunset-pier.

41 TACO EXPRESS

A taco truck, with as good Mexican food as can be found in town. 2318 N. Roosevelt, New Town, 305-509-1473, facebook.com/tacoexpresskeywest.

42 TWO FRIENDS PATIO

Fun, long-standing family-owned cafe with extensive American and seafood menu, excellent people watching and karaoke. 512 Front Street, 305-296-3124, twofriendskeywest.com.

43 WATERFRONT BREWERY

Classic brewery with solid food, plus pool table, skee ball, arcade games, rooftop deck. 201 William Street, 305-440-2270, thewaterfrontbrewery.com.

Like very thin pancakes?

I love crêpes.

With butter, sugar and lemon.

And raw fish?

Whatever you desire, dear.

Top Eating Picks - Lower Keys

GEIGER KEY MARINA RESTAURANT
LOW-KEY WATERFRONT SEAFOOD

A local's hide-out, Geiger Key is a laid-back experience under a tiki, on a secluded dock with plenty of nature. One night we watched a graceful shark swim by our table. It's owned by the same folks as the Hogfish, so the food is similar and equally delicious. 5 Geiger Road, turn oceanside at MM 11 onto Boca Chica, drive a ways then follow signs to the marina on the left, 305-296-3553, geigerkeymarina.com. *Favorites*: coconut shrimp, lobster BLT, hogfish tacos.

BAYPOINT MARKET
SUBS AND ICE CREAM

The owner of Baypoint once played in a Grateful Dead cover band, which explains the market's laid back, colorful vibe. This little purple convenience store makes subs and cheesesteaks. They also have good breakfast sandwiches, ice cream, and shakes. If you're in a hurry, call ahead, as there are usually only one or two people working, who can be overwhelmed with orders. Mile marker 15, Saddlebunch Keys, oceanside, 305-745-3882. *Note*: There is one picnic table out front for seating. *Favorites*: Porkroll-egg-cheese croissant sandwich, Italian sub.

BELLA LUNA
NEIGHBORHOOD ITALIAN WITH CLASS

Bella Luna opened in 2015 and quickly became a local favorite. With fresh ingredients and authentic recipes, it's hard to go wrong with any dinner selection. It's slightly upscale, but in a comfortable way, regardless of if you're dressing up or down for the evening. Mile marker 21.5, gulfside, Cudjoe Key, 305-453-6179, bellalunaflkeys. com. *Favorites*: chicken Parmesan, short rib ragu.

SQUARE GROUPER
CONTEMPORARY, INNOVATIVE AMERICAN FUSION

Anyone can find something they love on the menu. Inventive dishes from earth and sea range from lamb and steak to seafood stew and spaghetti squash. Order a large plate for a traditional dinner, or mix it up with a selection of small plates to share tapas style. They also take pride in being ingredient and environmentally conscious. The ambiance is a little upscale, though far from uptight — after all, the restaurant is a named after a prized local catch — floating bales of marijuana. Those are not on the menu, though. Mile marker 22.5, oceanside, Cudjoe Key, 305-745-8880, squaregrouperbarandgrill. com. *Tip*: Come early for dinner during the winter, or waits can be long. *Favorites*: Asian skirt steak, yellowfin-tuna-avocado egg rolls.

3

MY NEW JOINT — *COCKTAIL, TAPAS LOUNGE*

While theoretically part of the Square Grouper, My New Joint deserves its own listing. Located above the parent restaurant, this is a great place to go for socializing, snacking, or just hanging out. Colorful walls, comfy couches, dark corners, an expansive bar, and a shuffleboard table provide plenty of variety. So do the 150 beers, specialty cocktails and tapas, including fondue and a raw oyster bar. There's nothing else quite like this place in the Keys. Mile marker 22.5, oceanside, Cudjoe Key, 305-745-8880, mynewjoint420lounge.com. *Favorites*: oysters, communal salad bowl, soft pretzel, roasted cauliflower, lots of veggie options.

GALLEY GRILL — *CLASSIC DINER FARE*

This unassuming diner is a hidden gem of the Lower Keys, especially for breakfast. Besides plenty of bacon and sausage gravy, they also offer some refreshing vegetarian and gluten-free options. Their mix-match of coffee mugs can also lead to good entertainment. The only thing they're missing is hash browns, a rarity in the Lower Keys. Mile marker 25, oceanside, Summerland Key, 305-745-3440. *Favorite*: Hobo breakfast (eggs, cheese and gravy over potatoes).

NO NAME PUB — *LEGENDARY TAVERN*

Since the 1930s the No Name Pub has been a vital watering hole for local fishermen and world travelers alike, and many have left their names and messages here, scrawled on one of the thousands of dollar bills stapled to the walls. Once known for its rowdy, gambling, drug-smuggling crowd and upstairs brothel, today the No Name Pub is hailed for its famous pizza, fish dip and friendly locals. 30813 Watson Boulevard, Big Pine Key, 305-872-9115, nonamepub.com.

NO NAME PUB
BIG PINE KEY

Top Eating Picks – Lower Keys

BOONDOCKS GRILL — *CREATIVE PUB FOOD*
Despite its huge tiki, kitschy island theme, and flashing neon sign, this sports bar, pub and music venue doesn't settle for mediocre fare. It serves intriguing ingredients in both classic comfort food and innovative dishes. Bring the kids and cocktails onto their mini-golf course. Mile marker 27.2, gulfside, Ramrod Key, 305-872-4094, boondocksus.com. *Best deal*: Lunch special $9.98 half sandwich with soup or speciality salad. *Favorites*: bang bang shrimp, cream of crab with asparagus soup, steak and blue cheese chop salad.

SUGARLOAF PIZZA
Pizza, salads and subs to go, or to eat at the Sugarloaf Lodge tiki bar. Delivery. Mile marker 17, gulfside, 305-745-1929, sugarloaflodge.net.

SUGARLOAF FOOD COMPANY
Homemade pastries, hot and cold breakfast and lunch sandwiches, wraps, coffee, frozen dinners. Takeout, limited outdoor seating. MM 24, gulfside, Summerland Key, 305-744-0631, keylimepieshop.com.

FIVE BROTHERS GROCERY TWO
Excellent Cuban sandwiches and coffee plus convenience store, daily lunch specials. Mile marker 27, gulfside, Ramrod Key, 305-872-0702.

KIKI'S SANDBAR BAR & GRILLE
American pub and seafood with wildlife and water views, live music and a pet-friendly beach. 183 Barry Avenue, mile marker 28.5, gulfside, Little Torch Key, 305-872-4500, kikissandbar.com.

BAGEL ISLAND SANDWICH SHOP
Good breakfast and lunch sandwiches. Try the Reuben bagel. 205 Key Deer Boulevard, mile marker 30, Big Pine Key, 305-872-9912.

BUCKTOOTH ROOSTER
Menu is massive, creative American, and parking lot is always full. MM 30, gulfside, Big Pine Key, 305-916-5810, bucktoothrooster.com.

GOOD FOOD CONSPIRACY
Health food market and deli with an array of wraps (including gluten-free), salads, soups, smoothies and fresh juice blends. Mostly vegetarian with some free-range turkey and tuna options. Limited seating and good conversation at the bar. Mile marker 30.1, oceanside, Big Pine Key, 305-872-3945, goodfoodconspiracy.com.

BABY'S COFFEE
Fresh-roasted coffee, tea, smoothies, pastry-type snacks and a few sandwiches. Limited picnic table seating outside. Mile marker 15, oceanside, Saddlebunch Keys, 305-744-9866, babyscoffee.com.

Late Breakfasts & Weekend Brunches

It's common here to get up in time to miss breakfast, and those are often the same days it feels like a hearty breakfast would be key to surviving the day. If this sounds like you, then here's your salvation.

DAILY LATE BREAKFAST - OLD TOWN

Blue Heaven, 729 Thomas, 305-296-8666 (until 2 p.m.)
Sarabeth's, 530 Simonton, 305-293-8181, (2 p.m., closed Monday)
Camille's, 1202 Simonton, 305-296-4811 (2 p.m.)
Banana Cafe, 1215 Duval, 305-294-7227 (until 3 p.m.)
Croissants de France, 816 Duval, 305-294-2624 (until 3 p.m.)
Harpoon Harry's, 832 Caroline, 305-294-8744 (until 3 p.m.)
Frenchie's Cafe, 529 United, 305-396-7124 (until 3 p.m.)
Firefly Key West, 223 Petronia, 305-849-0104 (until 3 p.m.)
Havana-Key West, 703 Duval, 305-294-2626 (until 3 p.m.)
La Crêperie, 300 Petronia, 305-517-6799 (until 3 p.m.)
5 Brothers Grocery, 930 Southard, 305-296-5205 (until 3 p.m.)
Bagatelle, 115 Duval, 305-296-6609 (until 4 p.m.)
Blossom's Cajun Kitchen, 408 White, 305-294-9496 (4, closed Sun.)
Six-Toed Cat, 823 Whitehead, 305-294-3318 (until 5 p.m.)
Cuban Coffee Queen, 284 Margaret, 305-292-4747 (until 7 p.m.)
Fisherman's Cafe, 205 Elizabeth, 305-900-6878 (until 7 p.m.)
Denny's (the chain restaurant), 925 Duval, breakfast 24 hours
Sandy's Cafe, 1026 White, 305-295-0159 (until midnight)
The Sunshine Grill, 1110 White, 305-294-8089
> Thursday-Saturday 24 hours, Sunday-Wednesday to 9 p.m.

DAILY BREAKFAST/BRUNCH - NEW TOWN & STOCK ISLAND

Goldman's Deli, 2976 N. Roosevelt, 305-294-3354 (until 2 p.m.)
De Luna's Cafe, 5790 Maloney, Stock Island, 305-453-6654 (until 3)
Key Plaza Crêperie, 1105 Key Plaza, 305-517-6032 (until 5 p.m.)
IHOP (the chain restaurant), 3416 N. Roosevelt, breakfast 24 hours.

WEEKEND BRUNCHES: La Te Da (Sunday to 2 p.m.), Hot Tin Roof (Sun., 2:30), Louie's Backyard (Sat. & Sun., 2:30), Azur (Sun., 3), Martin's (Sun., 3), 2 Cents (Sat. & Sun., 3), The Cafe (Sat. & Sun., 4).

EXTRA FANCY: Luxury Sunday brunch on the private island resort of Little Palm, plan on $130 a person, catch the resort ferry at mile marker 28.5 on Little Torch Key, 16 and older only, reservations required, 305-872-2551. Or for slightly less fancy at a third the price, Bistro 245 near Mallory Square, Sunday for 70 feet of food with breakfast, seafood and more, goes until 2 p.m., 305-292-4320.

4

Bars & Drink

Fantasy Fest on Duval Street

IN THIS CHAPTER

About Key West drinking
Drinking Bingo
Rum primer
Cigar guide
The nightly circuit
Bar highlights Key West
Bar highlights Lower Keys

I used to love Wine, Women & Song

but my doctor said I had to slow down,

so I quit Singing.*

Out on a Saturday night, drinking may seem to be the biggest sport in the Keys. It is easily accessible, requires very little special training or certification, and is possible to pursue nearly 24 hours a day. From the roots of Spanish pirates, wreckers, rum-runners and drug smugglers, to modern-day spring breakers, snowbirds and hard-working locals, libations have long been a typical pastime on these little islands.

Duval Street in Key West is the epicenter of drink, and there is no shortage of places to enjoy a quiet, romantic glass of wine, or to simply get wasted. At night, starting after 10 or 11 p.m. up until closing time at 4 a.m., energetic, drunken Duval Street is a fascination of humanity where everyone is not only allowed but encouraged to be who they are. People of all shapes, sizes, colors, hometowns, and styles come for the "Duval Crawl," walking from bar to bar, either as happy drunks   or just observers of the scene. It's a phenomenon worth witnessing at least once in life, even if you don't like drinking or staying up late.

NOTE: SEE CHAPTER ONE FOR DRINKING LAWS & CUSTOMS.

Merriment doesn't just come from music and drinks here, though. Locals and visitors alike are social, happy and friendly, so it's easy to strike up a conversation and share some fascinating stories with people you don't know and may have nothing in common with. If that isn't enough entertainment, then we've created a little something more for you...

Encouraging a drinking game would be irresponsible, so here is a walking game we call "Inebriated Bingo," or more simply "Binge-O." Make copies of the game board on the next page for everyone in your group. As you progress through your evening, whoever spots a particular item and points it out first can mark off that item on their card. The winner is the first one to cover all of his or her squares in a straight line. The prize is up to you.

4

Rum, rum, Rum!

Rum is the unofficial drink of the Conch Republic. Celebrated by pirates, presidents and warriors, this fermented sugarcane comes in many forms, but typically is divided into light rums for islandy mixed drinks and dark rums for sipping or shooting.

MOJITOS: Mojitos are a favorite Cuban and Caribbean concoction and are best ordered from restaurants or bars that have enough time and care to make them properly from fresh ingredients, instead of sugary pre-mixes. Muddled mint, plenty of lime, white rum, and a bit of sugar are the main ingredients, with variations including club soda and pineapple juice. A good mojito should leave mint leaf pieces

*Thanks Capt. Carl "Fizz" Fismer for letting us use your wisdom!

4

BOOZERS	INSTRUMENTS	NATIVES	GARB	EXPRESSIONS	OBJECTS
B	**I**	**N**	**G**	**E**	**O**
bachelorette party	ukulele	rooster	picture of a marlin fish on a shirt	no working during drinking hours	coconut
man wearing tutu	washboard	iguana	treasure coin necklace	it's 5 o'clock somewhere	conch shell
sexy pirate	guitar	drag queen	naked boobs	you can't drink all day if you don't start in the morning	decorated bicycle (Conch cruiser)
two drunk people holding each-other upright	bucket	body paint model	mardi gras beads	growing old disgracefully	Captain Morgan
some-one singing Jimmy Buffett	drums	movie character	t-shirt with a cliché drinking saying	drinking rum before 10 a.m. makes you a pirate not an alcoholic	rainbow flag or walkway
Ernest Hemingway method actor	banjo	parrot	fedora	soup of the day: Jameson	pirate flag

stuck on your teeth. When you are enjoying a mojito with friends, proper etiquette dictates that you must inform one another when you see any of those big green things stuck in someone's teeth.

RUM-RUNNERS: As legend goes, rum-runners were invented in the Keys — both the drink and the profession — and include a lot of different kinds of juice, rum, and flavored liqueurs. Good. Potent. Another refreshing rum staple is the dark and stormy, made of dark rum and ginger beer.

CUBA LIBRE: It's hard to go wrong with a rum and Coke (a.k.a. Cuba Libre), especially when splurging for an upgrade from the house rum. When mixing your own, pick up some Ron Abuelo rum, a popular Panamanian añejo that is a great mix of quality, affordability and taste. It can be found at Summerland Wine & Spirits, Walgreens, and Winn-Dixie.

PAPA'S PILAR: For classy rum sippers or less-elegant rum shooters who still want good flavor and purity, nothing beats the gusto of Papa's Pilar, named appropriately after the gregarious and adventurous Ernest "Papa" Hemingway.

KEY WEST'S FIRST LEGAL RUM DISTILLERY: Though Key West has a long history with rum and rum-runners, oddly enough the distillery wasn't established until 2013. Stop in for house tastings of their signature spirits. All are made with Florida sugar cane, and some are creatively infused with flavors like coconut, Key lime, and vanilla creme brulee. 105 Simonton Street, keywestlegalrum.com.

THE RUM BAR: It might take a while to try all 230 varieties of rum elixir that head bartender Bahama Bob Leonard has collected through the years. The bar is set on the quiet end of Duval in the Speakeasy Inn, a historic landmark from the late 1800s, established by rum-runner and cigar magnate Raul Vaquez. Go back in time in the cozy, dark-wood-paneled bar, while sipping on a traditional tropical rum drink or a flight of sampler mini-shots. 1117 Duval Street, 305-296-2680.

4

I'm just a cuba libre in paradise…

Cigar Directory

To answer the perennial question — can you buy Cuban cigars in
Key West — no. As of this printing, it is still illegal to import tobacco
from Cuba into the U.S.A. But there is good news for aficionados.
Key West's history is deeply intertwined with both cigars and Cuba.
From fine stores to funky carts, here are a few interesting places.

CUBAN LEAF CIGAR FACTORY
Watch artisans hand roll cigars right on Duval.
They have some good affordable ones in their La
Liga line. 310 Duval Street.

KEY WEST HAVANA CIGAR COMPANY
Choose one from the walk-in humidor then relax
on the couch amidst old art and history. Part of the Speakeasy Inn and
rum bar, former home of a notorious rum-runner. 1117 Duval Street.

RODRIGUEZ CIGAR FACTORY
The real deal, this no-frills factory and store is owned by Cuban
rollers who've kept the family tradition alive since the town's cigar-
making peak in the 1880s. 113 Fitzpatrick Street.

CIGAR CITY, USA
If you've been searching for a mug and placemat set with cigar art
on them, rejoice, your quest is over. They also have an impressive
collection of cigar art and exhibits, an outdoor cafe and of course, a
plethora of smokables. 410 Wall Street, by Mallory Square.

CORK & STOGIE
Order wine or a craft beer, pull up a seat on the intimate patio,
challenge a friend to a game of backgammon, and enjoy your
masterful cigar at this family-run shop. Dog friendly. 1218 Duval.

KEY WEST CIGAR CLUB & SMOKE SHOP
Watch artisans masterfully roll cigars and find hard-to-get brands
in the humidor. They also have pipes and pipe tobacco, plus a large
selection of accessories. 335 Duval Street.

SCHOONER WHARF BAR
There's a small cigar cart here that's usually run by Eric, with help from
his long, gray beard and lively smile. 202 William on the seaport.

SUMMERLAND WINE & SPIRITS
Best cigar selection outside town. Mile marker 24.8, Summerland Key.

The Nightly Circuit

Duval can have slow nights. If you run into such a predicament, here's a local bar circuit that always has something going on:

Monday: Virgilio's $5 Martini Monday, and the hangovers can be lessened significantly if you opt for an upgraded drink.

Tuesday: Charlie Mac's Taco Tuesday, $2 pulled pork, $5 mahi. Hog's Breath Saloon for live music.

Wednesday: Schooner Wharf Bar and Smokin' Tuna Saloon for music, or for something completely different, the Green Parrot on the first Wednesday of the month for Ukulele Night. If you get lucky, you might see Street Singer Steve, a kind-hearted, burly, long-haired man strumming a tiny uke. If you get really lucky, he might just serenade you with one of his original songs, like, "I Kind of Like Stock Island."

Thursday: Durty Harry's to watch the house band the DurtBags.

Friday and Saturday: the Green Parrot is where the locals are listening to music.

Sunday: Wind down on the beach at Salute! for live music and the sunset. Every night there is also good jazz at the Little Room.

Self-Preservation Advice

Almost anything goes in Key West, but some self-preservation secrets are closely guarded by locals. Here are four to remember:

PACE YOURSELF. Duval doesn't really kick off until 10 p.m. or later, so if you drink early in the day, plan a nice, long nap and a hearty dinner to prepare for the night.

BEWARE OF SUGAR. Those blended drinks and Jell-O shots look really good, but they are very potent. Your body will remember them in the morning, even if your mind doesn't.

DRINK RESPONSIBLY OUTSIDE. Carrying drinks from bar to bar is widely practiced, though technically illegal. Just don't give authorities a reason to enforce it and they won't.

BRING NICE. Key West is a happy place. If someone tries to make it otherwise, be a wise ninja and diffuse or ignore their antagonism instead of escalating it.

Top Drinking Picks - Key West

Live music · Serves food · Dogs allowed · A little mature · Immature · Also nice for day drinking · Outside hangout · No smoking

I KEY WEST AIRPORT — *A PROPER WELCOME*

Whether you're arriving or headed home, if you're lucky enough to fly through EYW, then you'll be treated to a true Key West experience. The airport has almost as many bars as gates. Grab a cold one from the seasonal bar inside baggage claim or the restaurant-bar in the terminal. Once you've cleared security, inside the concourse you can order up a beverage, then walk three steps to the open-air, sandy patio and smoking lounge, complete with waterfall and shade umbrellas. It really is the best airport in the world. 3941 S. Roosevelt Blvd., 305-809-5200, eyw.com.

2 GREEN PARROT BAR — *THE LEGENDARY LOCALS BAR*

Claimed to be the town's oldest drinking establishment, it's been a second home to fishermen, vagabonds, hippies, sailors, bachelorettes, vacationers, and lovers of life of all sorts since 1890. It's most happening on Friday and Saturday nights, with some of the best live music in town. At other times, it's a good hangout with a pool table, dart board, jukebox, and free popcorn. The Parrot is a true locals hangout, that doesn't mind an influx of visitors. 601 Whitehead Street, 305-294-6133, www.greenparrot.com.

3 THE COURTHOUSE DELI BENCH
WORLD'S MOST SOCIAL SITTING BENCH

The "Bench" is Key West's version of Paris' Café de la Paix, where it is said if you hang out long enough you'll see everyone in the world worth knowing pass by. Just across the street from the Green Parrot Bar, the Bench is where a great deal of the Parrot's social scene takes place. Sit out here to listen to the live music while conversing with strangers. Anything might happen here, from a game of giant Jenga to someone pole dancing on the lamppost. Though there is no official bar at the bench, there are many purchased or undercover home-poured drinks in hand. Across Whitehead from the Green Parrot.

4 SCHOONER WHARF BAR

QUINTESSENTIAL LOCALS WATERFRONT BAR

With historic tall ships docked on one side and a bar and live music on the other, Schooner Wharf is a welcoming, laid-back island hangout. A long-time staple for locals and visitors alike, the bar also serves as an important anchor to the community, hosting many celebrations and events, plus contributing a couple of vessels to the Conch Republic Navy. The local bands are some of the best around, the dance floor is always active, the food is good, and the view from the upper deck is worth the climb. 202 William Street on the historic seaport, 305-292-3302, schoonerwharf.com.

5 CHART ROOM BAR

DIVE BAR TO THE STARS

Peanut shells litter the floor, treasure maps hang from the ceiling and years of secrets lie carved into the heavy wooden tables. It is in this tiny bar that Mel Fisher and his cohorts plotted and planned their way to finding the sunken Nuestra Señora de Atocha and the lost 1622 Spanish treasure fleet. Some say it's also where Jimmy Buffett and Bob Marley played their first gigs. Once adjoining a more modest motel, the Chart Room is now engulfed inside the luxurious Pier House Resort, but remains true to its roots, proudly serving zero blender drinks along with plenty of free popcorn, hot dogs and peanuts. It's often half-empty, and the bar tenders are not guaranteed to be friendly, but we come here for the ambiance, new friends, and a quieter place to converse. 1 Duval Street, 305-296-4600.

4

Note: Numbers by bar names correspond to map on page 66.

SCHOONER WHARF BAR

Top Drinking Picks - Key West

6 THE PORCH
CASUAL BEER AND WINE BAR

Your sure to see a few craft beards sitting at the bar enjoying The Porch's large selection of craft beer. Cozily nestled inside a historic Key West mansion, the dapper wooden-floored establishment is reminiscent of an Ivy League hangout, minus any pompous residue. Play Ms. Pac-Man inside or go outside to enjoy the actual porch, with tables facing a lush landscape, just steps from Duval. Need a stiffer drink? Traverse a few steps across the porch, to Caroline's Other Side, where classic cocktails meet leather couches and a fireplace. 429 Caroline Street, 305-517-6358, www.theporchkw.com.

7 VIRGILIO'S
LAID-BACK, ENERGETIC MARTINIS

Walk down the alley, then through a little gate in a big white fence, and it almost feels as though you're ducking into an old-time speakeasy. A short, narrow hallway opens up to a courtyard of cocktails, couches, live music, and dancing. Though it's attached to the chic La Trattoria Restaurant, the dress code in the back is whatever level of style your heart desires. Locals make Mondays a regular stop for $5 martinis. 524 Duval, 305-296-1075, latrattoria.us.

8 SMOKIN' TUNA SALOON
COMFORTABLE, OPEN AIR, MUSIC

When the bustle of Duval gets too much, the Smokin' Tuna is a welcomed down-to-earth oasis of comfort music, open air, and room to breathe. Two bars and a stage frame the secluded courtyard where people from 21 to 91 kick off their shoes and dance the night away. It's also a restaurant, known for its raw bar, seafood, and other tasties. 4 Charles Street, 305-517-6350, smokintunasaloon.com.

9 HOGFISH BAR & GRILL
LOCAL'S BAR ON THE WATER

It's not an oversight that we listed the Hogfish under both restaurants and bars. It earns a spot in each. The bar is where fishermen, treasure hunters and other hard workers go to unwind from the day, play pool, and weave their tales of the sea. Watch the boats come in, pull up a stool, make a few new friends, and munch on some of the freshest seafood bites around. 6810 Front Street, Stock Island, 305-293-4041, hogfishbar.com.

10 SLOPPY JOE'S, RICKS, IRISH KEVIN'S, HOG'S BREATH
THE NIGHTLIFE EPICENTER

Feel like a rock-n-roll bar, or maybe an Irish pub? How about a Harley motorcycle saloon, bumpin' nightclub, saucy strip club, or a bout of karaoke? You can have it all, in just a few hundred steps. This two-block strip of Duval is the Disney World of Key West — ground zero for the town's most famous party bars. Loud music and jubilant tourists spill from one doorway to the next most every night in a boisterous menage of intoxication and celebration. Even if this isn't your scene, a walk down this stretch at night is a must-do for people-watching. Duval, between Caroline and Front Streets.

11 CAPT. TONY'S SALOON
BRAS ON THE CEILING, HISTORY UNDERFOOT

What does a fisherman and gunrunner get when he retires? He gets to be the mayor of Key West, of course. And he gets a bar. Named after the late Capt. Tony, this bar is one of the town's most beloved dive bars. Originally the town's first icehouse and morgue back in the 1850s, in 1933 it opened as Sloppy Joe's Bar, the watering hole for Ernest Hemingway and a lot of other creative drinkers. In 1937 when the landlord raised the rent by $1, they packed up shop and moved it across the street to where Sloppy Joe's is today. But the spirit of Papa H. lives on here, and he surely would have appreciated the foosball table and all of the ladies who have since stapled their braziers to the ceiling. 428 Greene Street, 305-294-1838, capttonyssaloon.com.

4

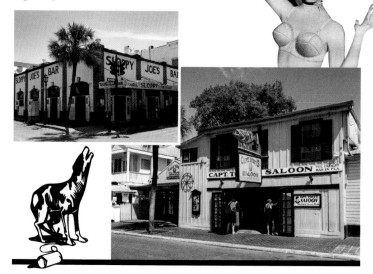

Top Drinking Picks – Key West

12 BOGART'S IRISH PUB & GRILL
COMFORT FOOD AND SPORTS PUB

Belly up to the wooden bar, watch the game and eat a meal that exceeds the quality of typical bar fare. Bogart's is mostly a classic Irish pub, but far from dreary. It's also a bit of a comfort stop in a land of island overload. Irish and American cuisine mix with Guinness on tap, live music and televised sports for a laid-back evening on the strip, but out of the stampede. 900 Duval Street, 305-296-0815, keywestcasablanca.com.

13 MARQUESA HOTEL BAR — *A MOMENT OF CLASS*

There are only a few seats, mostly filled by hotel guests, so it's not the place to plop it for long, but it's a fun duck away for a fine cocktail in an elegant setting, which is how my father and I found ourselves there one evening, sipping two dirty martinis and plotting our next adventure. 600 Fleming Street, 305-292-1919, marquesa.com.

14 GARDEN OF EDEN — *CLOTHING-OPTIONAL ROOFTOP*

Climb the staircase at the Bull & Whistle Bar, past the pool tables on the second floor, to the rooftop and take a look around. You'll either be in heaven, or you can do a brisk walk-through to the back staircase for a quick escape. Either way, you are free to do so fully dressed or in your birthday suit. 224 Duval Street, 305-296-4565.

15 LITTLE ROOM JAZZ CLUB — *LIVE, PEACEFUL*

Escape the coeds and revel in the soothing sounds of live jazz, seven nights a week. While you're there, enjoy some small-plate appetizers, fanciful drink concoctions, craft beer, and plenty of wine. 821 Duval, 305-741-7515, littleroomjazzclub.com.

16 DANTE'S KEY WEST
SWIMMING POOL, BAR, FOOD, PARTY

The swimming pool here comes with a waterfall, tiki bars and plenty of party atmosphere. People come here to eat good seafood too, but that is usually code for, "I like the view. It's straight out of a spring break movie." There's also beer pong, DJs, and a good happy hour. 951 Caroline Street, 305-293-5123, danteskeywest.com.

17 HOG'S BREATH SALOON

Looks like a biker bar, but it's friendly for all comers. Live music and dancing almost every night. One of the most popular bars. 400 Front Street, 305-296-4222, hogsbreath.com.

18 BULL & WHISTLE BAR

Live music downstairs. Pool tables upstairs. Good
people watching right on Duval. 224 Duval Street, 305-296-4565.

19 VINOS ON DUVAL
Comfy wine bar with cheese plates, seating in or outside and wine
delivery to local hotels. 810 Duval Street, vinosonduval.com.

20 COWBOY BILL'S
Country music fans, you have found near-vana. Besides music, there's
a mechanical bull, sexy bullriding competitions, line dancing, and $2
PBRs. 618 Duval Street, cowboybillskw.com.

21 THE GREEN ROOM
Friendly, laid-back, eco-conscious bar with a sustainable design,
energy efficiency, and all-natural original drinks. 501 Greene Street,
305-741-7300, thegreenroomkeywest.com.

22 DON'S PLACE
Darts, pool, video games, jukebox, and 10 sport-centric TVs inside.
Ping pong, cornhole, foosball, and tiki bar outside. Drive-through
liquor store. 1000 Truman Ave. (at Grinnell), 305-296-8837,
donsplacekeywest.com.

23 THE RUM BAR
More than 230 rums, excellent mixes, cozy, wood walls and a
good porch for people watching. 1115 Duval, 305-296-2680,
speakeasyinn.com.

24 AQUA NIGHTCLUB
DJs, nightly drag shows, and guaranteed party vibes permeate from
Aqua, a gay nightclub that is welcoming to and frequented by all
walks of life. 711 Duval Street, 305-294-0555, aquakeywest.com.

25 LOUIE'S UPPER DECK
Sit outside, watch the ocean, sip fine wines and martinis, contemplate
the meaning of life, and enjoy small-plate snacks. 700 Waddell Street,
305-294-1061, louisbackyard.com.

26 BOURBON ST. PUB
This legendary gay bar welcomes all comers at the front, but the
Garden Bar and pool area is reserved for men-only and is clothing-
optional. 724 Duval Street, 305-294-9354, bourbonstpub.com.

27 CAROLINE'S OTHER SIDE

Swanky and light-hearted craft cocktail bar with an extensive list of
fine rum, tequila, scotch, whisky, absinth, and more. 429 Caroline
Street, 305-517-6358, carolinescafe.com/other-side.

4

Top Drinking Picks - Lower Keys

PURPLE PORPOISE PUB
THE ULTIMATE LOW-BROW DRINKING ESTABLISHMENT
There are dive bars and then there's the Purple Porpoise. It's a glorious experience for those who like adventure, are not germophobic, don't wear expensive jewelry, and don't take themselves too seriously. If this sounds like you, don't miss this place. It's kind of like an abandoned building that someone put some coolers of beer and barstools in — yes sometimes they serve cans of beer out of an Igloo cooler. There is no top-shelf liquor, but there is skee ball and ping pong. Cash only. Mile marker 9.8, gulfside, Big Coppitt Key.

MANGROVE MAMA'S
ISLANDLY PATIO BAR

For a late-morning bloody Mary or an evening of live music, the colorful décor and characters make Mangrove Mama's a popular stop for those driving up or down the Keys in search of a quintessential island parrothead type of bar. Bands play classic covers from acts like Neil Young, the Allman Brothers and of course Jimmy Buffett, but come early as the party ends at 10 p.m. Originally the bar was a station on Flagler's Overseas Railway. Mile marker 20, gulfside, Upper Sugarloaf Key, 305-745-3030, mangrovemamasrestaurant.com.

SUMMERLAND WINE & SPIRITS
EXCEPTIONAL LIQUOR STORE

When you want your bar to be on your own terms, this is the place to get your ingredients. It's clean, peaceful, affordable and well stocked with a pleasantly uncommon selection of wine, beer, and booze. Summerland is an noteworthy liquor store for anywhere, but especially the Keys. Special orders are welcome. Hours: 9:30 a.m. to 8:30 p.m. all days except Sunday 10:30 to 8. Mile marker 24.8, oceanside, Summerland Key, 305-745-3900, keysliquors.com.

COCONUTS BAR
Even if Big Pine Key did have a lot of choices for drinking venues, the party would still inevitably end up here. It's just the right amount of dingy, complete with pool tables and a ring toss game. Coconuts is open to serve the town until around 4 a.m. every night, but after 11 p.m. or so, it's no place for the timid. The locals are like Gremlins, give them sustenance late, and who knows what sort of mischief they'll get into. Mile marker 30.5, gulfside, Big Pine Key, 305-872-3795.

MY NEW JOINT
EXPANSIVE BAR, COCKTAIL AND TAPAS LOUNGE

Between 150 beers, classic cocktails and new concoctions, the drink never gets old here. Mix in bar seating, comfy couches, superb munchies, dark corners, vivid décor, shuffleboard and live music, and it's clear why My New Joint is a perpetual favorite for locals and tourists. Mile marker 22.5, oceanside, Cudjoe Key, 305-745-8880, mynewjoint420lounge.com.

LOOE KEY TIKI BAR & GRILL

Island drinks, bar food, and a very affordable happy hour with $2 beers. 99-cent taco Tuesdays are especially popular with the locals. Mile marker 27.3, Ramrod Key, 877-816-3483, looekeytikibar.com.

KIKI'S SANDBAR BAR & GRILLE

Sit on the beach for a peaceful view, with hanging chairs and a dock to explore, or enjoy the air conditioning inside. Good margaritas. 183 Barry Avenue, Little Torch Key, 305-872-4500, kikissandbar.com.

GEIGER KEY MARINA RESTAURANT

For an afternoon or evening drink, saddle up to the tiki bar or gaze out at the wildlife in mangrove channels. The crowd here is especially laid-back and friendly. 5 Geiger Road, turn oceanside at mile marker 11 onto Boca Chica, drive a ways then follow signs for the marina on the left, 305-296-3553, geigerkeymarina.com.

4

NO NAME PUB
Known for the dollar bills covering the walls, the No Name Pub has wetted the whistles of all sorts of Keys characters for decades. 30813 Watson Boulevard, Big Pine Key, 305-872-9115, nonamepub.com.

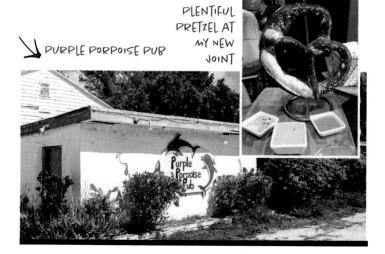

PURPLE PORPOISE PUB

PLENTIFUL PRETZEL AT MY NEW JOINT

5
Late Night

White Street Pier, Key West

IN THIS CHAPTER

Highlights for late-night things to do
Dinner served after 10 p.m.
Where to get food and other stuff 24-7
Insomniac activities
Where to watch the sunrise

The Cubans invaded ...
good for them

It was about 4 a.m. on a February morning when a Cuban border patrol boat pulled up to an upscale resort hotel. Four men, dressed in full Cuban military fatigues, tied their vessel to the dock and crept through the sleepy property, winding their way past the tropical grounds to Duval Street.

The scene on Duval was typical of closing time. The last drunks stumbled from the bars to the sidewalks, holding each other up, in cackling, inebriated-walking embraces. None gave the first glance to the Cubans.

"Estamos buscando la policía. Cómo sabes dónde están?" The men asked one drunken man, in an attempt to find a U.S. police officer.

5

"Don-dee... Este-fan..." the drunk pondered a couple of words he thought he might have picked out correctly. "Where is... Gloria Estefan?!"

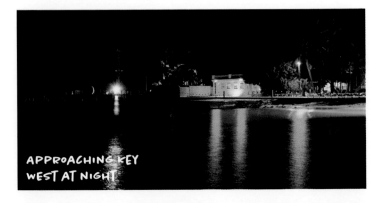

APPROACHING KEY
WEST AT NIGHT

The drunk suddenly looked quite pleased with himself over his masterful Spanish translation. "I don't know but when you find her, tell her I'm in room 307!"

As he walked off singing and air drumming "The Rhythm is Gonna Get You," the Cubans were left baffled in their tracks. Three hours ago, they had bravely fled Cuba on a daring escape mission, with hopes of defecting to the U.S. — only to find that nothing, not even a Communist military invasion, seems out of place at 4 a.m. on Duval Street.

The Cubans did eventually find a police officer, to whom they were able to surrender. Had they been able to kick back a bit longer, they would have enjoyed some of what Key West has to offer after closing time.

To educate is to give man the keys to the world, which are independence and love, and to give him strength to journey on his own, light of step, a spontaneous and free being. — José Martí, hero of Cuban independence, journalist, poet

5

Note: not José Martí

Note: Some creative license was taken with this story, but the Cuban military landing part is true.

Late-Night Things to Do

1 PIZZA: Mr. Z's is open until 4 a.m. and stumbling distance from anywhere on Duval. They are loved for their New York slices and authentic cheesesteaks, plus they deliver. Hey, you, there in Philly reading this. We can hear you mumbling about how there can never be a cheesesteak worth eating outside of your 50-mile radius. Don't judge before you bite. Mr. Z's has impressed many a cheesesteak snob — uh, connoisseur, especially at 3 in the morning. 501 Southard, Key West. 305-296-4445. mrzskeywest.com.

2 PEOPLE-WATCHING: The 24-hour Winn-Dixie supermarket is where it's at for people-watching and late-night grocery shopping. Winn-Dixie also has the added benefit of comprehensive after-hours emergency supplies, like Funyuns, ice cream, Band-Aids and Trojans. 2670 N. Roosevelt Boulevard, New Town, Key West, 305-294-3664.

3 OCEAN: Whether you're in the mood for romance, solace, nature, or an adventure with friends, the small Higgs Beach Pier might be one of the most under-appreciated late-night stops in the city. Take in the moonlight and sound of rolling waves and if you're lucky, catch a glimpse of bioluminescent sea critters. For a true adventure, sit on the end and sing "Show Me the Way to Go Home," like Richard Dreyfus and friends in *Jaws*, then go skinny-dipping. Don't jump, use the steps. The water is way too shallow for jumping. 1000 Atlantic Blvd.

5

Show me the way to go home,
I'm tired and I want to go to bed.

I had a little drink about an hour ago,
and it's gone right to my head.

WHEREVER I MAY ROAM,

on land or sea or foam,
you can always hear me singing this song,

SONG BY IRVING KING

Show me the way to go home.
SHOW ME THE WAY TO GO HOME.
Show me the way to go home.

P.S. Sharks are amazing creatures and not monsters.

BARS: Many bars are open until 4 a.m., especially downtown.

4 & 5 COFFEE: The Sunshine Grill and Sandy's Cafe, which are just a few feet apart, draw a crowd around the clock, but late nights bring maximum entertainment. At first glance, Sandy's looks a little grungy, since it's tucked into the corner of an aging laundromat and all. But that hasn't stopped it from gaining legendary status with Cuban and Mexican food until midnight. For hangover prevention measures, try a café con leche and a sausage-egg-and-cheese sandwich on Cuban bread. The Sunshine Grill is a cute, 50s diner with Keys' style, open 24 hours Thursday through Saturday. Nothing beats their American-South down-home cooking at 3 a.m. Try $5 biscuits and gravy, add a milkshake. Both are also late-night hangouts for hungry police officers, so practice your manners and plan your transportation responsibly. Sandy's: 1026 White, 305-295-0159, cash only! The Sunshine Grill, 1110 White, 305-294-8089, Sunday through Wednesday only open 7 a.m. to 9 p.m.

CLUBS: For the creatively challenged, there are strip clubs in town, including Bare Assets, The Red Garter and Living Dolls.

6 SUNRISE: If you're up late enough that you start to see a glow from the east, bicycle to the easternmost point of the island, where there happens to be a nice, wide sidewalk and scattered park benches from which to take in another of Key West's most least-seen attractions, the sunrise. Across from the airport, beach road, New Town.

FOOD: See the next page for a longer list of where to eat late night.

5

Note: Numbers by activity name correspond to map on page 82.

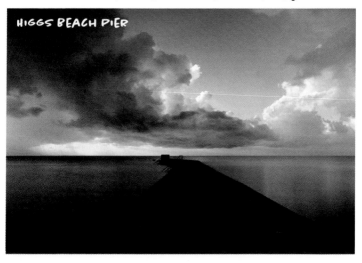

HIGGS BEACH PIER

24-Hour Supplies & Food

7 & 8 WALGREENS has two locations for shampoo, cheap flip-flops, beach towels, cigarettes, makeup, aspirin, and everything else you might need late-night. 527 Duval, Old Town, 305-292-2979; and 2805 N. Roosevelt, New Town, 305-292-9833.

9 CVS also has two locations, with all of the above, except no cigarettes. 520 Truman, 305-294-2576, 500 Duval, 305296-4251.

1 WINN-DIXIE supermarket for food, of course, and peaceful night shopping, 2670 N. Roosevelt, New Town, 305-294-3664.

11 DION'S QUICK MART Convenience store and gas station. The famous fried chicken isn't all night, but the rest of the store is. 1127 Truman, 305-294-7572.

12 CIRCLE K offers snacks, cigarettes and sodas in their Old Town convenience store, 1075 Duval, 305-294-8711.

13 DENNY'S restaurant serves the Grand Slam breakfast here, just like it does at all of its other 1,699 locations world wide, but when a hash brown craving hits, they are one of the only places in town where those can be found. 925 Duval, 305-294-5065.

14 IHOP restaurant serves its famous pancakes here like it does at all of its other 1,649 restaurants around the world, and they have hash browns too! 3416 North Roosevelt, New Town, 305-292-6319.

15 MCDONALDS... you guessed it, has Big Macs and hash browns here, too, like the rest of its 36,898 restaurants. You'll need a car to order late-night, as only the drive-through window is open. 3704 N. Roosevelt, New Town, 305-296-5800.

4 THE SUNSHINE GRILL diner diligently serves the community by curing hangovers and satisfying late-night munchie and dessert cravings, 1110 White, 305-294-8089. Open 24 hours Thursday through Saturday.

16 KEY WEST 24HR FITNESS: A cure for boredom, and love handles. Day, week, month, and yearly passes. 725 Caroline, 305-916-5500.

CONVENIENCE STORES & GAS OPEN 24, LOWER KEYS
Tom Thumb (no gas), 5690 Maloney, Stock Island, 305-296-5924
Chevron, 5220 Overseas Highway, Stock Island, 305-292-8600
Circle K, mile marker 11.9, Big Coppitt Key, 305-296-8811
Tom Thumb, mile marker 30.6, Big Pine Key, 305-872-9498

Food Served After 10 p.m.

Many restaurants in town are open until 10 p.m. and a decent amount until 11. But if you missed those dinner times, or are just perpetually hungry, there is still plenty of great food to be found into the wee hours. Times below are not guaranteed and vary according to how busy they are, either on a particular night or the time of year.

OLD TOWN
17 Caroline's Cafe: 310 Duval, 305-294-7511, open until 11:30
18 Amigos Tortilla Bar: 425 Greene, 305-292-2009, until midnight
19 Margaritaville: 500 Duval, 305-292-1435, until midnight
20 Hard Rock Cafe: 313 Duval, 305-293-0230, until midnight*
21 Mangoes Restaurant: 700 Duval, 305-294-8002, until midnight
22 Kojin Noodle Bar: 601 Duval, 305-296-2077, until midnight
23 Better Than Sex (dessert only): 926 Simonton, 305-296-8102, midnight
5 Sandy's Cafe: 1026 White, 205-295-0159, open until midnight
25 Jack Flats: 509 Duval, 305-294-7955, open until 2 a.m.
26 Wing Masters: 934 Truman, 305-293-0750, open until 2 a.m.
27 Lucy's: 320 Grinnell, 305-922-2616, Thurs.-Sat. 2 a.m., rest 12 a.m.
28 Clemente's Trolly Pizzaria: 629 Duval, 305-900-7035, 3 a.m.*
29 Angelina's Pizzeria: 208 Duval, 305-296-3600, open until 3:30 a.m.
1 Mr. Z's Pizza, 501 Southard: 305-296-4445, open until 4 a.m.*
30 Sandbar Sports Grill: 511 Greene, 305-916-5530, until 4 a.m.*
31 Gas Monkey: 217 Duval, 305-294-0103, Fri. & Sat. 4 a.m., rest 2 a.m.

FREE FOOD & FOOD CARTS
33 Key West Taco Dog: 208 Duval, Thurs. & Fri. 4 a.m., Sat. midnight
34 Green Parrot: free popcorn, usually 'til 2 or 3 a.m., 601 Whitehead
35 Hot Dog Cart: usually late-night near corner of Caroline & Duval
36 Chart Room: free popcorn, hot dogs and peanuts, 'til 2-ish, 1 Duval

NEW TOWN & STOCK ISLAND
24 Shanna Key Irish Pub: 1900 Flagler, 305-295-8880, until midnight
Hogfish Bar: 6810 Front, Stock Island, 305-293-404, until midnight
Mr Z's Pizza: 2798 North Roosevelt, 302-296-5306, until midnight*
Hurricane Hole: 5130 Overseas Hwy., Stock Island, 305-294-0200, 11ish
Kennedy Cafe: 924 Kennedy, 305-809-9000, until midnight

* Denotes delivery. There's also an independent delivery service in town that works with many restaurants, keywestfoodtogo.com. We have not used them, but have heard they are respectable.

5

6
Things to Do on Land

Hemingway House

IN THIS CHAPTER

Key West's most iconic attractions
Land attractions in Key West
Architecture
The green flash
Land attractions in the Lower Keys

Dear Daughter,

My wish list for visiting Key West (not necessarily in this order):

• Be the first one to show up naked at a clothes-optional bar.
• Go deep sea fishing without barfing.
• Tan my arms above the ends of my tee-shirt sleeves.
• Count the toes on Papa's cats.
• Understand Wallace Stevens's poem: *The Idea of Order at Key West*.
• Do my Christmas shopping at a gay porn shop.
• Take a long-distance swim to Fort Jefferson.
• Sail a hurricane on a Sunfish.
• Cruise the 90+ miles to Havana to listen to Cuban jazz.
• Sit in a deck chair on the beach with you, while drinking a gin and tonic, and watching the sun go down.   **Love, Dad**

That email came from my father, as he prepared for an upcoming visit. He's a world adventurer and a lover of humor. We gave it a good try. This was the end result, not necessarily in this order:

• Walked quickly through the clothes-optional bar, fully clothed.
• Went deep sea fishing, and barfed.
• Burnt our arms above the ends of our tee shirt sleeves.
• Counted to five toes, then got distracted by rum.
• Forgot to read Wallace Stevens.
• Also forgot the gay porn store.
• Missed the ferry to Fort Jefferson due to hangover, I mean weather.
• Saw some sailboats at the marina.
• Sat on the bench outside the Green Parrot bar, next to someone playing a ukulele.
• Boated out to a secluded sand bar and watched the sun go down while drinking tequila, with the authors of this book. A fine adventure.

Those are a few ideas for what to do in Key West and the Lower Keys, and here are some more.

The Big 10

Key West's Most Iconic Attractions

⸽ SUNSET CELEBRATION AT MALLORY SQUARE

Every evening a throng of street performers, artists, and revelers convenes on Mallory Square to celebrate the end of the day, or the start of the night, depending on your particular life view. The sunset celebration starts a couple of hours before the big event, and as the sun creeps toward the horizon, fire twirlers balance on unicycles, cats perform masterful tricks, and everyone enjoys local snacks and art. If the air is right, you might even see the elusive "green flash." Note: Parking is a pain, so best to walk, bike or if you must drive, pay for a spot in the Margaritaville Resort's parking garage (formerly the Westin). 400 Wall Street, Key West.

DUVAL STREET

Duval Street is the core of Key West. By day it teems with shoppers and cruise ship passengers, exploring art galleries, eating ice cream and buying T-shirts emblazoned with catchy drinking slogans. By night it transforms into a multi-block party where people of all walks of life are welcome to let their hair down. Watching the mix of people on Duval at night, realizing Key West's true "come as you are" spirit, gives one real hope for humanity, for peace, for tolerance, and for a place where   everyone can get   along.

Numbers by attraction name correspond to map on page 90.

6

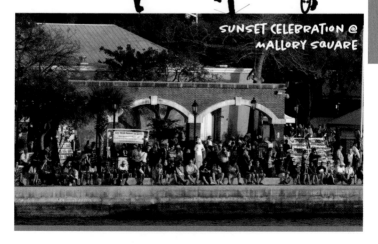

SUNSET CELEBRATION @ MALLORY SQUARE

2 SOUTHERNMOST POINT

It's hard to miss the Southernmost Point in the continental United States. Just look for a long line of tourists waiting to take their picture in front of a red and black cement obelisk. If you possess patience and spare time it can be an interesting place to socialize, but otherwise try going early morning, near sunset or at night, and you're likely to have the place to yourself. Don't forget to look past the cement toward the ocean, toward Cuba, which is only 90-ish miles away and closer than Miami. Trivia: The actual southernmost point on the island is closed to the public as it lies within the Key West Naval Air Station. But this one is pretty close. Corner of South and Whitehead Streets, Key West.

3 MILE MARKER 0

Near the other end of Whitehead Street is another popular photo op in the form of a small green-and-white sign that reads "Mile 0." It marks the end of the longest north-south road in the U.S., the termination of U.S. Route 1. The 2,369-mile ribbon of pavement starts near the Canadian border, links Boston, New York City, Baltimore, Raleigh and Miami, before it ends just one block past the Green Parrot Bar. Oddly enough, the road doesn't actually stop here,

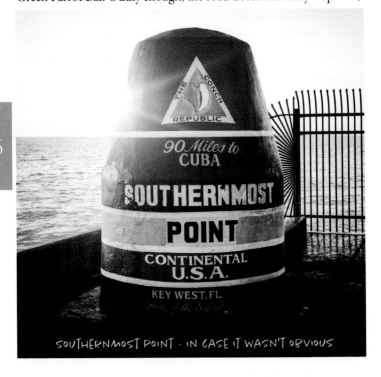

SOUTHERNMOST POINT - IN CASE IT WASN'T OBVIOUS

but continues for another few blocks. We have yet to get a straight answer as to why. But more importantly, with all ends come new beginnings. Just across the street from the end of the road is the start of U.S. 1, with another 2,369 miles of possibilities all the way to Fort Kent, Maine. We've never met our northern terminus friends, but hear they are excellent dogsled racers and Muskie fishers. Anyone reading this from Fort Kent want to house-swap for a few weeks, preferably in the summer? We've always wanted to see Maine. Corner of Fleming and Whitehead Streets, Key West.

4 MEL FISHER MARITIME HERITAGE MUSEUM

Gold doubloons, 80-pound silver bars and bronze cannons

Even our family can't resist the Mile 0 photo opp.

decorate the Fisher Museum, and tell tales of the sordid history of Spanish domination, piracy, the Middle Passage (a.k.a. slave trade), and one man's modern-day quest to bring up the sunken loot. Much of the treasure in the museum is from the Spanish galleons Nuestra Señora de Atocha and Santa Margarita, which sank 40 miles west of Key West during a hurricane in 1622. In 1985, after 16 years of searching, Mel Fisher found the wrecks, which have produced close to half a billion dollars in treasure so far. Mel was proclaimed the King of the Conch Republic in perpetuity, and to this day treasure hunters maintain a boisterous presence in the Keys. When you see someone walking down the street wearing a large silver coin, it's

6

very possible they not only found that one underwater, but some of the artifacts you just saw in the museum. For more on Keys treasure hunters, see the history section of this book. 200 Greene Street, melfisher.org, 305-294-2633.

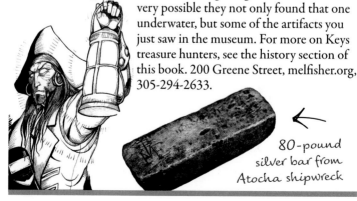

80-pound silver bar from Atocha shipwreck

5 ERNEST HEMINGWAY HOME & MUSEUM

small

Books, letters, writing desks, six-toed cats and the town's first swimming pool are just a few of the Papa relics to be found in the Hemingway Home. The larger-than-life personality spent much time in Key West, writing, drinking, fishing and leaving behind his legacy, as well as one of Key West's most-beloved and visited pieces of history. For more on Hemingway, see the next chapter. 907 Whitehead St., hemingwayhome.com, 305-294-2755.

6 THE CONCH TRAIN

For a crash-course in Key West history and attractions, relax with a tour on a colorful string of trolley cars, complete with a personable guide. For the last 50-plus years, 15 million souls have hopped aboard for the 90-minute tour on the self-proclaimed World Famous Conch Train. The Old Town Trolley also offers similar opportunities with a San Francisco look and more chances to get on and off for exploration. 303 Front Street, conchtourtrain.com, 888-916-8687. 1 Whitehead street, trolleytours.com/key-west, 305-296-6688.

7 HISTORIC SEAPORT

Stroll the wooden wharfs, eat some oysters and marvel at the modern super yachts and historic tall ships in this collection of picturesque waterfront marinas. As sport-fishing charters return, pelicans and giant tarpon gather for their share of the day's spoils. Adventurers hop aboard scuba and water-sports boats to explore the reef. Steel drums and island music waft from the many open-air seafood restaurants, bars and shops. For an apex experience, jump aboard one of the several historic, tall sailing ships for a sunset cruise. Between Greene, Caroline and Grinnell Streets, keywestseaport.com.

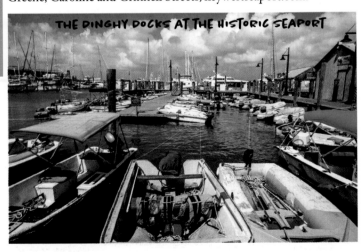

THE DINGHY DOCKS AT THE HISTORIC SEAPORT

CONCH TRAIN

8 HARRY S. TRUMAN LITTLE WHITE HOUSE

This historic house-turned-museum was frequented by Harry Truman and visited by other notable folks, including Thomas Edison, Dwight D. Eisenhower, John F. Kennedy, Jimmy Carter, and Bill Clinton. Truman's "The Buck Stops Here" sign is one of a handful of artifacts to be seen on a tour. All sorts of travel guides and websites list this as one of the town's most popular attractions, so we are listing it in the top 10. The oddity of it, however, is that we've never met anyone who has actually gone here and mentioned it. Maybe it's because Truman dropped two atomic bombs then ignited the arms race with Russia. More probably it's because politics aren't as relaxing as the ocean. 111 Front St., trumanlittlewhitehouse.com, 305-294-9911.

9 SMATHERS BEACH

Soft sand, shallow water and scantily clad college coeds draw spring break crowds to Key West's largest beach. Concessionaires offer up every water sport imaginable, from paddleboards to kayaks, jet skies to parasailing. During season, a steady stream of walkers, bicyclists and skaters roll by on the sidewalk making the people-watching unparalleled. The picturesque blue-green-water backdrop entices brides and grooms to say their vows. Drunken immaturity has probably kicked off a few divorces here, too. Did we say "drunken?" That's funny, because officially no alcohol is allowed on the beach. Or dogs. Note: For better snorkeling, head to Ft. Zachary Taylor or Higgs Beaches. S. Roosevelt Blvd., 305-809-3700.

6

SMATHERS BEACH

Land Attractions – Key West

Note: more attractions are in chapters 7 & 11.

10 FORT ZACHARY TAYLOR STATE PARK

In line with Key West's historically disobedient spirit, the town was one of only three Union strongholds in Florida during the Civil War. Fort Zach never saw battle, but its fortress walls, grassy courtyard and cannons poised for defense remain a trigger for the imagination. Still buried below the fort is one of the largest collections of Civil War cannons in the country. Save a couple of hours for exploring and relaxing at the park's beach. Fort Zach contains the best land-accessed snorkeling in Key West (see chapter 8). 601 Howard England Way, take Southard to the western end, bear left at the Coast Guard Cutter, then follow signs for the park. Small admission fee, dogs not allowed on beach. fortzacharytaylor.com, floridastateparks.org/park/Fort-Taylor, 305-295-0037, 305-292-6713.

11 HIGGS BEACH PARK

The sand on this locals' beach is some of the best in town, but once you've lazed around there is a lot to explore, including two piers, two memorials, a botanical garden, historic fort, playground, volleyball, bocci ball, tennis courts, dog park, bike path, yoga hut, and a good restaurant. A protected bay that gets progressively deeper makes swimming and snorkeling here especially safe for beginners and kids. Despite the laundry list of activities, the county-owned park remains a low-key hangout and a great place to people-watch for every kind of lively, curious and eccentric Keys character. 1100 Atlantic Boulevard.

HIGGS (ABOVE)

FORT ZACHARY TAYLOR

6

12 SCHOONER WESTERN UNION

Key West is home to a dozen or so tall sailing ships. The Western Union is the most celebrated. The 130-foot vessel is the official flagship of Key West and the state of Florida. Built in 1939, it was the last tall ship constructed in town and is one of the oldest working wooden schooners in the country. It was originally tasked with defending our waters from German U-boats. Afterward, it maintained communication cables between Key West, Cuba and the Caribbean. It lent humanitarian aid during the Mariel Boatlift and training for troubled youth, before starting an easier life as a sunset cruise charter. Today lack of funding has left it in a state of ultra deterioration. With luck, by the time you read this it will be majestically sailing once again, but who knows. Possibly at 202 William Street, docked in a slip.

START LOOKING FOR THE GREEN FLASH WHEN THE SUN IS A LITTLE LOWER THAN THIS, BUT BEFORE IT SETS.

The Green Flash

The Green Flash is a phenomenon that a few lucky people witness. Right as the sun dips below the horizon, a small burst of brilliant green emanates from it. Some call it a well-hyped legend, but it actually does exist and is proven through physics. There are a few tricks to seeing one. First, it must be a very clear evening with little haze or cloud cover close to the horizon. Second, don't stare at it until the last two seconds. Have a friend tell you when the tip of the sun is just about to disappear, then quickly look. Voila! Jules Vern immortalized it in his 1882 novel *Le Rayon Vert* (The Green Ray).

6

> "A green, which no artist could ever obtain on his palette, a green of which neither the varied tints of vegetation nor the shades of the most limpid sea could ever produce the like! If there is a green in Paradise, it cannot be but of this shade, which most surely is the true green of Hope."

The green flash is pretty cool, but there are many other things worth having eyesight for, so please use common sense and don't burn out your eyes looking at the sun.

13 SOUTH BEACH

This tiny, friendly beach sits tucked behind the Southernmost Hotel at the end of Duval. It draws a mixed crowd of lazy sunbathers and vivacious socializers. The blend of international visitors is obvious thanks to an influx of Speedos and occasional topless females (that's allowed here). Non-hotel guests are welcome to rent umbrellas and chairs, which gains access to the pool area and the attendants, who are quite attentive, delivering drinks and snacks. This is one of only two beaches in town where drinking is legal, as long as it's purchased on the beach or from the adjacent Southernmost Beach Cafe.

14 WEST MARTELLO TOWER & GARDENS

Inside this unassuming yet charming red-brick building hides one of Key West's most enticing secrets — two acres of exotic tropical gardens straight from a fairly tale. Paths wind under giant strangler fig trees, through butterfly gardens, and past orchid pavilions, absurdly spiky trees from the Amazon, giant cacti from Africa, and rare native flora. Iguanas spy from hidden perches while roosters proudly declare their prowess. Gazebos and benches allure picnickers and romantics. It's free to visit, thanks to the diligent volunteers and green thumbs of the Key West Garden Club, who first began converting the old Civil War fort ruins into a tropical paradise in the '50s. 1100 Atlantic Blvd. at Higgs Beach, keywestgardenclub.com, 305-294-3210.

15 BUTTERFLY CONSERVATORY

Hundreds of butterflies mingle amongst tropical birds and flowering plants. Learn about the lives of these delicate flying creatures, and see caterpillars in action. 1316 Duval Street, (305) 296-2988, keywestbutterfly.com.

Strangler fig at West Martello. Look closely to see the 8-foot-high walkthrough archway, for perspective on the true size of this arboreous fellow.

6

16 AFRICAN CEMETERY AT HIGGS BEACH

Symbols of endurance, interconnectedness, hope, faith, and peace now grace the earth over one of Key West's greatest tragedies. In 1860 survivors from three illegal slave ships were brought to Key West. Despite the community's efforts to save them, it was just too late for many of the nearly 1,500 prisoners who soon died from malnutrition and disease as a result of their voyage. One hundred and thirty years later, historian Gail Swanson found their stories in dusty archives. By 2002, with the help of ground-penetrating radar, some of their graves were located on Higgs Beach. Today the touching and inspirational memorial offers more than just homage to the 12 million Africans taken as prisoners during the Middle Passage — but as a positive space for introspection, learning and celebration of the potential goodness of humanity. Corner of White Street and Atlantic Boulevard, africanburialgroundathiggsbeach.org.

"One day we'll all find out that all of our songs was just little notes in a great big song!" — Woody Guthrie

17 KEY WEST AIDS MEMORIAL

As the sunset illuminates the ocean, palms sway in a gentle breeze and laughing seagulls glide by, it's impossible to imagine the weight of sorrow represented in the more than 1,000 names etched into the granite AIDS Memorial. They are the friends, family and neighbors of this little town, which was hit especially hard by the disease. But the monument also stands as a symbol of Key West's philosophy "One Human Family" — as the number of people stricken with AIDS grew through the '80s and '90s, the community was not only overwhelmingly supportive of their own, but also embraced countless others who came to Key West seeking refuge, acceptance and love. The tradition continues every December 1, when many join in a candlelight march and reading of the names. The memorial is at the corner of White Street and Atlantic Boulevard, keywestaids.org.

6

Someone flies a kite by the African Cemetery.

Architecture

The personalities of the diverse settlers of Key West live on through the architecture in Old Town. With almost 3,000 wooden structures dating from around 1886 to 1912, it is among the largest historic districts in the country. Bahamian shipwreck salvors mingled with New England sea captains, Cuban cigar makers, and Haitian carpenters. Each added their particular aesthetic, giving the town an architectural mix from elegant Victorian mansions to quaint shotgun houses and cottages, bedecked in tropical gardens, gingerbread lattice, and white picket fences. Today, some spend years studying the architecture and history-laden buildings, others just enjoy the pretty houses while walking and biking. Either way, here are a few of note.

18 CURRY MANSION INN

William Curry sailed from the Bahamas to Key West, young and broke in 1837. Over the next 40 years he built an empire, as well as his mansion. When Florida's first self-made millionaire wasn't salvaging or building ships, he imported goods, including the new product condensed milk, which soon made Key West history with the creation of Key lime pie. Today the mansion is a B&B, open to daily tours. 511 Caroline Street, currymansion.com, 305-294-5349.

19 THE OLDEST HOUSE

Usually people find this gem while looking for a place to hide from the rain or sun. However, this unassuming house on Duval leaves a big impression with most, with its 1829-era antiques, family portraits, Key West stories, and enthusiastic staff. Out back are benches in gardens, perfect for peaceful reflection. Better yet, the whole experience is free. 322 Duval Street, oirf.org, 305-294-9501.

6

PELICAN PATH

If you love architecture and history—really, really love it—you still probably won't have the time or stamina to complete this self-guided walking tour of 51 historic Key West buildings and their stories, which were diligently and thoughtfully put together by the Old Island Restoration Foundation. The good news is, there's no penalty for visiting only a few. Download the printable map here: oirf.org/images/pelicantour.pdf. Use your phone to hear more detailed narration of each site by calling 305-507-0300.

20 AUDUBON HOUSE & TROPICAL GARDENS

You can buy prints here that artist John Audubon made during his time in the Keys (1832), though John never visited this house. Instead, the 1840s mansion was home to wrecker Capt. John Geiger. The gardens pay tribute to its namesake, while the furnishings give a glimpse into the life of the upper class in 19th Century Key West. 205 Whitehead Street, audubonhouse.com, 305-294-2116.

21 BAHAMA VILLAGE

Immigrants from the Bahamas began settling this neighborhood in the 1800s, while trying their fortunes at fishing, sponging, turtling and wrecking. Sadly but not surprisingly, the community was historically marginalized for generations, but today is appreciated once again for its vibrant heritage, art, architecture, tropical gardens and Caribbean foods. The apex of Bahamian spirit explodes onto the streets each October during the Bahama Village Goombay Festival, a family-oriented weekend of street processions, wild outfits, vending trucks and dancing to the music of Caribbean Junkanoos. Southwest edge of Key West, between Whitehead Street and the Truman Annex.

EXAMPLES OF KEY WEST ARCHITECTURE

6

More Stuff to do on Land

22 KEY WEST LIGHTHOUSE

The only American lighthouse within a city's limits, this one dates to 1847 (the one from 1826 was rebuilt after falling to a hurricane). It was operated mostly by female lighkeepers. Through tragedies and triumphs, hurricanes and wars, the stories that unfolded here piled up until its deactivation in 1969. Now you can climb the 88 steps to the top to take in a panoramic view of the island and sea, before exploring the museum and lighthouse keepers' quarters. 938 Whitehead Street, kwahs.org, 305-294-0012.

23 KEY WEST FIREHOUSE MUSEUM

Through hurricanes and the depression, from horse-drawn hose carriages to modern fire trucks, the firefighters of Station No. 3 passionately protected the people of Key West. The 1907 firehouse, one of the oldest in the state, was deactivated in 1998 but still holds treasures including a coal pit, antique pumpers and alarms. 1026 Grinnell Street, keywestfirehousemuseum.com, 305-849-0678.

24 EDWARD B. KNIGHT PIER (FORMERLY WHITE STREET PIER)

Bicycle or walk this long, spacious pier, affectionately dubbed the "unfinished highway to Havana." Fish for snook and snapper. Chill on a bench. When the sun starts to sink, there's no need to relocate to the official sunset celebration, since most of the year you'll get as good a view from here. With its south-facing position, it also is a great place to watch the sun come up. South end of White Street.

25 COAST GUARD CUTTER INGHAM

This maritime museum and National Historic Landmark honors veterans of WW II and Vietnam. Those who served aboard this ship committed considerable acts of bravery and heroism throughout both wars, as well as saved hundreds of refugees during the Cuban Mariel Boatlift. There are some steep stairs in this time capsule, so you'll have to make your own little sacrifice to see it. Truman Waterfront, end of Southard Street, uscgcingham.org, 305-292-5072.

FLORIDA KEYS OVERSEAS HERITAGE TRAIL

Seventy-six miles of paved bicycle and walking paths run up and down the Keys, through mangrove and salt flats, past nesting ospreys, ocean vistas and families fishing from historic bridges. The path is especially fun to explore during cooler winter months, or at night on a longboard. Eventually the trail will run all 106 miles from Key Largo to Key West.

CURBSIDE SHOPPING

When people no longer have need for a possession, they'll often move it to the curb, where someone will be thrilled to find it. It's a good community system, and an environmentally friendly one. We like to believe this works with the fortuitous timing of the Keys. One year we invited our families down for Thanksgiving. We only had a few forks and knives, and weren't sure how to utensil up the crowd. The next day we found three boxes of fancy silverware. Thank you, people in Key Haven who curbed it, whoever you are.

26 KEY WEST BOTANICAL GARDEN

Grab a tour or self-walk through the woods to see an exotic array of trees, palms, flowers, butterflies and tropical species that can only live in a frost-free environment. Closed-toe shoes recommended. ADA. 5210 College Road, Stock Island, kwbgs.org, 305-296-1504.

27 KEY WEST CEMETERY

It may seem in poor taste to chuckle at a headstone, but at least a few of the 100,000 people buried here intended to have the last laugh. Here are a few of the classics, as interpreted by some dancing farm animals and a hobo:

"Devout fan of singer Julio Iglesias."

"Born in Nassau 1783. Died at Key West 1891, aged 108 years... A good citizen for 65 years."

"The best flan maker."

"I told you I was sick."

"If you are reading this, you need a new hobby."

6

The cemetery also has a somber side, of course, with monuments to those aboard the U.S.S. Maine, which blew up in Havana Harbor, and those who fought in the 1868 Cuban Revolution. Like Key West itself, the plots are a proper intermingling of working class and barons, from all walks of life and religious beliefs. A few lucky Yorkies and a pet deer also made the cut. A self-guided tour points out notable graves, including Florida's first millionaire, politicians, infamous criminals, and of course Sloppy Joe Russell, the inventor of drunks... or at least of Key West's most famous drinking establishment. 701 Pauline Street, friendsofthekeywestcemetery.com.

28 SIMONTON BEACH

It's not extravagant, but Simonton is the closest public beach to the busy end of Duval Street. The sand is soft and the water deep enough for swimming. There are restrooms and a seafood-taco bar that also often puts lounge chairs on the sand. Dogs are welcome and drinking is allowed if purchased at the bar. 0 Simonton Street.

29 ECO-DISCOVERY CENTER

This natural history museum teaches kids of all ages about the native plants, animals and ecosystems of the Keys through exhibits and its 2,500-gallon reef tank. It is also a nice oasis from the hubbub of downtown, especially since it's free and air conditioned. 35 E. Quay Road, floridakeys.noaa.gov/eco_discovery.html, 305-809-4750.

30 KEY WEST WILDLIFE CENTER

You might see folks from this rescue around town, netting birds stuck inside stores, freeing pelicans from fishing line, and helping other creatures in mortal danger. Or, you can pay them a visit and walk their indigenous nature trail, plus see the aviary of gypsy chickens who were picked up on nuisance violations and are awaiting deportation and adoption. Free, but donations are appreciated. 1801 White Street, keywestwildlifecenter.org, 305-292-1008 info and rescue hotline.

DRY TORTUGAS: Only a ferry, seaplane or private boat will land you at this remote national park. These pristine islands 70 miles west of Key West are an adventure paradise, with natural beaches, two lighthouses, snorkeling and bird watching. There's also the largest masonry structure in the Americas, Civil War-era Fort Jefferson, built of more than 16 million bricks. If you have a day, this is one of the greatest journeys in the Keys. There's also a primitive campground for extended stays. nps.gov/drto, drytortugas.com, 305-242-7700, 800-634-0939.

6

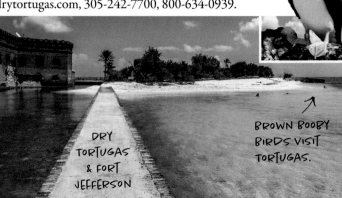

DRY TORTUGAS & FORT JEFFERSON

BROWN BOOBY BIRDS VISIT TORTUGAS.

3 | KEY WEST TURTLE MUSEUM

Tiny but with a huge heart, this museum on the historic turtle kraals docks is dedicated to our gentle, water-living friends. Exhibits tell the story of the once-major Keys turtle industry, the turtles' demise, and how many worked passionately to bring them back from the brink. Free. 200 Margaret Street, keywestturtlemuseum.org.

AIR TOURS

The Keys are exceptionally beautiful from above. Fly over Key West, past lighthouses, and watch turtles, dolphins and other ocean wildlife, Key West Seaplanes, 305-294-4014, keywestseaplanes.com. Air Adventures helicopter tours, 844-246-3594, fly-keywest.com.

Land Attractions - Lower Keys

BAHIA HONDA STATE PARK

Accented by the dramatic ruins of one of Henry Flagler's Overseas Railroad bridges, the beaches of Bahia Honda are indisputably among the most scenic in the Keys. What does draw some contention is how to pronounce the name. Some say it Ba-hee-ah. Others say Bay-ah, including the voices on the recorded exhibits in the park. Whichever you choose, you probably will not face ridicule from the sea-grape-lined paths, the white beaches, shallow blue-green expanses of water, and fishing pelicans. Bahia Honda contains a hearty infrastructure as well, with kayak rentals, food concessions, a marina, boat ramp, nature center, and campgrounds. They also offer free beach wheelchairs. Recently the first known leatherback sea turtle nest in the Keys was found here. Dogs not allowed on beach. MM 36.8, floridastateparks.org/park/Bahia-Honda, 305-872-2353.

BAHIA HONDA

6

NATIONAL KEY DEER REFUGE & VISITOR CENTER:

One of the Key's most iconic endangered species, the darling Key deer live primarily on the islands of Big Pine and No Name, where they roam throughout their namesake National Wildlife Refuge, foraging on mangroves and other plants. They are also often seen in neighborhoods. The best place to start on a Key deer voyage is at the Visitor Center, where an enthusiastic staff will point you toward the day's sighting hotspots. When you see one, don't feed it. It encourages them to hangout in the street near traffic. Plus, human food is not only unhealthy for the deer, but it will bring a host of angry words and gestures from locals. For more on Key deer, see "nature" chapter 15. See page 195 for the Blue Hole. Leashed dogs allowed on trails. As of this printing, the center is at 179 Key Deer Blvd., but by the time you read this it may be at MM 30.6, also on Big Pine Key, 305-872-0774.

PERKY BAT TOWER: A mile down an unmarked dirt road, a wooden tower stands alone. There's no plaque to commemorate Richter Clyde Perky, but it was here in 1929 that the ambitious developer tried to solve the mosquito infestation in the Keys. To put the problem into perspective, around that time an entomologist had caught 365,696 in a single trap one night. Bats can eat 1,000 an hour, so Perky reasoned that if bats had a place to live nearby, they might make life much more tolerable at his fishing resort. He bought construction plans from Texan bat researcher Dr. Charles Campbell and with $10,000 he built a bat lodge equipped with "all the conveniences any little bat heart could possibly desire" including a louvered bat entrance, a central guano removal chute and honeycombed cypress walls for roosting. After spreading around

Campbell's patented pheromone-enhanced guano to entice them into their new digs, Perky released hundreds of bats. But they all just flew away. Out of 14 bat towers constructed around the world using Campbell's plans, Perky's bat tower is one of only three remaining. If you have no interest in history, you might still like watching the ospreys who have made the top of the tower home. Turn gulfside at Sugarloaf Airport, mile marker 17, back about a mile.

The human race has one really effective weapon, and that is laughter.
—Mark Twain

GRIMAL GROVE: A revitalized colony of rare tropical fruit trees and other plants, Grimal Grove is not just an edible tourist stop, but also serves as a community arts and education center. Tour, buy fruit trees, honey, and other sweet delights. If you're lucky, you might be there during one of their events, like the arts and chocolate festival or the tropical fruit fiesta. 30770 Overseas Highway, Big Pine Key, growinghopeinitiative.org, 305-923-6663.

NO NAME BRIDGE: Watch Key deer, manatees and other wildlife, swim, fish, snorkel, bike, Rollerblade and enjoy the social scene at this locals hangout. Pontoon and bicycle rentals plus the best kayak eco-tours on-site, too. Watson Boulevard at Bogie Drive, Big Pine Key.

JUMPING BRIDGE: Here's a local hideout. We know you'll act responsibly here because you wouldn't want us to get in trouble for sharing a secret. If you dare, jump off the old bridge into the canal below. The jump is maybe 15 to 20 feet down into water that's about 15 to 20 feet deep. The currents can be strong, so pay attention and swim to shore in a timely manner. Even if you don't want to jump, there are usually friendly locals and lots of nice shoreline for a picnic. Wear sandals or water shoes, though, because too often some dim-witted muttonheads decide to decorate with smashed beer bottles. It's also a nice place to snorkel or just lounge in the water. Turn oceanside at mile marker 17 on Lower Sugarloaf Key. Follow it until the big 90-degree bend to the right. The path is on your left, down a road closed to motorized traffic. It's a few-minute walk from there to the bridge. This is a public area, and you are allowed to be here, but for some reason the county put up no-parking signs for a hundred yards around the path, and once in a while they do enforce that with excessively expensive parking tickets. So just park beyond those signs.

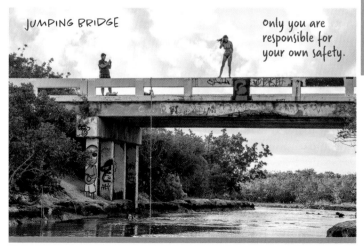

JUMPING BRIDGE

Only you are responsible for your own safety.

6

SKYDIVE KEY WEST

From two miles in the air, the beauty and intricacy of the islands, channels, reefs and waters that make up the Keys take on a whole new meaning — that is if you can keep your eyes open while plummeting at 120 m.p.h. (193 km) First-timers are welcome on tandem jumps, and this operation has a stellar safety record. 5 Bat Tower Road, Sugarloaf Key, mile marker 17 gulfside, skydivekeywest.com, 305-396-8806.

BOCA CHICA BEACH

This isolated beach has no food or bathrooms. It observes no leash laws or clothing obligations. In fact, the beach is a mere modest strip of sand, sometimes clogged with seaweed and rocks. But if you like exploration more than amenities, and are not offended by naked people and free-running dogs, here lies your adventure. Follow the beach trail as it winds past an evolving artistic "castle" made of driftwood and limestone. Soon after, the hike gets more challenging, as you traverse woods and wade through flooded channels to abandoned Cuban refugee boats. Note: Please respect the fragile freedom of this beach, visit under your own responsibility, and don't come if you are easily offended, unable to respect the live-and-let-live spirit that built the Keys, or want to blame others if you get lost or drown. To get here, turn onto Boca Chica Road at mile marker 11. Follow the road to the cement barriers at the end. Walk about a half mile down broken pavement behind the Naval air runways before seeing the beach.

VETERAN'S MEMORIAL PARK

With a picturesque mini-tiki picnic area, small beach and sandbar, the Veterans Memorial Park makes for a perfect pause when driving up or down the Keys. Parking is right at the beach for quick access to the sand and water. A Cuban-refugee boat and plaque tell a story of a turbulent-yet-hopeful history. Sometimes locals sell fresh coconuts in the parking lot, adding to the refreshment of the stop. There are restrooms. Mile marker 40, on the oceanside.

PROBABLY NOT WHAT HUNTER S. THOMPSON MEANT BY, "BUY THE TICKET, TAKE THE RIDE," BUT THEN AGAIN, HE DID HANG OUT ON SUGARLOAF KEY. SEE PAGE 118.

7

Arts, Literature & Events

IN THIS CHAPTER

Literary attractions & history
Art museums
Film & theater
Live music
Art galleries
Events & Fantasy Fest
Movies filmed in the Keys
Keys characters

Key West's legacy of
Disorderly Writers

In the 30s, a handful of famous writers frequented Key West, and often they would hang out at the grand old hotel Casa Marina. One fateful night Ernest Hemingway and poet Wallace Stevens both ended up at the lobby bar. They knew of each other's work, but neither had the inclination to strike up a conversation. Hemingway saw Stevens' work as sissy, pacifist poetry. Stevens, a lover of philosophy, was appalled by Hemingway's ever-swelling ego and fondness for slaughtering animals. After some time and booze, however, it became too difficult for the pair to ignore each other, so they started lobbing the occasional insult across the bar. As their rum intake escalated, so did the banter. Hemingway compared

Stevens' creativity to that of a melancholy jellyfish. Stevens told Hemingway that his writing sounded like an imitation of Ernest Hemingway. The two could stay civil no longer. Hemingway took a swing at Stevens, and they ended up rolling on the ground, knocking over several bar stools and a vintage bottle of rum. Stevens, who had a free hand near Hemingway's crotch shouted, "I could begin to fight dirty!" Hemingway, who had the same advantage, shouted, "I could too! But look, we both like

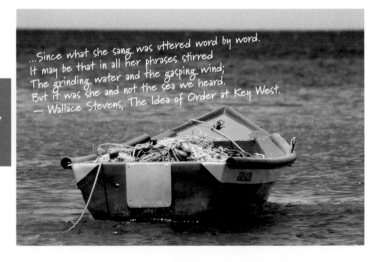

...Since what she sang was uttered word by word.
It may be that in all her phrases stirred
The grinding water and the gasping wind;
But it was she and not the sea we heard.
— Wallace Stevens, The Idea of Order at Key West.

7

sex, most likely me more than you. So let's stop this nonsense." They stopped and got up, and then Hemingway hit Stevens over the head with a chair, sending him to the hospital. After he got out, Stevens still wrote poetry, but no one could understand it. Or so goes the story, as imagined and once told by a modern-day appreciator of both authors' works. Strangely enough, we could not find much supporting evidence to prove this specific tale. But it is commonly accepted that, during their mutual time together in 1930s Key West, the two authors did exchange physical blows now and again, though were able to remain affable friends.

There is solid evidence about a drunken altercation between Wallace Stevens and fellow poet Robert Frost at the Casa Marina in 1935. It didn't come to blows, but it did create a lifelong riff between the two. Frost's biographer, Lawrance Thompson, summed up their argument:

"The trouble with you, Robert, is that you're too academic."
"The trouble with you, Wallace, is that you're too executive."
"The trouble with you, Robert, is that you write about—subjects."
"The trouble with you, Wallace, is that you write about—bric-a-brac."

The trouble with both was that not only did they dislike each other's creative styles, they forevermore made fun of each other in front of audiences and created problems for the hosts of functions at which they were both guests.

But the old man always thought of her as feminine and as something that gave or withheld great favours, and if she did wild or wicked things it was because she could not help them. The moon affects her as it does a woman, he thought.
— Ernest Hemingway, The Old Man and the Sea.

Half the world is composed of people who have something to say and can't, and the other half who have nothing to say and keep on saying it.
— Robert Frost

STEVENS   HEMINGWAY   FROST

7

BIO PHOTOS: FAIR USE, EN.WIKIPEDIA.ORG

Literary Attractions

Numbers by attraction correspond to map on page 90.

32 **HEMINGWAY HOUSE** was home to Ernest, and is now the casa for 50 or so six-toed cats, the first in-ground swimming pool in Key West, and the author's "last penny." For those who like Papa's work or mutant felines, this should be a pilgrimage destination. For dog people and illiterates, you will probably be better off spending your entrance fee on a bottle of the Hemingway-inspired Papa's Pilar rum. hemingwayhome.com, 907 Whitehead Street, 305-294-1136. Other Hemingway haunts include the Casa Antigua, where he and Pauline first stayed and fell in love with Key West, 314 Simonton; and 729 Thomas, where he relocated his home boxing ring to make room for the pool. That address now belongs to Blue Heaven Restaurant.

33 The popular **SLOPPY JOE'S BAR** hosts the annual Hemingway look-alike contest. He often planted his cheeks at Sloppy Joe's, both at its current location as well its former address across the street at the present-day **CAPT. TONY'S BAR.** Rumor has it he built his house by the lighthouse so no matter how drunk he got, he just had to focus on walking toward the light. It's not recommended to try that today, as buildings and trees now block the path. What is recommended is trying to impress a member of the opposite sex by throwing a quarter into the mouth of the plaster grouper (large fish) above the entrance to Captain Tony's, while people at the Mexican restaurant across the street make fun of your talents. 201 Duval and 428 Greene Street.

34 **ROBERT FROST** spent 16 winters in Key West at his cottage at

GROUPER ↘

410 Caroline Street, which is also home to one of the first water wells in town. The main house there was the home of Jessie Porter, whose exotic garden was a center of Key West society and a gathering place for writers. Later, the place became a museum, which closed in 2010. It was reborn as a cottage, inhabited by some free-spirited artists and musicians. But as Frost once put it, "Progress goes on visibly around us mounting from savagery to barbarianism to civilization to sophistication to decadence and so to destruction." Appropriately the cycle continues. The compound now houses a real estate office.

7

35 & 36 PLAYWRIGHT TENNESSEE WILLIAMS lived in Key West from the 1940s to '80s, and wrote notable works here. He had a house here too, but admirers can only walk by the front, as it is a private residence. In the '50s Williams and his love Frank Merlo offered their residence as a dressing room for Burt Lancaster and Anna Magiani during the filming of Williams' Academy Award-winning film *The Rose Tattoo*. To tour Williams' history here, walk courteously by the house at 1431 Duncan Street, visit an exhibit dedicated to him at 513 Truman Ave., 305-842-1666, and catch a play or movie at his namesake theater at the Florida Keys Community College, 5901 College Road, Stock Island, 305-296-1520. Another Williams destination is the St. Mary Star of the Sea Catholic Church on Truman, where he was baptized.

Hemingway vs. Williams
An unstoppable force meets a movable object

Though the potent Ernest Hemingway and the sensitive Tennessee Williams both shared contemporary acclaim, the two men met only once. It happened in 1961 in Havana, Cuba. Journalist George Plimpton arranged for the meeting at La Floridita restaurant. Williams was hesitant. After all, the 6-foot-tall Hemingway could be fierce, and his ultra machismo was surely an indicator of his homophobia. Conversely, there's no telling what Hemingway imagined of the 5-foot-6-inch emotionable playwright. But while their personalities could not be further apart, both did share a passion for weaving yarns about struggles with sexual identity and prowess.

Ultimately, it was a cordial affair. The two had much in common to discuss, including their love of Key West and their shared friends, who included a bullfighter and Hemingway's late wife, Pauline. The two also shared tips for keeping their overworked livers and kidneys running. Had it had more time, their acquaintance probably would not have blossomed into a beautiful friendship. but that was never to be tested. Hemingway killed himself just several months later. Williams was able to last another two decades, during which time he wrote dozens more screenplays, poems and books.

7

Literary Attractions

37 THE CHART ROOM: By the 1970s Key West was growing some pretty interesting characters. During that time residents and frequent visitors included Jimmy Buffett, Hunter S. Thompson, Tom Corcoran, Tom McGuane, Jim Croce, Jerry Jeff Walker, Tennessee Williams and Bob Marley, most of whom were friends but not all of whom were famous yet. All of them did enjoy drinking at the Chart Room Bar. It is there Buffett first set up with a little amp and mic in 1971 and began to write the soundtrack of the Keys.

38 JIMMY BUFFETT'S influence in Key West is most obvious with his **MARGARITAVILLE** store, bar and restaurant at 500 Duval, the original location of the now sprawling international franchise. But when he came to Key West in 1971, he was a struggling musician busking for drinks and change. He began performing at the Chart Room and in bars along Duval, writing songs inspired by local characters. He liked Key West and Key West liked him. One of his first apartments was 704 Waddell, which he loaned out to Hunter here and there. It is now a private residence and time-share complex, presumably with quieter tenants than it had 40-some years ago.

Ninety-two in the Shade writer **TOM MCGUANE** lived in several places around town. Some of his friends included Hunter and Buffett. Despite having no filmmaking experience, he directed the movie based on his acclaimed book, which filmed in Key West. The real-life drama that ensued was stranger than his fiction. The cliff notes, to the best of our research and knowledge: he struck up a romance with one of the female leads and married the other. His wife slept with one of the male stars, then married the other, Peter Fonda. Down the road some, Tom married Buffett's sister. Not sure who all lived happily every after, but the '70s must have been quite a time to be creative in Key West.

Free-spirited developer **DAVID WOLKOWSKY** started the Pier House and its bar, the Chart Room, where he entertained the artists, as well as prime ministers, Rockefellers and Vanderbilts. He then built a compound on Ballast Key, a 10-minute helicopter ride away, which became the true hideout for the gang.

SILVERSTEIN   BUFFETT   CAPOTE

7

39 TRUMAN CAPOTE stayed at the **PIER HOUSE** and Ballast Key, and also drank at the Chart Room. The writer and actor was once visiting his contemporary Tennessee Williams when a legend was made. There are numerous versions of the tale, but it basically goes something like this: They were in a crowded restaurant or bar, and a woman who might or might not have been drunk and who most likely didn't know either were gay, approached the table, pulled up her "little top," handed Capote an eyebrow pencil and asked him to sign her belly button. Williams egged him on. He signed. Her husband became angry. He was definitely drunk when he approached the table, handed Capote the eyebrow pencil, unzipped his fly and hauled out his dangle. By now the room was deathly silent. He said, "Since you're autographing everything, how'd you like to sign this?" Pause. Capote: "Well, I don't know if I can autograph it, but perhaps I can initial it." The room filled with laughter. The man returned to his table. History was made.

Children's author, cartoonist and songwriter **SHEL SILVERSTEIN** used to stay in a Greek Revival house and writing studio on William Street. His son was born in Key West, to Conch Train driver Sarah Spencer, who inspired his song "The Great Conch Train Robbery." **MANY OTHER WRITERS** have lived in and been inspired by the Keys, including Judy Blume, George Cooper, Elizabeth Bishop, Richard Wilbur, Ralph Ellison, J. James Merrill, Philip Caputo, Carl Hiaasen, and hundreds more we forgot to list.

40 CASA MARINA: If you read the intro to this chapter, then you already know to have a drink at the Casa Marina hotel bar. Besides the aforementioned characters who frequented the place, it is likely many of the other writers drawn to Key West did as well — though we don't know which, if any of them, got drunk and caused a scene at the bar. 1500 Reynolds Street, 305-296-3535.

THE CHART ROOM

7

HUNTER S. THOMPSON often stayed at the **SUGARLOAF LODGE** at mile marker 17. Today the hotel is quiet and serene, which was often not the case when their celebrity guest paid extended visits. It is here he was said to fornicate so loudly it would scare the other guests, and where he put a dead pig's head decorated in lipstick in the owner's toilet, then commemorated the affair with his short story *Tales of the Swine Family*. The lodge is a wonderful place to stay, or just stop for a drink at the tiki bar.

IF YOU'RE GOING TO BE CRAZY, YOU HAVE TO GET PAID FOR IT OR ELSE YOU'RE GOING TO BE LOCKED UP. - HUNTER S.

Hunter vs. Papa

Hunter S. Thompson never met Hemingway, though he claimed to have a great deal of respect for the author. He demonstrated that respect one day by stealing the elk antlers above Hemingway's front door. Hemingway didn't know they were stolen. He had already been dead three years, plus when he was alive he'd never heard of Hunter. Hunter was not yet famous. He hadn't even discovered the drug culture yet. He was just a 27-year-old reporter for the National Observer, on assignment to write about why Hemingway settled in Idaho after so much time in Spain, Cuba and Key West. For years the antlers hung in Hunter's Colorado garage. He was somewhat embarrassed about the whole ordeal and had talked about driving up with his wife to return them. Eventually, though, 41 years went by and sadly Hunter ended up shooting himself Hemingway style. After another 11 years, his widow Anita decided to finally make the journey, and in 2016 drove the antlers back to the Idaho estate. Reportedly, the Hemingway family was not angry, but rather happy and amused. The antlers didn't get to go back above the door, however, but instead got shipped to Hemingway's grandson in New York.

7

I WOULDN'T RECOMMEND SEX, DRUGS OR INSANITY FOR EVERYONE, BUT THEY'VE ALWAYS WORKED FOR ME. - H.S.T.

Art Museums

41 FORT EAST MARTELLO
Besides being home to Robert the Doll, one of Key West's most
famous paranormal stories, the Civil War-era Fort East Martello
houses one of the Keys' first art and history museums. Come here
to see the imaginative welded sculptures of Keys artist and character
Stanley Papio, along with early island life, industries, haunted history,
and Cuban migration. Of course, the actual fort itself is its own
wonder. Run by the Key West Art and & Historical Society. 3501 S.
Roosevelt, by the airport, kwahs.org, 305-296-3913.

42 KEY WEST MUSEUM OF ART & HISTORY AT THE CUSTOM HOUSE
Climb the steps of the historically preserved former U.S. Custom
House and follow the path once trod by wreckers, rum-runners,
politicians and most other citizens of the Southernmost town when
it was the richest and largest city in Florida. Then enter the modern
museum's local, national and international exhibits of art and history
housed in one of the finest examples of Richardsonian Romanesque
architecture in the country. 281 Front St., kwahs.org, 305-296-6616.

43 SAN CARLOS INSTITUTE (LA CASA CUBA)
Though it's right in the middle of the action on Duval Street,
even many locals don't know about this wondrous art museum,
library, theater, and school. Explore two floors of exhibits and learn
about Cuban history in Key West from its early independence to
today's refugees. Founded in 1871 by Cuban exiles, it has served
as a vital resource ever since. If you are around when there is a live
concert, it is not to miss. It is free, but donations are very appreciated
since it is only open when there are enough volunteers available to
staff it. 516 Duval Street, institutosancarlos.org, 305-294-3887.

7

Film & Theater

44 TROPIC CINEMA - FILM

The Tropic Cinema triggered a resurgence of art and culture in Key West when it opened in 1999. Today, a sultry statue of Marilyn Monroe welcomes moviegoers to this stylish retro venue, known for its mix of hip indies, mainstream features, and local art exhibits. 416 Eaton Street, 877-761-3456, tropiccinema.com.

45 KEY WEST THEATER - MUSIC, FILM, THEATER, COMEDY

The town's newest arts venue raised the bar for the live music scene in Key West, drawing national acts like Big Bad Voodoo Daddy, Robert Cray, and Jay Shimabukuro. Housed in the historic 1848 1st Baptist Church, the performing arts center also entertains with original plays and films. 512 Eaton Street, 305-985-0433, thekeywesttheater.com.

46 OUTDOOR CINEMA - FILM

There are three places to catch a flick under the stars. The Bayview Park Movie Series is free and family friendly, even for Fido. Movies are the first and third Friday of the month from October through May. The Marker and the Gates hotels both hold "dive-in" movie nights at their outdoor pools, with food and drink specials. kwoutdoormovies. com, gateshotelkeywest.com, themarkerkeywest.com.

47 LA TE DA - CABARET, MUSIC

From Cher to Bette Midler, Marilyn Monroe to Tina Turner, there's one place to find all of the stars under one roof — La Te Da's Cabaret. Of course, being a cabaret, all of these lovely, iconic ladies are brought to you by the impersonation and singing talents of a few gentlemen, such as Christopher Peterson and Randy Roberts. Also on site, the Piano Bar offers its own blend of live music and entertainment. 1125 Duval Street, 305-296-6706, lateda.com.

48 801 BOURBON BAR & AQUA KEY WEST - CABARETS

Follow the rainbow crosswalk to the 7-foot-tall, glitteringly clad "ladies" hanging around the entrance to 801. If they are able to entice you through the door, then the 801 Bourbon Bar cabaret inside will not disappoint. Prepare for a naughty, indecent, whimsical cacophony of drag performances, including Key West's Grande Dame of Drag, Sushi. 801 Duval Street, 305-294-4737, 801bourbon.com. Right nearby, the "ladies" of Aqua hit the dance floor under the direction of Inga, a perpetual darling of Key West. 711 Duval, 305-294-0555, aquakeywest.com.

49 WATERFRONT PLAYHOUSE - THEATER

Once the sun sets on Mallory Square, theater appreciators can mosey next door to the 150-seat home of the Key West Community Players. The Players formed in 1939 and played anywhere they could find space, including the Red Barn Theatre and the U.S.S. Gilmore Navy ship. With the help of Tennessee Williams, they moved into the historic ice warehouse, now known as the Waterfront Playhouse, where they've continued to entertain with a mix of hit plays, indie gems and theatrical world premieres. 310 Wall Street, 305-294-5015, waterfrontplayhouse.org.

50 RED BARN THEATRE - THEATER
The space is tiny, but the plays and musicals performed inside consistently receive expansive praise. Hidden behind the buzz and bustle of Duval lies this cultural oasis. Outside, enjoy a peaceful drink from their reasonably priced bar, before taking your seats in the renovated 1829 carriage house. Regional and local premieres. 319 Duval Street, 305-296-9911, redbarntheatre.com.

FRINGE THEATER
A spirited community uprising of talent created this troupe who perform prolifically around town at temporary venues, bringing "theater by the people for the people" that's light on its feet, genuine, and affordable. fringetheater.org, 305-731-0581.

TENNESSEE WILLIAMS THEATER - THEATER, FILM
Part of the Florida Keys Community College, this performing arts center offers a little bit of everything, from local plays to cabarets and even the classic Nutcracker. 5901 College Road, Stock Island, 305-295-7676, twstages.com.

MEDIA: There are many free publications to be found throughout the Lower Keys in news boxes, convenience stores and restaurants that list current arts and entertainment schedules, which include the Key West Weekly, the Keynoter, and Konk Life.

7

Live Music

OLD-TOWN BARS WITH LIVE MUSIC - ORIGINALS VS. COVERS
Music overflows onto the sidewalks throughout Old Town. Some bars
prefer bringing in acts who write and perform their own songs, while
others cater to crowds craving classic comfort music and island tunes.
Either way, the Key West's talent pool of musicians runs decently
deep. For consistently good original bands, both local and national,
try the Green Parrot, Smokin' Tuna Saloon, Schooner Wharf Bar, the
Little Room Jazz Club, and Blue Heaven. For some classic '80s, '90s
and '00s rock and pop plus island-life-themed hits, we suggest Willie
T's, Captain Tony's, and Margaritaville. If you want the rockin'-est
party and crowd combination, then head to the big four: Durty
Harry's, Irish Kevin's, Sloppy Joe's, and the Hog's Breath Saloon.

WHOANDWHEREINKEYWEST.COM runs an excellent site to easily
look up what live music is happening today. And tomorrow. And
tomorrow's tomorrow.

The Durtbags

If you love cover bands, Billy Idol, Green Day and AC/DC, you
must see the Durtbags. If you hate cover bands and all popular music,
you must see the Durtbags — the show can be some of the best
people-watching in Key West. The band has performed nearly every
night for a decade at the touristy bar Durty Harry's, part of the Rick's
complex. What makes them remarkable isn't their ability to replicate
more than 1,000 songs that have defined several generations,
but rather that every night they make a new batch of strangers
completely joyful. Most revelers wander in, get a drink from the bar,
then jump right in, busting out dance moves they haven't tried in a
decade or two, singing the familiar lyrics and truly just letting it all go
as they get caught up in the moment. From grandmothers to spring
breakers, the band
knows how to keep
everyone happy.
Just don't
ask them
to play
Freebird,
unless you
are willing to
pay the mandatory
$400 tip.

ART GALLERIES

There is no shortage of interesting and inspiring local art to be found, from peaceful island scenics to modern metal sculptures, pottery, and jewelry. There are around three dozen galleries on the island. See chapter 10 for shopping highlights, pick up a copy of the Key West Art Guide, keywestartguide.com, or try this good independent summary of them: keywesttravelguide.com/arts/galleries. For more art try the Lower Keys Artists Network, artistsinparadise.com; Florida Keys Council of the Arts, keysarts.com; and The Studios of Key West, tskw.org.

Artists Inspired...
for better or worse

From sweaty Cubans stacking walls of sea-encrusted lobster traps to herons wading in pristine sunset-colored waters, this little string of land has inspired artists through time immemorial. Key West-born folk artist Mario Sanchez carved and painted local scenes here for more than 70 years. Many of marine landscape painter Winslow Homer's inspirations sprang from the islands. John Audubon also created art in the Keys. On a visit in the 1830s, he painted 22 species of local birds, including flamingos, terns and pelicans. The less-glamourous side of that story is that in an era before photography, the celebrated conservationist and naturalist had a propensity for killing his subjects and stringing them up with wires into aesthetic poses from which to draw and paint. Alas, the balance between sharing something beautiful and leading it to its destruction may have eluded Audubon as much as it does adventure travelers today. Whether hero or misguided pioneer, Audubon did maintain more wisdom than many of our modern-day policy makers, when he noted both, "A true conservationist is a man who knows that the world is not given by his fathers, but borrowed from his children." And, "To repay evils with kindness is the religion I was taught to practice, and this will forever be my rule."

7

← NOT DRAWN BY →
AUDUBON

Event Highlights

January

KEY WEST LITERARY SEMINAR: readers and writers converge from around the world for readings, lectures, and conversations. kwls.org.

 KEY WEST FOOD & WINE FESTIVAL: eat, drink and be... stuffed and tipsy; keywestfoodandwinefestival.us.

QUANTUM KEY WEST RACE WEEK: watch competitive sailboat races from some of the world's top teams; keywestraceweek.com.

BIG PINE & LOWER KEYS NAUTICAL FLEA MARKET: an exciting opportunity to buy your dive gear, fishing poles, treasure coins, clocks shaped like boat wheels, and mermaid art all at one location. There's also live music, food vendors, and raffles; lowerkeyschamber.com.

FLORIDA KEYS CHALLENGE: Multi-day kayaking expedition, often in the Lower Keys, conservation and sport; paddleflorida.org.

FLORIDA KEYS SEAFOOD FESTIVAL: yum; monroe.ifas.ufl.edu/environment/env_seafood_fest.shtml.

KEY WEST CRAFT SHOW: national juried show, local artists, many booths, more than 30 years running. keywestartcenter.com.

February & March

OLD ISLAND ART DAYS: international juried outdoor fine art festival set up downtown, in 52nd year; keywestartcenter.com.

T. WILLIAMS BIRTHDAY CELEBRATION: the Keys celebrate this local icon with verve, and a month-long string of films, parties, painting and writing contests, lectures, and tours; twkw.org/events.

KEY WEST HOUSE TOURS: see pretty homes and gardens. Also December, January; oirf.org.

CONCH-SHELL-BLOWING CONTEST: open to everyone and judged on quality, duration, volume and novelty. Register and buy your instrument at the door of this half-century long event; oirf.org.

KEY WEST GARDEN CLUB FLOWER SHOW: featuring the flowery jewels grown here, usually March; keywestgardenclub.com.

NATIONAL WILDLIFE REFUGES OUTDOOR FEST: Wildlife, hikes, birding, paddles, photography, talks and more; favorfloridakeys.org.

7

April

CONCH REPUBLIC INDEPENDENCE CELEBRATION: a gathering of colorful locals with even more outrageous events, including races, a parade, a pirate ball, and a harbor battle with stale Cuban bread, eggs, and toilet paper; conchrepublic.com.

TASTE OF KEY WEST: local chef creations and wine along the waterfront; aidshelp.cc.

COW KEY CHANNEL BRIDGE RUN: the only zero K bridge run in the world, with costumes, beer, awards, and, oh yeah, a run, walk or relay race across the 300-foot-long bridge separating Key West and Stock Island; cowkeybridgerun.com.

KEY WEST PADDLE CLASSIC: SUP races, clinics and parties; paddleguru.com/races.

7 MILE BRIDGE RUN: 1,500 people run across the bridge. It's fun, but don't try to drive up or down the keys this morning; 7mbrun.com.

May

KEY WEST SONGWRITER'S FESTIVAL: musicians from across the country come to strut their talents at nearly every bar; keywestsongwritersfestival.com.

SUNSET CELEBRATION TALL SHIPS: tall masts, tours and sunset sails mix with daily festivities at Mallory Square; mallorysquare.com.

CINCO DE MAYO: many places but especially Schooner Wharf, with pepper eating and Mexican hat contests. schoonerwharf.com.

HARRY S. TRUMAN LEGACY SYMPOSIUM: historians and experts discuss the lasting effects of the president's policies. Also, the only Key West event that doesn't use the words "parties" or "drinking" on their marketing materials; trumanlittlewhitehouse.com.

June

KEY WEST AFRICANA FESTIVAL: retreat, academic conference and festival illuminating Key West's Afro-Caribbean heritage... and yes, Harry S. Truman event fans, even these guys mention sampling the Key West bars; keywestafricanafestival.com.

7

KEY WEST PRIDE: parades, street fairs and revelers in rainbow flags celebrate the success of the city's "One Human Family" philosophy; keywestpride.org.

SWIM AROUND KEY WEST: guess what happens at this event, which started more than 40 years ago; swimaroundkeywest.com.

July

MEL FISHER DAYS: treasure hunts and street fairs celebrate Key West's famous treasure-hunting family; melfisherdays.melfisher.com.

INDEPENDENCE DAY: celebrate July 4 with fireworks and parties in Key West and Big Pine Key.

HEMINGWAY DAYS: hundreds of Papa look-alikes roam the streets, while anglers compete for marlin and everyone else gets a great excuse to drink excessively; fla-keys.com/hemingwaymedia and sloppyjoes.com/papa-look-alike-contest.

UNDERWATER MUSIC FESTIVAL: swim the reef while boats pipe music underwater, mermaids frolic in the octopuses' garden, and other costumed folks play nautical-themed musical instruments, all for promoting reef protection; lowerkeyschamber.com/festival.

LOBSTER MINI-SEASON: in the reverse spirit of the underwater music festival, during the last Wednesday and Thursday of July hoards of mainlanders descend on the Keys to "get their bugs" before the commercial season opens a week later; myfwc.com.

August

KEY WEST LOBSTERFEST: food and fiestas kick off lobster season; keywestlobsterfest.com.

September

WETSTOCK: nothing like Woodstock, except for live music and an occasional naked person. Locals school in boats near Picnic Island off Ramrod Key to drink beer, swim, and be silly. On or near Labor Day.

KEY WEST BREWFEST: beer dinners, beer brunches, beer happy hours, beer pool parties, beer tastings, beer breath, beer goggles… it's all here; keywestbrewfest.com.

KEY WEST WOMENFEST: kinda like Key West Pride, but for lesbians and friends from every walk of life who want to convene for social events, relaxation, concerts, and food; womenfest.com.

BIKE WEEK: a.k.a. Phil Peterson's Poker Run, where thousands of motorcyclists ride into Key West for some R&R and T&A; pertersonsharley.com.

October

ZOMBIE BIKE RIDE: just before Fantasy Fest, locals dress like zombies and parade their bicycles to Duval, where they then wander around and usually end up drinking; zombiebikeride.com.

GOOMBAY FESTIVAL: food, arts and music fill the air in Bahama Village at this family-friendly, island-themed street party at the beginning of Fantasy Fest; fantasyfest.com.

FANTASY FEST: free spirits, painted body parts, costume parties, parades, street fairs, revelry, and general debauchery fill the air, the streets, and the gutters of Duval during the legendary party that lasts the final 10 or so days of October; fantasyfest.com.

November

KEY WEST WORLD POWERBOAT CHAMPIONSHIPS: watch fossil fuels get combusted almost as fast as they do during a Space Shuttle launch, as the world's fastest boats race around the island and spectators watch from shore and boat; superboat.com.

KEY WEST FILM FESTIVAL: indie films and their makers share local, national, and international movies, some of which are actually entertaining; kwfilmfest.com.

INTERNATIONAL SAND ART COMPETITION: famous sculptors get to play in the sand and make castles at Casa Marina; sandartkeywest.com.

7

BIG PINE & LOWER KEYS ISLAND ART FESTIVAL: how locals shop for Christmas presents; lowerkeyschamber.com/art_fair.

KEY WEST GARDEN CLUB PLANT SALE: Come for homemade lunch and leave with too many plants to fit in the garden. The week before Thanksgiving; keywestgardenclub.com.

December

KEY WEST "BIGHT" BEFORE CHRISTMAS: lighting of the Harbor Walk, city parade, dog photos with Santa (sometimes they let kids in on it too), and more all month; keywestchristmas.org.

KEY WEST LIGHTED BOAT PARADE: Everything from 5-foot dinghies to 120-foot tall ships strut their illuminous creations, while onlookers drink rum and watch from the Schooner Wharf Bar; schoonerwharf.com.

LOWER KEYS LIGHTED BOAT PARADE: if you're not in it, watch it from Kiki's Sandbar on Little Torch Key. No website, but info will be in the printed version of the Lower Keys newspaper News-Barometer.

NEW YEAR'S EVE: Times Square-esque countdowns welcome in the new year, with "drops" around town of various items, including a conch-shell, key lime pie, pirate wench, and drag queen celebrity in a big red high-heeled shoe.

Movies Filmed In the Lower Keys

From Bogart to Bond, Hollywood has long intertwined itself with the Keys. The Seven Mile Bridge co-starred with Schwarzenegger in *True Lies,* and was also in *2 Fast 2 Furious* and *License to Kill*. In that Bond film, the opening aerial sequence took place above the Sugar Loaf Shores Airport, and today a plane from the film is still parked out front. Speaking of the airport, parts of Wesley Snipes' *Drop Zone* were also filmed there. *License to Kill* filmed prolifically around Key West, including Mallory Square, Hemingway House, the airport, and what is now Thai Island Restaurant. Other notable films in Key West include Tennessee Williams' *The Rose Tattoo*, Goldie Hawn in *Criss Cross*, Peter Fonda in *92 in the Shade, Speed 2, Tomorrow Never Dies, Jackass Number 2,* and *Office Space* — when Milton escapes at the end to his tropical paradise, that's on Sunset Key, just off of Mallory Square. Also, MTV's *The Real World 2006* house still stands in Key Haven just outside of town. The colorful 6,000-square foot, 10-bedroom palace can be rented as a vacation home. On the flip side, the romantic comedy *Fool's Gold* claims to take place in Key West, but some details don't add up, like the backdrop of mountains. The "Key West" part was actually filmed in Port Douglas, Australia, about 9,358 miles away.

7

What is Fantasy Fest?

Fantasy Fest is a 10-day street party that draws between 25,000 and 75,000 revelers each October, sometimes tripling the population of Key West. It all starts with the fashionable Zombie Bike Ride and Goombay street festival, followed by a week of costume contests, street parties and galas. The final Friday brings the Masquerade March, a social walking spectacle that anyone can join. Saturday's apex parade is complete with theme floats hurling projectiles like Mardi Gras beads, candy, and condoms. Every night it's an adventure and a grand social experiment — people of all sizes, shapes, colors, ages, and orientations wander around Duval Street. Some don elaborate costumes, others artistic body paint, some are just, well, unimaginatively revealing, and others simply wear their everyday street duds. What is amazing is watching so many people drop their inhibitions to just have fun, each in their own way. It's awkward, tantalizing, disturbing, and beautiful all mushed up together with a lot of smiles, laughter, dance, and booze. Like it, ignore it, or immerse in it, it is remarkable and vital that something like this exists in our otherwise orderly and regulated world.

7

Free to Be You and Me

When you encourage children to use their most vivid imaginations to dress themselves, you'll get some pretty interesting and entertaining results. Since everyone in the Keys is allowed to be who they want, there are a lot of adults here who also have some pretty interesting outfits and personas. Some do it for a living (if you find them entertaining, please tip them). Many do it simply because it makes strangers smile, or as a form of self-expression. Some, well, who knows. We don't know all of their stories, but when we see them we are reminded of the quirky, glorious diversity of the Keys — and how we all contribute to our Island of Misfit Toys. While you're enjoying your stay here, see how many you can identify.

LIGHTED, MUSICAL TRICYCLE MAN: Mr. Chapman rides around town on his tricycle spreading smiles with festive lights and a boombox churning out songs like Super Freak and other funky classics.

BANJO VADER: in the 5 years he's been in business, the man behind the Darth Vader mask playing a neon-lighted banjo on Duval has become one of the most classic icons of the Key West busker scene.

SITAR SPIDERMAN: on some evenings, Spiderman is spotted sitting cross-legged on Duval, playing the sitar, usually not far from Vader.

PARROTS: several people are happy to let you take a picture with their parrot in exchange for a few bucks. But if you see a kind-faced woman with long-grey hair and a parrot or two, that's probably Nancy Forrester, a local legend who runs the parrot rescue.

SOUTHERNMOST MAD MAX: just a man riding a bicycle, usually shirtless, sporting a mohawk, with a spear gun strapped to his back, pulling a cart piled with a random collection of belongings flying a Conch Republic flag.

THE HAPPY DRUMMER: with a huge smile and a full drum set, this guy joyfully bangs away on the side of U.S. 1 in the Saddlebunch Keys between Big Coppitt and Baypoint.

JIMMY HENDRIX: for years Kenyatta Arrington entertained thousands with his original lyrical guitar songs, and a style and appearance similar to those of Hendrix. Sadly he died in 2016, and Key West is a less colorful place without his presence.

THE INSPECTOR: also known as the Walking Man, this gentleman sports a scruffy beard, a cigarette dangling from his lips, an official-looking walking stick and a construction safety jacket. At first we thought he was an inspector for public utilities or roads, but in reality he seems to just walk many miles daily, back and forth along several Keys near Summerland.

VIOLIN GUY: for years this kind, slight-of-figure man with greying hair has stood under La Concha and played to passers-by.

SCHOONER'S CIGAR MAN: with a gloriously long, white beard and infectious smile, you'll find Eric, a.k.a. Monkey, a.k.a. Monster, selling hand-rolled cigars from a cart at the Schooner Wharf Bar.

FREE ICE CREAM MAN: not at all creepy, despite the nickname, this jovial soul shows up with a cart to some local events, dolling out free ice cream and smiles.

CAT MAN: with a French accent, a couple of performing felines and a knack for making audiences giggle, this man and his cats are one of the longest-running shows at the Mallory Square sunset celebration.

7

Lower Keys

GULF OF MEXICO

FLORIDA BAY

DRY TORTUGAS &
MARQUESAS KEYS

16 19

KEY WEST
N.W.R.

15
6

5
SAND KEY

2
1
KEY WEST

STOCK ISLAND

THE VANDENBERG

7

ATLANTIC OCEAN

GREAT WHITE
HERON N.W.R.

THE BACKCOUNTRY

9

SADDLEBUNCH KEYS

10
SUGARLOAF

HAWK CHANNEL

8

14
AMERICAN SHOAL

18
SUMMERLAND

11 13

12

KEY
DEER
N.W.R.

17

LOOE KEY REEF

4

STRAITS OF FLORIDA

BIG PINE KEY

BAHIA
HONDA
STATE
PARK

3

TOWARD
MARATHON,
KEY LARGO
& MAINLAND
FLORIDA

8

Things to Do – Water

IN THIS CHAPTER

Beaches
Snorkeling from shore and boat
Scuba diving, reef spots
Watercraft rentals
Kayaking, standup paddleboarding
Sunset & eco-tours

Water — Life of the Planet

...and the Vacation

Aqua, teal, blue, crystal-clear, jade, translucent, serene, magnificent. These are just a few adjectives to describe the waters encircling the Keys. Just one step off the dock brings an entirely different world, filled with an abundance of aquatic life. But trying to describe the excitement of smelling the salty air, the elation of watching a fiery sunset from a boat or the peaceful relaxation of meandering through underwater civilizations, always ends up sounding like a worn-out postcard slogan.

The thing is, there is no way to convey the emotion of watching a 400-pound green sea turtle swim through a barrier reef, seeing the smile of a child who just caught her first fish, or gliding 300 feet above the water in a parasail. They are simply moments that must be experienced to understand.

The water is amazing. It's the epitome of what makes the Keys such an extraordinary corner of the world. There are divine and preposterous animals, fish with colors and shapes that don't even look possible, and a

ANGELFISH

8

> **❝How inappropriate to call this planet Earth when it is clearly ocean.❞**
> **Sir Arthur C. Clarke**

multitude of activities that revolve around this vivid liquid. Regardless of your level of experience and comfort in the water, you will find something to enjoy, even if it's just smelling the ocean air and being rejuvenated and energized by the warm sun on your skin.

Stewardship

Before we dig into all the fun details of enjoying the water, we must first be the fun police for a moment and set forth the rules. As most are aware, our seas are greatly affected by human interaction. Pollution, global warming, changing sea levels, and sadly, careless tourism, are all factors that are taking a major and rapid toll on the health of our planet's oceans and waterways. Globally, coral reefs act as nurseries for a quarter of the world's fish. Helping preserve reefs is vital. Besides their inherent right to exist, they are a primary source of food and income for at least a half-billion people. Their medicinal values are just starting to be explored, but some reef organisms are already proven treatments for cancer and HIV. We sincerely ask you to keep in mind that you are visiting a vast coral reef, which requires respect. Your efforts will help preserve precious sea life so that our children and theirs can enjoy the amazing oceans!

MANATEE

LITTER: Please do not litter, at your home or ours, but especially near the water. A small piece of trash or cigarette butt carelessly tossed off a boat could end up choking a cormorant, a wonderful sea turtle, or any other number of majestic creatures who call these waters home.

CHEMICALS: Rinse your bug spray and perfumes off prior to going swimming and use a reef-friendly sunscreen. Nearly all widely sold sunscreens have chemicals in them that destroy coral and other marine life. Chain stores here don't usually carry reef-safe brands and even many "natural" brands contain these poisons. Dive and health-food stores around town should have true reef-safe options, or prior to your travels order some online. Mote Marine endorses Tropical Seas brand, which we've found to work well without leaving a white zinc-oxide residue.

WALK WITH CARE: Be aware of your surroundings in the water. Try to avoid stepping on anything other than sand to not crush small marine plants and animals. At the reef, it is especially vital not to touch anything. Brushing against a coral or sponge can cause severe damage that won't heal for years, if ever. This is good advice to keep you safe as well, as there are a few creatures who, if touched, might send you home with a bad rash or worse.

Shh... don't tell the urchin you can see him. He spent a long time working on his clever leaf-grass-shell disguise.

8

WATER DEPTH: Whether on a boat or WaveRunner, be aware that depths change rapidly with underwater terrain and tidal fluctuations. Coral heads and other life lurk just millimeters below the surface. Hitting them not only damages the craft, but causes trauma to fragile sea life and results in unspeakable monetary fines if authorities see you.

WILDLIFE: Turtles, manatees and other sea life are too often injured or killed by boat propellers. Keep a keen lookout. Floating seaweed (sargassum) clumps are also home to baby sea life, so avoid motoring through. Boating too close to birds agitates them, causing them to abandon their food or even their nest. If they notice you, that's probably a sign you're too close. Instead, get some good binoculars or a telephoto lens for wildlife watching that's safe for everyone.

If you see injured wildlife, report to FWC at (305) 470-6863.

BUI: Just like in a car, authorities give fines and jail time to people boating drunk or recklessly. Please mitigate your alcohol intake while on the water. Clear water, abundant shallows, rocky patches, and the freedom of being on vacation can easily cloud one's judgement, even without an excess of the sauce. Plus, too much drink almost always leads to dehydration and sunburn. Stay safe. We want you to be around to visit again!

"The Sea, once it casts its spell, holds one in its net of wonder forever." - Jacques-Yves Cousteau

A note for water beginners

If you're a greenhorn swimmer or intimidated by the water, it doesn't mean you should steer clear. Even Cousteau had to take a first step into the liquid that covers 70 percent of our little planet. Visiting the Keys without a snorkel or boat ride is like traveling to Bangkok and not trying opium. Just kidding. Sorry Bangkok, we know you have cleaned up your ways. Partly. But seriously, going to the Keys and not sampling the reef is a tragedy, especially because it may not always be here. If you muster up the courage, the adventure will leave you feeling a great bit different about your accomplished life, and you might just end up with a new love.

Water Activities

Snorkeling from the Beach in Key West

Playing in the water is fun, until you take a peak underneath. After that, swimming without a mask and snorkel will seem pretty dull. What's underneath is a whole new world. You don't need any particular skill set to don a mask and snorkel, but do make sure to read our safety precautions page in this chapter. A mask-snorkel combo can be purchased for under $30 or rented for much less at most beaches. It's worth a try, even if you end up sharing one set with friends and family. Note: for first-timers, getting the hang of breathing underwater might take a little bit of practice, so just be patient. It won't take terribly long to become proficient but will feel awkward at first. The most important thing to remember is just to relax.

Just off the beaches, you're likely to see many fish, like yellow-striped sergeant majors, yellowtail snapper, angelfish and the brilliant multi-colored parrotfish. Nurse sharks, crabs, snook and urchins are just a few of the critters commonly found around rock piles. Floating slowly around an area, even of super-shallow water, will also reveal an intriguing host of tiny creatures going about their daily business.

I HIGGS BEACH

This is a fantastic spot to snorkel, especially for beginners as it's a protected cove with a gently sloping seafloor. Start at the base of the pier and swim under it to see an array of tropical fish. As you near the end, you'll see the remains of a submerged retaining wall. At that end the fish are usually a little larger and there's a greater chance of spotting a ray or nurse shark. There is free parking, and vendors rent chairs, umbrellas, masks, and sometimes kayaks. This beach also has a volleyball court, restrooms and rinse showers, plus a walking pier with stairs into the deeper water. Don't miss the restaurant Salute! on the beach. No alcohol is allowed on the beach, but it is served at the restaurant. 1100 Atlantic Boulevard.

8

Bahia Honda

Fishing has its own chapter, no. 13. Beaches for lounging are in land attractions, chapter 6.

Numbers by attraction name correspond to map on page 132.

2 FORT ZACHARY TAYLOR STATE PARK

This is our favorite Key West beach snorkeling spot. The beach starts with nice shady pine trees at the top, followed by a band of soft sand. Down by the water, though, there are larger rocks and broken shells, so a pair of water shoes makes life much more pleasant. Standing on the beach and looking toward the sea, you'll see three large rock piles about 150 feet or so offshore. An abundance of sea life congregates there, and you'll probably stay entertained for hours just circling around them. Use caution, however, as sea urchins are definitely nestled into the crevices. Water depths range from about 8 to 20 feet. Fins are nice to have here, as strong tidal currents are sometimes present. On windy days, take extra caution not to get dashed against the rocks by waves. Those who are not decent swimmers can swim near the beach, but might not feel comfortable out by the rocks. There are public restrooms, rinse showers, a full-service snack bar and an entire Civil War-era Fort to explore. Again, alcohol is prohibited on the beach, but you can buy it at the snack bar and drink it on the deck. Small entrance fee. 601 Howard England Way.

SNORKELING ROCKS OFF OF FORT ZACHARY TAYLOR'S BEACH

8

Snorkeling from the Beach Outside of Town

3 BAHIA HONDA STATE PARK

People often vote the beaches at this full-service state park the best in Florida, and a day here is sure to enhance your appreciation of the Keys. There are so many excellent snorkeling areas, from beginner to advanced, that it could be a chapter all in itself. So for now we'll just recommend getting advice from a park employee or doing a bit of self exploration. Bahia Honda is also loaded up with history and the ruins of Flagler's railroad. The park encompasses 292 acres with hiking trails, 80 camp sites, a full-service marina, two boat ramps, a nature center, picnic pavilions, food, gifts, and kayak rentals. If you plant to camp here, make reservations well in advance. Small admission fee. Mile marker 36.8, oceanside, 305-872-2353.

ROADSIDE SNORKELING

As you drive up or down the Overseas Highway, you'll pass numerous parking areas on the sides of the road. Some are well-suited for pulling over and busting out your snorkel gear for a dip, while others are not. If you see cars parked and people out picnicking, chances are that's a decent spot. Many of these have rocky shores, which are great for swimming along to see a variety of tropical fish, shellfish, and if you are very fortunate, maybe even a small octopus. Please remember the importance of paying attention to where you step, and to enjoy the beauty with your eyes only.

Diving with a Purpose

A while back a diver from Nashville wanted more than a look at pretty fish, so he started Diving with a Purpose, a nonprofit that works with NOAA to train its members in underwater archeological techniques. The group's members, who are primarily African American, converge on the Keys annually to assist in documenting historic shipwrecks, as well as to volunteer with the Coral Restoration Foundation's coral propagation efforts. If you think you might want to dive with a purpose or help plant coral, see divingwithapurpose. org, and coralrestoration.org. For other volunteer vacation ideas, try: counting fish, fishcount.org; activities with the National Wildlife Refuges, favorfloridakeys.org; the Key West Tropical Forest and Botanical Garden, kwbgs.org/volunteer.aspx; the historic tropical fruit community of Grimal Grove, growinghopeinitiative.org; lionfish derbies, reef.org/lionfish/derbies; or just bring a bag and pick up trash you find on the beach and in the water.

Eco & Sunset Tours

There is nothing like a relaxing boat ride. The air, the sky and the spectacular vistas are not just a treat for the senses, but food for the soul and healing for the spirit. During the day, boats whisk visitors into the backcountry, for dolphin watching, paddleboarding, kayaking, and nature tours. As the day comes to a close, you can take Key West's enchanting sunset one step — or knot — further by watching it from the open water. Each evening a fleet of ships depart the historic seaport toward the glowing horizon. Sail on a tall-masted schooner, snuggle up on an intimate private sailboat, or booze-cruise it out on a party barge with live music.

We've highlighted two of our favorites below, and there is a more comprehensive listing at the end of this chapter. Our recommendations are based on friendly staff, safety and respect for the environment. Many operators also offer day, dinner, and full-moon night cruises.

HONEST ECO
Billy, Rob, Jen, Evan and Bosco will show you a great time while imparting wisdom, friendship and local knowledge. To us they are also a shining example of people who shape their lives based on a true commitment to the planet and humanity. Both of their boats maintain small groups, and their guides operate at a leisurely pace, going out of their way to make each guest feel at home. They offer three types of tours:

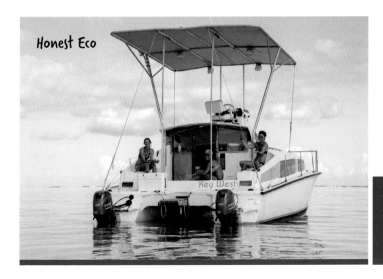

Honest Eco

8

Dolphin Watch is a four-hour tour into the lives of dolphins while learning how they live, play, sleep, and mate. These are not dolphins who are captive or bribed with food, but those who are free in their natural habitat. After spending some time observing these wonderful, intelligent creatures, you'll get treated to a dip at a protected, secret snorkeling spot. Kayak and snorkel trips are four hours of exploring mangrove islands where you get to watch their wild inhabitants both above and below the water, while learning about the Keys' unique ecosystem. SUP yoga mixes the coordination of paddleboarding with the relaxation of yoga on a trip into the national wildlife refuge. Teaching is geared toward each student's individual level. Located at the historic seaport and Garrison Bight Marina, 305-294-6306, honesteco.org.

SCHOONER JOLLY II ROVER

Set out to sea with the friendly yet piratical crew aboard this classic square-rigged schooner. Join them for a two-hour daytime or sunset cruise around Key West. Adventurous guests help raise the ship's 10 signature red sails, fire the cannon, and even take a turn at the helm of the 80-foot vessel. The crew provides water, bottle openers and cups, you provide your additional beverage and food of choice. The Jolly II Rover also offers private charters and Boy Scout adventures. Key West Historic Seaport, behind the Conch Republic Seafood Company at the foot of Greene and Elizabeth Streets, 305-304-2235, schoonerjollyrover.com.

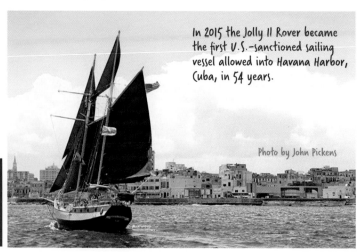

In 2015 the Jolly II Rover became the first U.S.-sanctioned sailing vessel allowed into Havana Harbor, Cuba, in 54 years.

Photo by John Pickens

8

Diving and Snorkeling

Shimmering schools of grunts swoosh by yellowtails and arms of coral where parrotfish chomp loudly. Great barracuda keep a close eye on the social scene, while a buried ray suddenly darts off, leaving a poof of sand. Obviously, the reef is a great place to dive, and can keep anyone entertained for a lifetime. It's also a safe and comfortable place to complete open water dive training, as most of the reef never exceeds 30 feet. There are treats for more advanced divers, with both natural and premeditated shipwrecks, the latter for the creation of artificial reefs. There are night dives to be experienced, advanced certifications to earn and, once a year, the cosmic-looking wonder of coral spawning.

Because of the shallow waters, most of the reefs here are also good for snorkeling. Some are even as shallow as a foot in places. Marine life you are likely to see include angelfish, triggerfish, grouper, spiny lobster, barracuda, surgeonfish, jacks, butterflyfish, snapper, parrotfish, stingrays, lionfish, hogfish, sea turtles, nurse sharks, octopuses, and a multitude of other colorful reef fish. Once in a while, even manta rays and whale sharks make an appearance.

In the next pages are a few of our favorite places to dive and snorkel. If you don't have your own dive boat, there are many good operators who offer daily trips and equipment rentals, some of which can be found in the back of this chapter.

Curious Ray

8

4 LOOE KEY REEF - ASTOUNDING REEF DIVING

One of the most beautiful reefs in the Keys, Looe Key lies about 5.5 miles south of Ramrod Key. Water depths range from 3 to 30 feet. The visibility is usually excellent, making it great for snorkelers and divers. Finger-like canyons of coral spread out to sea on the deeper end, while coral and sandy floors make up the shallower leeward side. More than 150 species of fish spend at least some of their lives in and around this hospitable 200-by-800-yard expanse. The reef is named after the HMS Looe, a British frigate that foundered on the reef in 1744 and sank along with a captured French ship it was towing. A ballast pile can still be found on the eastern end. Fishing and lobstering are strictly prohibited, which makes for even better wildlife viewing. Please take extra care not to harm this many-thousand-year-old civilization. Operators in Big Pine Key, Ramrod Key, and Bahia Honda State Park make daily trips.

5 SAND KEY - SNORKELING HAVEN

Sand Key lies about 7 miles southwest of Key West and is known for its snorkeling accessibility. Diving is also nice off of the oceanside, with a steep drop-off. The site is easy to locate, since it has a 110-foot lighthouse over it. The sands around the islet are often changing, so it's never the same dive twice. The best snorkeling is near the lighthouse on the sides and back, where reef fish congregate in finger canyons and depths run between 15 and zero feet. It is also nice in the grass and sand areas before the lighthouse, where turtles abound. The lighthouse, originally built in 1827, faced the full fury of many storms, being destroyed several times. In 1846 it disappeared without a trace, along with its keeper and his family. Major restoration was underway in 1989 when a fire broke out, gutting the internals. Today, the iron structure still stands but the light now resides on a 40-foot-tall tower nearby. On calm days, access to Sand Key is relatively easy by rental boat, WaveRunner, and nearly any dive operation in Key West.

Goliath grouper and friends at Looe Key

8

6 COTTRELL KEY AREA - WHEN IT'S BLOWING

If you've booked a charter or rented a boat and the wind is blowing too much for oceanside exploration, the area near Cottrell is a great spot to visit. It's nestled in the Key West National Wildlife Refuge, about 9 miles northwest of the city. Below the water lies a mix of soft sponge patch reef and seagrass. In some spots sits a shallow underwater sandbar, which is great for relaxing on. The reef itself starts west of the lighthouse ruins. It's common to see conch and sea urchin, as well as larger marine life like grouper, rays, dolphins, and sharks. Navigating back here requires close attention and charts. The ruined lighthouse, now just a collection of rusted beams crested by magnificent frigatebirds, is also called the Hemingway stilts, as it is rumored to have been one of the author's favorite fishing spots. Wading birds like great white herons and roseate spoonbills make for good bird watching. You cannot explore the islands themselves, as Cottrell Key and the nearby Little and Big Mullet Keys are protected by a 300-foot no-access zone.

7 USNS GENERAL HOYT S. VANDENBERG - EPIC WRECK DIVE

More adventurous divers never get bored exploring the 523-foot-long Vandenberg. The U.S. Navy transport ship was intentionally sunk in 2009 to create an artificial reef habitat. The ship that once monitored Soviet missile launches during the Cold War and tracked space launches off of Cape Canaveral is now the world's second-largest artificial reef, making a peaceful home for a multitude of sea life that becomes more abundant every year. The Vandenberg's new home is about 7 miles south of Key West in around 150 feet of water. The top of the superstructure lies about 40 to 45 feet down, which gives a little idea about the immensity of this vessel. Diving to the upper point is considered a light-intermediate dive, while diving to the bottom and exploring penetrable areas is reserved for those with advanced skills. Because of the depths, strong currents and complex structure, it is very important to dive within your skill limitations and with an experienced guide. The sinking was quite a feat in itself. It took a decade of planning, around $8.6 million and 75,000 man-hours to clean up and remove toxic substances from the ship — and after all that, it took just 1 minute and 45 seconds for it to sink to the bottom. Nearly every dive charter in Key West makes regular trips to the Vandenberg, and the ship plays occasional host to art exhibits, contests, treasure hunts, and other events.

Underwater sandbar & Cottrell Key

8

Non-Motorized Watersports

KAYAKING, CANOEING, STANDUP PADDLEBOARDING (SUP)

Shallow water and hundreds of small mangrove islands make the Lower Keys ideal for exploring via paddle. Above, wading birds hunt for fish in water so shallow they appear to be walking on top. Below, rays, fish, and young sharks quietly patrol the crystal-clear channels and seagrass beds. In places, rivers winding through the mangroves are so narrow it's like going through a tunnel. These hidden paradises are vital nursery ecosystems, which host all sorts of life and protect the little fish until they're large enough to explore the giant sea. Rentals are available all around Key West and the Lower Keys, and many companies offer eco-tour and other paddling adventures (see the end of this chapter for recommendations). For self-guided adventures, here are a few of our favorites, but also pick up a copy of the *Florida Keys Paddling Guide* by local eco-guru Bill Keogh. Make sure to bring mosquito spray, as sometimes they get feisty in the mangroves.

8 SUGARLOAF LODGE

Rent a kayak at the marina by Sugarloaf Lodge at mile marker 17. Drop it in the water there and paddle up the bay toward the anchored boats. Before too long you'll see a few channels going into the mangroves. Take any one of them, and they'll lead to smaller and smaller channels to explore. This is a great location for families, as the mangroves offer protection from winds and heavy boat traffic.

9 GEIGER KEY

The waters around Geiger Key marina are stunning, and there are kayak and SUP rentals right on-site. Turn to the left, or right, or straight... it doesn't matter, it's all beautiful and secluded, plus there's a good restaurant for post-paddle refreshments. To get there, turn oceanside onto Boca Chica Road by at the Circle K at mile marker 11. Follow the road until you see a sign for "marina" pointing to the left.

Mangrove tunnel

8

10 SAMMY CREEK LANDING AT SUGARLOAF CREEK

There are no rentals here, so you need a vehicle to transport your craft. If you have one, launch at the little boat ramp, turn right under the bridge, and explore away through narrow channels leading to back bays too shallow for boat traffic. To get here, turn oceanside at the blinking light on Sugarloaf (mile marker 17), follow it all the way back, around the 90-degree turn, then back some more. The park is on the left before the bridge.

SAILING: The Key West Community Sailing Center is a great place to get a boat or learn to sail. They don't rent boats, but when you become a member, you can use the boats in their fleet, which include styles from Sunfish to 18-footers with a full keel. They offer education and safety courses, and cater very well to junior sailors, too. keywestsailingcenter.org, (305) 292-5993, 720 Palm Ave.

WINDSURFING & KITEBOARDING
Although not yet widely popular sports here, oftentimes the winds are ideal for windsurfing and kiteboarding, and there are outfitters in town who offer rentals and lessons.

PADDLE PRECAUTIONS
If you decide to head out on your own, do a little research about the area, even if that just means a quick check on Google Earth to get your bearings. When you start out, note the direction of the current and wind. It can be very difficult to get back to land if you've worn yourself out paddling with the current, then must fight it to return. There are smartphone apps for tides, which are handy tools, along with weather apps and radar. You'll also want plenty of water, sunscreen, hats, sunglasses, and long-sleeves for bugs and sun.

WASSUP WITH SUP?
Standup paddleboarding, or SUP, is a sport gaining a lot of momentum in the Keys. It's like standing on a long surfboard while using a paddle to propel yourself over the water. It's a good workout and a way to increase your balance. Because you stand above the water, you also get a better view of the marine life. If you are extra adventurous, you might like SUP yoga, or naked SUP. Yep, of course there's an outfitter that offers it in the buff. It is Key West, after all.

8

Motorized Watersports

PARASAILING

If you've never seen parasailing, it's essentially a parachute that's towed behind the boat, lifting you up to 300 feet in the air. It's quite a rush, and the view is unparalleled. Though it sounds like a sport reserved for adventurers, it's safe and suitable for families (kids 6 and up) and water newbies. You don't even have to get wet or know how to swim, though you can request a dunk if you want to cool off. Typically people ride tandem, as the minimum weight for the sail is 250 pounds. In some cases three people can ride one at once, if weather conditions are favorable and the whole lot of you doesn't exceed 450 pounds. There are several businesses who offer trips, which typically take an hour or two. We particularly like Larry and the Parawest crew, a smaller family-run operation who offer free shuttles from anywhere in town aboard their pimpin' golf cart. parawestparasailing. com, (305) 292-5199, 700 Front Street at the A&B Marina.

SNUBA

A blend of snorkeling and scuba diving, with Snuba you breathe underwater through a pressured air hose. No prior diving or snorkeling experience is necessary, just a 20-minute safety orientation. The minimum age is 8. There is only one Snuba outfit in town, Snuba Key West, snubakeywest.com, 305-292-4616, Garrison Bight Marina on Palm Avenue, between North Roosevelt and Eisenhower Drive, next to Thai Island.

Not in the Keys...

But maybe they're headed this way.

| | PERSONAL WATERCRAFT

Jet skis, WaveRunners, Sea-Doos or whatever you choose to call them, are a popular past-time here. These zippy little beasts can seat one, two, and sometimes three people. Tours around Key West are widely available, and cover 20-plus miles in an hour. You can also rent them for your own adventure. Many areas of the backcountry are closed to them, however, because of the damage they can cause. Check with the rental outfit on regulations and never speed near a reef. Our favorite place for rentals is the laid-back **FLORIDA JET SKI RENTALS** on Summerland Key, because of their prices, quality of equipment and lovely owner. Look for the sign that says "Free Beer" around mile marker 24.5 and turn oceanside into the parking lot. Friendly and courteous will set you up on her late-model WaveRunners and give you the low-down, as well as rent you a mask, fins, and snorkel if you need. She rents by the hour, half-day, full-day, or even multiple days. From there, there are many bays that are fun to zip around, and on a calm day you can even head out to Looe Key Reef. When you return from your adventure, if you are nice and courteous as well, you can rinse off on her dock shower with complimentary, locally made coconut salt scrub, and enjoy your free beer. 305-396-7255, flkeysjetskirentals.com.

MOTORBOAT RENTALS

If you're already a boater, then renting your own means the freedom to explore, fish, dive, and snorkel when and where you want. Beyond the snorkeling and scuba locations in this chapter, here are a couple of suggestions for other places to explore:

THE BACKCOUNTRY offers good fishing and scenic expanses. It also hides tidal sandbars frequented by locals, such as those around Snipe Keys. At low tide, the white sand becomes exposed. People set up chairs. Children run across the soft surface. There are a number

Keys backcountry

8

of these around, but you'll have to gain a local's trust to get there, as they are guarded secrets and difficult to navigate to without running aground. A GPS or nautical chart is imperative, as numerous shoals hide just underneath what look to be passable expanses of water.

12 **PICNIC ISLAND** awaits between Ramrod Key and Little Palm Resort. More than a tiny island, it's a shallow, sandy underwater expanse popular for anchoring up and hanging out. The water is four or so feet deep and the location is relatively sheltered. On weekends, there's usually a pretty good social scene here, too, reaching its climax over Labor Day Weekend's Wetfest — when locals congregate for a bit larger and more organized party.

13 There are a number of places that rent boats, but as with the jet skis, we're just going to give you our favorite — which happens to have two locations, one of which is next to Nicole and her WaveRunners. We refer friends to **BIG PINE KEY BOAT RENTALS** all the time, and for good reason. Maya, the charming owner, maintains a large fleet of newer-model boats and is impeccable about maintaining her equipment. Every boat has a T-top or Bimini for shade. Boats also come with GPS units, charts, dive flags, and Coast Guard-required safety equipment. Rates for daily and weekly rentals are reasonable, especially considering the quality of the vessels. Be sure to tell Maya that you read about her in our guidebook, please, and take good care of her boats! Big Pine Key: 305-849-0139, mile marker 33. Summerland Key: 305-745-1505, mile marker 24.5. bigpineboatrentals.com.

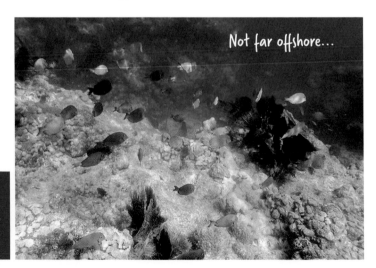

Not far offshore...

8

Abandoned Water...The Keys' Enduring Lighthouses

For almost two centuries, a string of lighthouses have been standing sentinel over the Keys' treacherous shoals and reefs. Eight of them were built in the open water, miles from land. These monumental feats of engineering, and the stories of the brave keepers who lived on them, can be found in the history chapter 14. Today their lights don't shine, but their proximity to the reef makes them popular areas for fishing and diving. Unfortunately, climbing them is illegal.

14 **AMERICAN SHOAL:** This striking red, 124-foot tower stands around 7 miles south of Sugarloaf. There are no mooring balls, though there are usually a few boats anchored nearby for snorkeling and fishing. First lit in 1880, in 2016 American Shoal made news again for being the brief hiding spot for 21 Cuban refugees, who were spotted by the Coast Guard just shy of succeeding on their 90-mile float.

5 **SAND KEY LIGHTHOUSE:** Elsewhere in this chapter we go into detail about the stunning snorkeling at this 110-foot structure near Key West. The shoal is high enough to serve as a roost for large congregations of seabirds, such as pelicans, terns, and magnificent frigatebirds. Note: it is illegal to fish at Sand Key.

15 **NORTHWEST PASSAGE:** A group of twisted iron sticks rise eerily above the water 8 miles northwest of Key West. They are all that remain of the lighthouse that saved countless ships from 1855 to 1921. At 47 feet tall, it was never the grandest of lighthouses, but in the 1930s it was a favorite fishing spot for author Ernest Hemingway, earning it the modern-day title of the Hemingway Stilts. The surrounding area is a scenic hangout to watch for sharks, large grouper, dolphins and seabirds.

Sand Key

American Shoal

Northwest Passage Ruins

8

A Lonely Outpost

16 DRY TORTUGAS NATIONAL PARK & FT. JEFFERSON NATIONAL MONUMENT

An enchanting and pristine wilderness beckons. It's a world filled with sea life and birds, yet to be overrun by the breadth of Key West civilization 70 miles to the east. Seven remote islands and 100 square miles of open water make up the Dry Tortugas, which is one of the nation's most remote national parks. Intrepid travelers arrive by seaplane and ferry to dive and snorkel, as well as explore the ruins of the fort and lighthouse. Today the clear, blue waters are inviting, but that wasn't always the case.

The struggle of man and nature here goes back more than 500 years. Ponce de León was the first westerner of record to come across them. In 1513 he named them the Tortugas, or turtles in Spanish, due to the extreme number of turtles on and around the islands. Soon he added the word dry, after learning there was no source of fresh water to be found. As New World travel and trade expanded, the nearby waters became a frequented route, and soon the Tortugas grew to a location of legend.

> "His stories were what frightened people worst of all. Dreadful stories they were — about hanging, and walking the plank, and storms at sea, and the Dry Tortugas, and wild deeds and places on the Spanish Main," wrote Robert Louis Stevenson in his classic story "Treasure Island."

It wasn't just the lack of water that made them ominous, but the shoals and reefs that sent hundreds of ships to their doom, many of which still lie in the waters here. Despite the dangers, seafarers continued to approach the islands to collect turtles for sustenance, a practice that over time decimated their numbers.

Today humans are much kinder to the turtles, and though not present in their pre-Columbian numbers, one-third of the world's loggerhead turtles still nest in the area, along with more than 100,000 sooty terns, boobies, pelicans, frigates, and hundreds of other winged and shelled wonders.

Historically, the islands' location also made them a strategic outpost from which to control Atlantic and Gulf shipping lanes. Inevitably the U.S. chose to fortify it by building Fort Jefferson on Garden Key. This six-sided fort made from more than 16 million bricks is the largest masonry structure in the Americas. Even today the feat of transporting all of those bricks, laborers, and their food and water to this remote island would be an ambitious undertaking, but in 1846 it was monumental. Construction continued for the next 30 years, and was never technically completed, though for a time the fort housed a couple thousand people, mostly military personnel and prisoners.

A ferry and seaplanes make daily trips, weather permitting. The ferry is a comfortable catamaran that travels around 20 to 30 m.p.h., departing Key West at 8 a.m. and returning around 5:30. Seaplanes get you there faster, with a stunning view, but a higher price tag.

Dr. Samuel Mudd was imprisoned here, then pardoned after saving many from a yellow fever outbreak.

Park: 305-242-7700, nps.gov/drto.
Ferry: Yankee Freedom, 800-634-0939, drytortugas.com.
Seaplane: Key West Seaplane Adventures, 305-293-9300, keywestseaplanecharters.com.

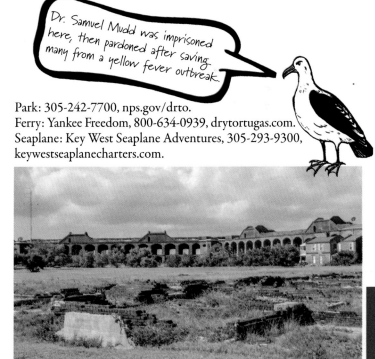

Astute Apps for Boating

We like to encourage turning off technology while on vacation, but while boating, there are a few apps essential for safety and planning.

WEATHER/RADAR: Most weather apps offer radar, temperature, heat index, humidity and forecasts, plus some combination of the enhanced weather features below. The three most popular here are WeatherBug (free), MyRadar Radar Pro NOAA Weather Radar ($1.99) and the Weather Underground (free). Especially in the summer, storm cells can materialize out of nowhere, putting up a wall of dark thunderstorms where there was blue sky just a few minutes ago. It's vital to check radar prior to departure and while underway.

LIGHTNING: NOAA's app includes lightning proximity maps as does WeatherBug's, which calls it "Spark."

WIND: Windspeed dictates whether it's a great day on the water or a social day at the bar. Most weather apps include windspeed, but a lot of locals here use Windfinder (free) or Windfinder Pro ($1.99).

TIDES: Speaking of tides, they can vary greatly between the Atlantic and Gulf, even though it's a short distance. Knowing the tide in specific locations is vital to safe navigation, as well as to figure out when those alluring backcountry sandbars will be exposed. Try Tide Charts Near Me (free) or TideTrac ($2.99).

HURRICANE: Several apps keep track of forming tropical depressions and send push notifications when one is brewing. Try Hurricane by American Red Cross (free) or Hurricane Pro ($2.99).

GPS CLUSTER: Compass readings, latitude-longitude coordinates, and speed. Our favorite is My Coordinates Pro ($3.99), but there are tons.

WATER NAVIGATION: Serious boaters never thought they'd see the day when mounted GPS navigation units gave way to apps on tablets and smartphones, but that day... well it hasn't entirely come yet, but it is arriving. Some apps work nearly as well as traditional units, with far greater affordability and portability. Downloading nautical and sonar charts, tracking journeys, and marking waypoints are just a few of the features. Many swear by Navionics, which offers a free app plus in-app chart purchases. Garmin's BlueChart Mobile is another good one, since tracks and other information can be exchanged between the app and the traditional Garmin. Garmin's app is also free, with in-app chart purchases.

The Arbutus

19 From an airplane, the Quicksands look like an underwater desert, an expanse of white sand spreading gracefully beneath a layer of bright blue water. It was here that Mel Fisher found much of his loot from the Spanish treasure galleons Atocha and Santa Margarita. It was also here that he lost one of his own boats — the Arbutus. The 187-foot converted Coast Guard ship served as a sentry to the treasure site, its inhabitants keeping a watchful eye for would-be looters. Eventually the tired old vessel's hull gave out and she sank west of Key West, where she still sits three decades later, a ghostly, rusty shell jutting upright in 25 feet of water. Above the seas, frigatebirds now stand sentry on its decaying mast, while giant barracuda patrol its underwater decks. Though her picture graces the back cover of Jimmy Buffett's "Songs You Should Know By Heart" album, she is far from famous. Only a few seafarers know her name and fewer can recount tales of her heyday. There aren't many shipwrecks shallow enough to snorkel around, so if you can find a way to get there, the Arbutus is a grand adventure.

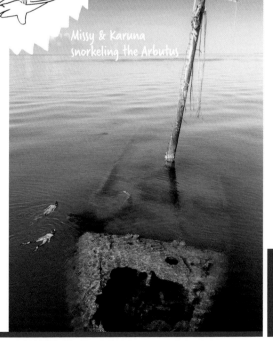

Missy & Karuna snorkeling the Arbutus

"What would the ocean be without a monster lurking in the dark? It would be like sleep without dreams."
–Werner Herzog

8

Water Safety

The ocean can feel as peaceful as a featherbed one moment, and unleash the fury of a thousand Krakens the next. Currents, tidal shifts, sudden wind and weather changes, mechanical failures and health emergencies can quickly compound into a life-threatening situation. Luckily, most water outings end with smiles. Here are a few basic precautions.

BUDDY UP: always have a buddy and keep a close eye on them.

CURRENTS: when getting in the water, from a boat or the beach, float for a minute to see how strong and in what direction the current is headed. Always swim against the current first.

DIVE FLAGS: prominently display a red-and-white diver-down flag whenever anyone from your party is in the water.

SAFETY GEAR: have a life jacket for each person, safety flares, a noise-making device, and anchor and navigation lights when running at night.

WEATHER FORECASTS: check weather forecasts and advisories before disembarking and while on the water. Also look at the sky often.

SKILL LEVEL: inform your guide about your swimming skill level and any medical conditions prior to departure.

NAVIGATION: make yourself familiar with your navigation equipment and pay attention to recommendations from rental outfitters.

WILDLIFE: don't touch or pester anything underwater or above water, as you may unwittingly destroy it, or it might sting or bite you.

WATERPROOF: on any boat, it's no guarantee there will be a place to keep valuables dry. Bring a plastic bag or dry sack to protect your stuff.

SPEED: just because a watercraft will go a certain speed, doesn't mean it's wise to go that fast, especially under certain conditions. Play it safe.

SUSTENANCE/SUNBURN/DEHYDRATION: always bring extra water and snacks. Drink the water. The sun at this latitude (24^0 N) is intense. Wear sunscreen, a long-sleeve cover-up, hat, and sunglasses.

BATTERIES: charge your phone prior to leaving and bring extra batteries for navigation and communication devices.

MOTORS: in shallow water, trim up the motor to avoid hitting bottom. If you do hit, you'll see a sediment trail behind your boat. Immediately cut and raise the motor, then pole yourself into deeper water.

TIDES: in the backcountry, it's easy to go somewhere during high tide and then be unable to return once the tide goes out. Remember, the full and new moon create the most dramatic high and low water levels.

POLARIZED SUNGLASSES: a high-quality pair of polarized glasses is a game-changer when it comes to seeing shallows and hazards underwater. Remember: brown, run aground; white, you just might; blue, sail on through; green, nice and clean.

RADIO CHANNEL: weather VHF 2; Coast Guard emergency VHF 16.

EMERGENCY NUMBERS: Emergency 911; Florida Marine Patrol *FMP; FWC Injured Wildlife and Violations 888-404-3922; Coast Guard 305-292-8856; Monroe County Sheriff non-emergency 305-289-2351; Seatow 305-901-5744; TowBoatUS 305-872-3092.

8

Favorite Aquatic Adventurers – Key West

HONEST ECO - ECO TOURS
Join them for four-hour eco-tours of dolphin watching, kayaking, snorkeling, and SUP yoga. Two boats, small groups, comfortable. 231 Margaret St., 305-294-6306, 711 Palm Ave., 305-294-6306.

JOLLY ROVER - SUNSET SAILS
Sunset sailing at its finest, TripAdvisor acclaimed, and in their off-time they teach the Boy Scouts. Come for drinks, relaxation, good company. Elizabeth Street, 305-205-2235, schoonerjollyrover.com.

DANGER CHARTERS
Half and full-day sails on 65-foot schooners small enough to access the backcountry for snorkel and kayak trips. Also hailed for their wine and sunset sails. See a tropical array of sea birds, spotted eagle rays, bull sharks, and if you're really lucky, the illustriously rare red-footed booby, or maybe just nude sunbathers. 245 Front Street, 305-304-7999, dangercharters.com.

SCHOONER WOLF SAILING CHARTERS
When the flagship vessel of the Conch Republic Navy isn't defending the island from riffraff, the 74-foot topsail schooner hosts pirate, military and traditional weddings, family gatherings, day rides, sunset sails, full moon charters, and memorial sails. The ship is patterned after the blockade runners who roamed the waters of the Caribbean in the 19th century. Historic seaport, 305-296-9694, schoonerwolf.com.

NOMADIC SUP STANDUP PADDLEBOARD
Looking to get an even suntan? Why not try an au naturel (in the buff) paddleboarding adventure. If you'd rather not crawl out of your shell or clothes, good news, these guys also guide fully clothed ecological explorations, sunset paddles and off-the-map private boat tours. Either way, you'll have a blast. They will also pick you up in style in a groovy paddle-van. 711 Eisenhower Drive, 305-395-9494, nomadicsup.com.

Nurse sharks are the most docile of sharks. They have small teeth and rarely bite people, except for those who poke them and pull their tails. You can't really hold that against them.

8

Favorite Aquatic Adventurers – Key West

MELLOW VENTURES: BACKCOUNTRY OUTFITTERS

If it's tacos and aquatic adventure you crave, Mellow Ventures is the answer. They offer trips on their 26-foot catamaran, as well as paddleboard and bicycle rentals. They also rent out a small boat fleet for overnight slumber parties and paddle-yoga retreats. As for the tacos, they make them at the restaurant inside their retail store. 1605 North Roosevelt Boulevard, 305-745-3874, mellowventureskeywest.com.

LOST REEF ADVENTURES

Lost Reef opens up the ocean for divers and snorkelers, with trips to the sparkling reefs at Sand Key and Sambos, and shipwrecks such as the Vandenburg and Joe's Tug. With a 30-plus-year record of safety and fun, they are also a great group of folks from whom to get your open water or advanced certifications, or try their one-day discover scuba course for beginners. They even certified one of your authors back in 2004. 261 Margaret Street, 305-296-9737, lostreefadventures.com.

PARAWEST PARASAILING

"Get high" is their motto, and by that they mean 300 feet in the air above the clear Keys waters. Fun for adrenaline junkies and even the timid at heart, the guides at this family-owned business know how to cater to both adventure and safety. If you're too spooked by heights, you can also just chill out in the boat, sip on a strawberry lemonade and wave to your high-flying pals. 700 Front Street, 305-292-5199, parawestparasailing.com.

13 BIG PINE KEY BOAT RENTALS
They maintain a large fleet of newer model boats with GPS units, charts, dive flags, shade, cushions, safety equipment, and reasonable rates. Mile marker 33, Big Pine Key, 305-849-0130; mile marker 24.5 Summerland Key, 745-1505, bigpineboatrentals.com.

11 FLORIDA KEYS JET SKI RENTALS
Rentals come with a mask, fins and snorkel. Book by the hour, half day, or full day. Newer models, rinse-off showers with salt scrub, friendly and prepared with happy prices. Mile marker 24.5, oceanside, Summerland Key, 305-396-7255, flkeysjetskirentals.com.

17 BIG PINE KAYAK ADVENTURES
Retreat to Big Pine Key for tranquil paddling amongst patient great white herons, peaceful Key deer, and elegant nurse sharks. Capt. Bill Keogh gives half and full-day kayaking nature tours through pristine mangroves, plus shallow-water skiff tours and short and long-term kayak rentals. Capt. Bill isn't just a naturalist, educator and professional photographer, he also wrote the *Florida Keys Paddling Guide* and *Keys Adventure Guides*. 1791 Bogie Drive, Big Pine Key, 305-872-7474, keyskayaktours.com.

18 CUDJOE KEY BOAT RENTALS
Dylan and Shelby rent nicely maintained boats with exceptional smiles. Deck, center console, and catamarans are available by the day, week or month. If you also bring a smile, they might be your guides on a charter fishing, snorkeling, or sightseeing tour. Based at Cudjoe Gardens Marina, fast access to the ocean, backcountry, Looe Key reef and American Shoal lighthouse. Tell them you read about them here! 477 Drost Dr., 305-204-4376, cudjoekeyboatrentals.com.

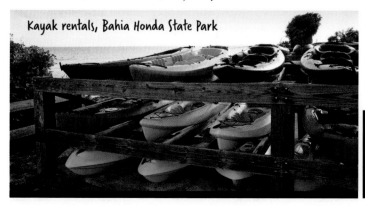

Kayak rentals, Bahia Honda State Park

8

FORT ZACHARY TAYLOR S.P.

MALLORY SQUARE

WISTERIA (CHRISTMAS TREE ISLAND)

HISTORIC SEAPORT

FLEMING KEY

See page 171 for lower Keys map.

DUVAL

OLD TOWN

WHITE

PALM AVE.

HIGGS BEACH

WHITE STREET PIER

DREDGERS KEY

N. ROOSEVELT / U.S. 1

KENNEDY

FLAGLER

NEW TOWN

SMATHERS BEACH

AIRPORT

S. ROOSEVELT / A1A

ATLANTIC OCEAN

GULF OF MEXICO

COLLEGE ROAD

STOCK ISLAND

KEY HAVEN

5TH STREET

FRONT

MALONEY

OVERSEAS HIGHWAY U.S. 1

= PUBLIC BOAT RAMP

9

Marinas, RVs & Camping

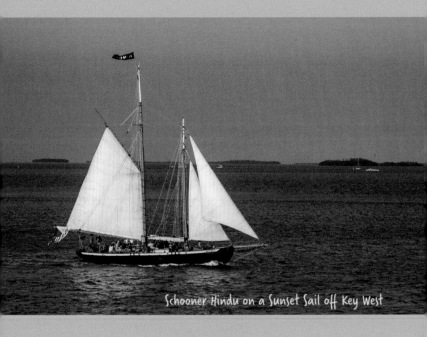

Schooner Hindu on a Sunset Sail off Key West

IN THIS CHAPTER

Transient boaters' guide to marinas
RV and tent guide to campgrounds

9

Marinas, RVs & Camping
... for transient boaters and landlubbers

Coming to the Keys in your floating or rolling home is an adventure never to be forgotten. Although we certainly don't have an unlimited supply of marina slips and campgrounds, possibilities are ample with enough forward planning and reservations. Read on for a comprehensive list for Key West and the Lower Keys.

MARINAS: There are a few types of marinas: transient, liveaboard, and those that offer both types of slips. As the world is in continual change, so too are marinas, and it is wise to contact them directly to confirm amenities and availability prior to heading for the Keys.

CAMPING: There are no legal public places to park an RV or pitch a tent overnight in the Lower Keys outside of official campgrounds. Police are quick to enforce this, especially with RVs. But there are some excellent campgrounds, most offering RV sites as well as tent spaces. During the winter and spring, the RV spots are in scarce commodity for those who didn't book reservations well in advance.

Restaurant

Swimming pool

Fitness center

Cable/Wi-Fi

Ships store

Fuel dock

Bait & tackle

Laundry, showers

Waste pumpout & or RV hookups

Mechanic services

Dogs allowed

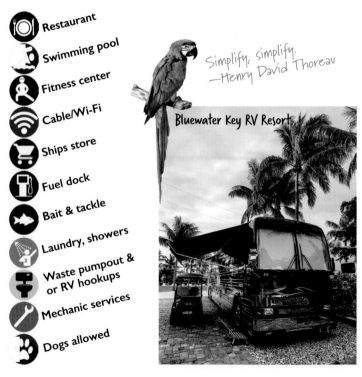

Simplify, simplify.
—Henry David Thoreau

Bluewater Key RV Resort

Marinas: Key West

1 A & B MARINA

A & B is pretty much in the middle of the Key West action, steps from the historic seaport and a gluttony of restaurants, shops, and entertainment. Refreshingly, the marina truthfully represents itself on its website. Transient slips, boats to 190 feet, 30/50/100 amps, diesel only. 700 Front Street, Key West, 800-223-8352, aandbmarina.com.

2 THE GALLEON MARINA

Upscale marina in the heart of the Old Town hubub. On-site resort hotel, nice ocean views, private beach, all new dock decking. Transient and seasonal slips, boats to 140 feet, 30/50 amps. 619 Front Street, Key West, 305-292-1292, galleonmarinakeywest.com.

3 KEY WEST YACHT CLUB

KWYC is a top-notch, old-school style club. They have a great restaurant and staff, a nice gazebo with a TV, and a convenient spot, 2 miles from Duval and less than 1 to New Town's supermarkets. Member of the Yachting Clubs of America. Boats to 58 feet. 2315 N. Roosevelt Blvd., Key West, 305-896-0426, keywestyachtclub.com.

4 MARGARITAVILLE KEY WEST RESORT & MARINA

Formerly the Westin, it was recently purchased and renamed. It's a nice marina with a large hotel tucked peacefully behind Mallory Square. The only down side is that cruise ships dock between your open-water view and the hotel. Fortunately, this is only a few days a week, and they are usually gone in time for the sunset. 245 Front Street, 305-294-4000, margaritavillekeywestresort.com.

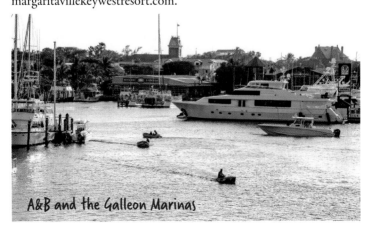

A&B and the Galleon Marinas

Marinas: Key West & Stock Island

5 CONCH HARBOR MARINA

At the northern end of the historic waterfront, it's a nice marina near an abundance of restaurants and bars, plus its own Conch Harbor Club. Transient and monthly slips, boats to 200 feet, 100 amps. 951 Caroline Street, Key West, 305-294-2933, conchharbormarina.com.

6 KEY WEST BIGHT MARINA

Location! Next to Conch Harbor, this City-run marina gets many a return visitor, with consistent reviews of friendliness and relative affordability. Transient slips, boats to 140 feet, 30/50/100 amp. 201 William, Key West, 305-809-3984, keywestbightmarina.com.

7 GARRISON BIGHT MARINA

Though it does not offer transient or liveaboard slips, this marina is a convenient stop for boating supplies and snacks. Gasoline only. 711 Eisenhower Drive, 305-294-3093, garrisonbightmarina.net.

8 KEY WEST CITY MARINA

At the no-frills municipal marina the rates are low, but so is the availability. It's almost in Old Town, about a mile from the historic seaport, and offers transient and liveaboard slips. Just a note, a photo on their Google search page shows a pool; problem is, there is no pool. 1801 N. Roosevelt, Key West, 305-809-3981, cityofkeywest-fl.gov.

9 KEY WEST MOORING FIELDS
The city rents out 149 moorings between Fleming Key and Sigsbee Park. Of course this is more affordable, but doesn't include power or other amenities. Depending on where you tie up, the skiff ride can be a few or 15 minutes, and can be choppy on a stormy day. Liveaboard, transient, free pump-out service. 305-809-3981, cityofkeywest-fl.gov.

10 COCONUT MALLORY RESORT & MARINA
This marina is in New Town, and not really walking distance to shops and bars, but it is a peaceful retreat from the relentless traffic

Lobster trap buoy, Sugarloaf

of downtown. They only rent slips to resort guests, who also get to enjoy a clubhouse, barbecue, playground and Jacuzzi. 1445 S. Roosevelt, Key West, 866-316-1843, mallorykeywest.com.

Stock Island

Note:
Stock Island is not the same island as Key West. It is right next door, but we wanted to point this out as several places in Stock Island use "Key West" as their address, though Old Town is five or more miles away. Historically Stock Island has been a spirited community of commercial fishermen and the hard-working folks supporting the rungs of the Key West service industry. Quite recently, Stock Island has become embroiled in chronic gentrification. It also has an emblematic layer of drug dealers and users. Most feel safe here inside marinas and campgrounds, but there are parts that should be treated as unsafe for pedestrians after the sun sets.

11 KEY WEST HARBOUR MARINA

This is a very nice marina with a tasty restaurant, pool, and a small picturesque beach with cocktail service. It's a 10 to 15-minute drive from Old Town. Of all of the marinas on Stock Island, this would be our choice. It's secluded at the end of the road, with no adjacent neighborhoods, easy ocean access, and peaceful water views. Transient and liveaboard slips, boats up to 110 feet, 30/50/100 amp power. 6000 Peninsular Ave., Stock Island, 305-292-3121, reservations at opentable.com, floridamarinaclubs.com.

12 STOCK ISLAND MARINA VILLAGE

Another top choice, Marina Village gets rave reviews for transformation. What was once a dirty, working marina with derelict vessels has reawakened into a pleasant, airy, friendly, clean, deep-water marina with excellent ocean access, floating docks, a new hotel, dog park, organic community garden, shuttle service to Key West, and leather-clad captain's lounge with a flat-screen TV. The downside is an adjacent working boatyard where locals paint, repair, and work on their vessels. Transient and liveaboard slips, boats up to 300 feet. 7005 Shrimp Road, Stock Island, 305-294-2288, stockislandmarina.com.

13 SAFE HARBOUR MARINA

This is a classic Florida fishing community marina. It is not fancy, no glitz and glamour here, but you'll get basic facilities and the beloved Hogfish Bar & Grill. This is another area not fit for long night walks, but it is secluded, being on a dead-end road. Transient and liveaboard slips, boats from 35 to 160 feet, 30/50 amp power. 6810 Front Street, Stock Island, 305-294-9797, safeharbourmarinakw.com.

Note: Numbers in front of marina names correspond to map on page 160.

Marinas: Stock Island

14 OCEANS EDGE KEY WEST HOTEL & MARINA

We haven't visited this marina yet, due to it being closed for transition from a working waterfront to an upscale tourist property. We are certain it is very nice, and everything is shiny new, but immediately outside of the entrance lurks a big industrial building. Beyond is a lobster yard, and a little farther is somewhere I would not bicycle or walk through past sunset. If you are arriving via water, and will have a car to get to Key West, then it would be fine. Transient slips, boats up to 140 feet, 30/50 amp power. 5950 Peninsular Ave., Stock Island, 844-885-7855, oceansedgekeywest.com.

15 COW KEY MARINA

This is a small marina, at the edge of a decent residential neighborhood on Stock Island. At press time the marina was closed for renovations and change of ownership. Jet ski, paddleboard, kayak rentals. 5001 5th Ave., Stock Island, 305-292-9111, cowkeymarinakeywest.com.

16 HURRICANE HOLE MARINA

Just over the bridge from Key West in a protected lagoon, they rent slips for short and long-term, but no liveaboard. The on-site restaurant is good and there's a bait-and-tackle store, dive shop, and paddleboard rentals. Boats up to 34 feet, gasoline only. 5130 Overseas Hwy 1, Stock Island, 305-294-8025, hurricaneholekeywest.com.

17 SUNSET MARINA

This is on the "nice" side of Stock Island, off the bayside not far from Key West. Its name doesn't lie, the west-facing view brings daily dazzling sunset vistas. Being bayside means a longer trip to the open water. Conversely, it means a calm-water skiff ride to the bars on the historic seaport. It's very near the golf course, and the Sheriff detention center, but feels safe and you can't see indications that a jail is nearby. Transient slips, boats to 120 feet, 30/50/100 amps. 5555 College Road, Stock Island, 305-296-7101, sunsetmarinakw.com.

Key West Mooring Fields

Marinas: Lower Keys

See page 171 for Lower Keys map.

Note: These are local, small marinas mostly for personal fishing and pleasure vessels, not destinations for cruisers or liveaboards.

18 BIG PINE FISHING LODGE

This marina is mostly used by guests of the RV park and lodge, but it offers a sizeable gift shop with snacks, bait and tackle, and other necessities. Gasoline only. Big Pine Boat Rentals is on-site (chapter 8). Mile marker 33, Big Pine Key, 33042, 305-872-3868, bpkfl.com.

19 OLD WOODEN BRIDGE MARINA & RESORT

This friendly, down-home-type marina caters to small boats and people who love to fish. There are on-site boat rentals, kayak eco-tours and rentals, and 14 efficiency cottages. It's a great jump-off for exploration in the backcountry. Gasoline only. 1791 Bogie Drive, Big Pine Key, FL, 33043, 305-872-2241, oldwoodenbridge.com.

20 DOLPHIN MARINA AND COTTAGES

The ferry to Little Palm Island launches from here (chapter 2). They offer limited transient docking, have a small bait, ice and beer store and on-site boat rentals. There are also 12 cottages (tiny dogs only). About 30 minutes from Key West. Mile Marker 28.5, Little Torch Key, 33042, 800-553-0308, dolphinmarina.net.

21 CUDJOE GARDENS MARINA

A nice little neighborhood marina, Cudjoe Gardens is family run and eco-friendly. They have a decent-size store with bait, beverages, beer, ice, and other basics for a day on the water. There are boat and kayak rentals on-site, plus offshore charters and a mechanic. Boats up to 40 feet, excellent open-water access. Make sure you tell Allen, the owner, that you found him in our book! Mile marker 21, oceanside, 477 Drost Drive, Cudjoe Key, 33042, 305-745-2352, cudjoegardensmarina.com.

22 SUGARLOAF KEY, KEY WEST KOA

This small marina is used mostly by guests of the campground or those passing by who need to restock on gasoline and store supplies. Boat rentals, easy ocean and backcountry access. Mile marker 20, oceanside, 251 State Road 939, Sugarloaf Key, FL 33042, 305-745-3549, koa.com/campgrounds/sugarloaf-key.

Cudjoe

9

Marinas: Lower Keys

23 SUGARLOAF MARINA

Right next to Sugarloaf Lodge, here you'll find a basic ships store supplies plus bait and tackle, as well as kayak sales, rentals, and tours. If you are looking to launch your runabout to explore the back country off Sugarloaf Key, or kayak through mangrove creeks, this is your place. Gasoline only. Mile marker 17, gulfside, Sugarloaf Key, 33042, 305-745-3135, sugarloafkeymarina.com.

24 GEIGER KEY MARINA

This marina accommodates guests of the RV park. There's a small bait store with the basics, but the real highlight for non-guests is pulling up to the dock to have lunch. This is also a great place to launch (or rent) kayaks and paddleboards to explore clear, shallow lagoons and meandering mangrove paths. Mile marker 12, oceanside, 5 Geiger Road, Geiger Key, FL 33040, 305-296-3553, geigerkeymarina.com.

25 BOCA CHICA N.A.S. MARINA

Boca Chica is a U.S. Navy base, so entry is granted only to active and retired military personnel and their guests. If you fit the bill, this is nice place to liveaboard for a day, season or year, so long as you can tolerate the decibels of frequent fighter jet flyovers. Mile marker 7, oceanside, 33040, 305-293-2402, cnic.navy.mil/keywest.

Camping: RVs & Tents

26 BAHIA HONDA STATE PARK

Chances are you've drooled over pictures of the pristine beaches and clear waters of Bahia Honda, even if you didn't know it. It contains the Keys' most celebrated stretches of sand and is a favorite location for photo shoots. Campsites for both RVs and tents usually require a reservation months in advance, but if you plan well, your backyard will be a water lovers' wonderland. Boat ramps, transient dockage and a few cabins are also available. Less than 10 minutes to stores at Big Pine Key and 45 minutes to Old Town Key West. floridastateparks. org/park/Bahia-Honda, mile marker 36.8, oceanside, 305-872-2353.

22 SUGARLOAF KEY/KEY WEST KOA

As one of the busiest KOAs in the country, what the Southernmost KOA lacks in secluded campsites, it makes up for in personality and the social scene. When you're done playing in the pool, hot tub, tiki bar and ocean swimming hole with water trampoline, walk to the marina to rent a boat, or charter a sunset cruise or reef snorkeling trip.

Camping: RVs & Tents

This is another of our favorites at which to house company. Old Town is 25 minutes, but there's no need to stop the libations — jump on the campground shuttle or bus. RV and tent camping, plus Airstream cabin rentals. koa.com/campgrounds/sugarloaf-key, 251 County Road 939 (turn oceanside at MM 20), Sugarloaf Key, 305-745-3549.

27 BLUEWATER KEY RV RESORT

Those bringing their own house can park in luxury at one of Bluewater Key's private, lushly landscaped lots. Request a waterfront with a souped-up tiki hut. Some come equipped with bars, couches and flat-screen TVs. The regular snowbirds here trend toward an older crowd, but with their exuberant socializing they sometimes prove the saying, "You can only be young once, but immature forever." 20 minutes to Old Town. bluewaterkey.com, mile marker 14, oceanside, 305-745-2494.

28 SUNSHINE KEY RV RESORT & MARINA

Sunshine offers RV and tent sites on 75-acre Ohio Key, with fishing, a pool, clubhouse, store, bocci ball, tennis, basketball, horeshoes, volleyball, pickleball, ping pong, and marina on-site. Near Bahia Honda. rvonthego.com, mile marker 38.8, 877-570-2267.

24 GEIGER KEY RV PARK & MARINA

Relax in waterfront seclusion, next to a great bar and restaurant with live music. Marina has boat slips, laundry, showers, and fishing, Paddleboard and kayak rentals on-site. geigerkeymarina.com, 5 Geiger Key Road, 305-296-3553.

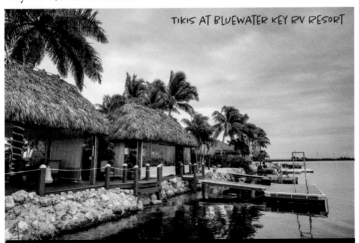

TIKIS AT BLUEWATER KEY RV RESORT

9

Camping: RVs & Tents

18 BIG PINE KEY FISHING LODGE & MARINA

Leave the boat in a slip and enjoy a rooftop pool, water aerobics, game room, nature trail, playground, barbecues, store, and beach. RV and tents. bpkfl.com, mile marker 33, oceanside, Big Pine Key, 305- 872-2351.

29 LAZY LAKES RV RESORT

Here you'll find short and long-term RV sites on 28 acres with a 7-acre saltwater lake, pool. There are some waterfront sites, plus horseshoes, a clubhouse, and a fishing dock. Mile marker 20, oceanside, 311 Johnson Road, Sugarloaf Key, lazylakesrvresort.com, 305-745-1079.

30 BOYD'S CAMPGROUND

Boyd's is well groomed, awash with amenities, offers some waterfront sites, and is right on the city bus line. This is a safer Stock Island location, but still beware of walking outside of the complex at night. Luckily it is spacious enough inside the park for nice strolls. boydscampground.com, 6401 Maloney, Stock Island, 305-294-1465.

31 LEO'S CAMPGROUND

The closest campground to Key West has limited frills, but it is friendly and on the bus line. RVs, tents, daily, monthly, hookups, tent rentals, Wi-Fi, barbeque, showers, laundry, sun deck, and dog park. Same night-walk warning as Boyd's. No dogs in tent area. leoscampground.com, 5236 Suncrest, Stock Island, 305-296-5260.

32 EL MAR RV RESORT

No frills, some waterfront. Electric and water hookups, pets under 25 pounds. No on-site management, minimum 26-foot RVs only. People like the price vs. proximity to Key West, but it sits between two trailer parks and not in a good spot to venture out from at night. 6700 Maloney Ave., Stock Island, 305-294-0857, elmarrvresort.com.

9

TO MAINLAND

BAHIA HONDA STATE PARK

BIG PINE KEY

KEY DEER N.W.R.

SUMMERLAND

U.S. 1

HAWK CHANNEL

= PUBLIC BOAT RAMP

SUGARLOAF

THE BACKCOUNTRY

SADDLEBUNCH KEYS

ATLANTIC OCEAN

OVERSEAS HIGHWAY

GULF OF MEXICO

GREAT WHITE HERON N.W.R.

STOCK ISLAND

KEY WEST N.W.R.

KEY WEST

Shopping & Provisions

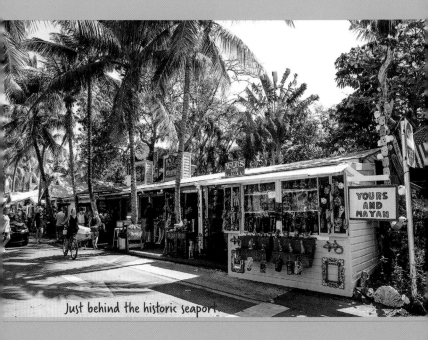

Just behind the historic seaport.

IN THIS CHAPTER

Art gallery highlights
Gift highlights
Bookstores & learning
Local products
Provisions & necessities

... of course Key West is the place to get your

Abstract Cock Art...

you know, artful roosters & other classic Keys gifts

Shopping in a tourist town invokes images of kitschy T-shirts, fudge, and overpriced knickknacks that are brought home, then quickly relegated to a box of junk in the closet. Key West certainly has its fair share of $5 T-shirt shops and nice-yet-predictable chain fashion stores, but there is also an impressive number of family-run businesses selling imaginative gifts and useful items found nowhere else.

In this chapter you will find bits on art, gifts, oddities, and our favorite products made in the Keys. There is also information on where to get provisions, such as specialty groceries, beverages, and health food.

Art Galleries

1, 2 & 3 There is no limit to breadth of art here, but there are some perennial Keys themes worth noting: roosters, sea creatures, birds, Cuba, cats, and tropical everything. There are dozens of art galleries along Duval and throughout Old Town. Three of our favorites, which exhibit local artists, are 7 Artists and Friends at 122 Duval, Art Gone Wild at 619 Duval, and Alan S. Maltz photography at 1210 Duval, all of which feature vibrant colorful works and some noble and goofy animals. The Key West Art Guide, can be found in most galleries, and gives a good feeling for what each offers as well, keywestartguide.com.

Numbers by store name correspond to map on page 172.

Keys-Centric Gifts

4 **KINO SANDALS:** In the '60s, a husband-and-wife team began making sandals that are now worn by people around the world. See the durable, fashionable, and comfortable shoes being handcrafted at their Old Town factory. They also make purses and the *Cuban Conch Cookbook*. Buy them around town or at the factory, 107 Fitzpatrick Street, Kino Plaza, Old Town, Key West, kinosandals.com.

10

SMILIN' BOB'S FISH DIP: Hungry musician-anglers turned their home recipe into a national hit, but it surely tastes best in a Keys breeze with sand in your toes. Made with wild amerjack and kingfish caught right here, this dip has long been coveted by locals and is now available in many Whole Foods, Publix, Safeways, and other supermarkets around the country. It's crafted on Summerland Key and found most everywhere down here, smilinbobs.com.

THE KEYS SALT SCRUB: These local salt scrubs are divine, whether you want softer, rejuvenated skin or just to easily wash off some grease after working on the car. Handmade in small batches, the blend of salts, coconut and essential oils are all natural, plus chemical and cruelty free. They also serve as a nice, lasting reminder of the feeling of the Keys. Find them in many stores around town as well as at thekeyssaltscrub.com.

PICKLE BARON OF KEY WEST: We aren't sure how a classically trained Swiss chef ended up making pickles in Key West, but good fortune is not to be questioned. He says he was inspired by Caribbean tastes, colors and aromas, and cucumbers are the perfect medium to soak up those flavors. Key West is also warmer than the Alps. Either way, he is prolific, with an array from classic dills to sliced jalapeños in sweet candy brine. "Eat pickles, live forever," is his slogan. Sounds good. Find them around town and at local farmer's and artisan's markets, picklebaronofkeywest.com.

5 **KEY WEST DISTILLING:** Rums, whiskey and vodkas crafted slowly and with care, just like the Key West lifestyle. Find the award-winning spirits at liquor stores and bars in town, and at the distillery. 524 Southard, kwdistilling.com.

Keys-Centric Gifts

6 KEY WEST ALOE: Nothing helps a sunburn like fresh aloe. With this knowledge they launched their wares in 1971, and today make the largest selection of aloe vera-based products in the world. Their cleansers, shaving gels, shampoos, sunburn salves, and everything else is vegan as well as free of animal testing, gluten, and parabens. They are sold around town and at their store, 1075 Duval, keywestaloe.com.

KEEZ BEEZ RAW HONEY: The Keys have more species of native flowers than anywhere else in the U.S., making this honey deliciously varied, and the bees ultra healthy. It's free of pesticides and bears vitamins, enzymes and antioxidants (most big-brand store honey is ultra-filtered and contains no pollen, meaning it technically isn't even honey). The local buzzers produce their honey from Keys flora including mango, avocado, sea grape, and black mangrove. Find it in grocery and gift outlets around town, or at keezbeezhoney.com.

NELLIE AND JOE'S KEY LIME JUICE: The yellow bottle you see in every respectable liquor store, supermarket, and bar in the U.S., Europe and Asia, is actually a Key West original. It started right here, when young local Nellie presented Henry Flagler with a bouquet of flowers as he stepped off of his momentous inaugural railroad journey to Key West in 1912. The family founded the business in 1968, when they began filling long-necked beer bottles with juice in their Key West kitchen. Eventually they got so big they had to move the factory to Pompano, Florida, but the juice's heart still lives in the Keys. Available everywhere, keylimejuice.com.

7, 8, 9, 10 & 11 KEY LIMES: Speaking of the little tart ones, Key lime products are plentiful here. Try the Key Lime Pie Factory at 412 Greene or Kermit's Key Lime Shoppe at 200 Elizabeth and 802 Duval for cookies, lip balm, taffy, salsa, tea... and of course pie. Other famous pie stops include Blue Heaven at 729 Thomas Street, Pepe's at 806 Caroline, and the Hogfish Bar on Stock Island.

BABY'S COFFEE: Some ambitious caf-fiends ride their bicycles from Key West 15 miles up to Baby's for a morning cup of coffee. Others just drive. The family business uses only pure mountain arabica beans roasted in the Keys. For the decaf, they use Swiss Water Process, which decaffeinates without chemicals. They also have a cool logo. Mile marker 15, oceanside, Saddlebunch Keys, babyscoffee.com.

Local Favorites & Specialties

12 ISLAND DEODORANT

Give a loved one a stick of deodorant, and they might take it as an insult. On the contrary, a gift of Island Deodorant shows how much you truly care for someone's long-term health. It's organic and free from toxic aluminum and other chemicals, and the strangest part is it actually works really well. They have a baking soda-free formula as well, for those with senitive skin. Made in Key West, available at Date & Thyme or online at islanddeodorant.com.

10

COAST: This creative compound built out of materials recycled from the ashes of a dilapidated boatyard always draws a diverse crowd with its monthly-or-so concerts. A conglomeration of hippies, hipsters, artists, wanderers, and other free spirits congregate here to build things like houseboats and skateboards, sell their wares, fix things, do art, host kids' camps, and even train pigeons. They are self-admittedly a bit difficult to put into a box and explain — indeed their motto is simply "Live By It" — but they are friendly and are up to date on their rabies vaccinations, so don't hesitate to check them out and buy a cool T-shirt or hat. 6404 Front Street, Stock Island, coastprojects.com.

The cost of a thing is the amount of life which is required to be exchanged for it. — Henry David Thoreau

KEY WEST NATIONAL WILDLIFE REFUGE

Odds & Ends Worth a Note

REEFSAFE SUNSCREEN: New research shows the damage even a tiny bit of certain chemicals can do to reefs and water systems, and nearly every big brand contains them. A few companies have made it a point to eliminate these toxins, and Florida-based Tropical Seas earned the endorsement of the non-profit marine research organization Mote Marine. It works well, and doesn't leave a white residue. Find it at dive shops in town or tropicalseas.com.

COSTA DEL MAR: These guys make sunglasses in Daytona Beach that have practically become dress code for being on a boat in the Keys — not just for fashion, but because the lenses are keenly sharp with polarization vital to spotting shoals and sea life under the water. Get them in pretty much any sunglass shop in town, costadelmar.com.

The Guerrero Project

One of our favorite documentaries shot in the Keys, *The Guerrero Project* tells the story of the search for a pirate Spanish slave ship that sank here, and what finding it means to people today. It's a compelling story, wrought with dramatic history, local treasure hunters and historians, but we particularly like it because one of the authors directed it. DVDs are available at some places around town that sell this book, and at theguerreroproject.org.

ROYAL TERN AT SUNSET, LOWER KEYS

Bookstores, Science & Nature

13 KEY WEST ISLAND BOOKS
Eclectic and expansive with a staff dedicated to finding you a good read, it's easy to get lost in this independent bookstore. Browse new, used and rare titles, plus a great section from local authors. 513 1/2 Fleming Street, kwislandbooks.com, 305-294-2904.

14 BOOKS & BOOKS @ THE STUDIOS OF KEY WEST
The town's newest indie bookstore also serves as a community center for those who write, make art, or just enjoy reading. Browse books, magazines and gifts, meet artists, buy art supplies, and enjoy local art in the studios. 533 Eaton Street, booksandbooks.com, 305-320-0208.

15 FLORIDA KEYS ECO-DISCOVERY CENTER
Nestled in the corner of the natural history museum, the center's gift shop is an experience all in itself, with an excellent collection of Keys nature and history books, science projects, and educational toys. 35 East Quay Road, floridakeys.noaa.gov/eco_discovery, 305-809-4750.

KEY DEER BOOKSTORE
Besides giving the daily lowdown on where to spot Key Deer, the kind folks here stock an impressive collection of local and worldly wildlife and science books and gifts. Located in the Key Deer Visitor Center and run by the Friends and Volunteers of Refuges. Proceeds benefit Keys National Marine Wildlife Refuges. As of this printing the center is at 179 Key Deer Blvd., but by the time you read this, it may have moved to mile marker 30.6, also on Big Pine Key, 305-872-0774, favorfloridakeys.org/key-deer-bookstore.

Interesting Gift Stores

16 **WANDERLUST:** Inspired by travelers and beach culture, and packed with local art, affordable women's clothing and jewelry. 310 Petronia Street in funky Bahama Village, wanderlustkw.com.

17 **90 MILES TO CUBA:** Nautical antiques, new and classic postcards, and plenty of art from Key West and Cuba. 616 Greene Street, 90milestocuba.net.

LOW KEY TIE DYE: Great place to shop and meet new friends. Clothing and more for everyone from retired hippies to free-spirited Millennials. 31109 Avenue A, Big Pine Key (near mile marker 31), gulfside.

10

Interesting Gift Stores

18 **SALT ISLAND & GALLERY:** This art gallery, spice shop, and homeopathic apothecary awakens all five senses and offers a bit of everything: handcrafted Keys goods, a revolving fine art gallery, jewelry, local honey, candles, books, and of course an array of fancy salts. 830 Fleming Street, saltislandprovisions.com.

19 **SOUTHERNMOST RESORT WEAR & GIFTS:** This is the best souvenir store on the island, just a couple of blocks from the Southernmost Point. They offer classic and inventive Key West-themed gifts, clothing and merchandise. 1103 & 1105 Whitehead Street.

20 & 21 **MEL FISHER'S TREASURES:** Touching a silver coin lost to the sea for four centuries changes one's perception of the world. Wearing that coin as jewelry also makes for a great conversation starter. Find jewelry, shipwreck artifacts and a shelf full of good reads about real-life pirates, hurricanes and modern-day treasure hunters. 200 Greene Street & 613 Duval, melfisher.com.

22 **SALTWATER ANGLER:** Plan on spending a while exploring their extensive collection of fly and light-tackle rods, reels, fish art, and stylish high-performance clothing for guys and gals. 243 Front Street, saltwaterangler.com.

23 **MALLORY SQUARE SUNSET CELEBRATION MARKET**
As if the sunsets at Mallory Square weren't impressive enough, there's always an array of remarkable art, accompanied by its makers. 400 Wall Street, sunsetcelebraton.org.

Be content with what you have; rejoice in the way things are. When you realize there is nothing lacking, the whole world belongs to you. — Lao Tzu

Simonton Beach, the closest sand to shopping.

Interesting Gift Stores

24 KEY WEST TREASURE CHEST: Find coins here from the 1784 El Cazador shipwreck, which is a little-known yet pivotal event in the U.S. gaining the Louisiana Territory. There is also coin jewelry and artifacts from other famous shipwrecks, replicas, and maintain a great bookshelf. 700 Front Street, facebook Key West Treasure Chest.

25 LEATHER MASTER: A toy shop for the naughty and sexy, with lingerie for men and women, leather accessories, makeup, wigs, and body art. 418 Appelrouth Lane, leathermaster.com.

26 PARADISE TATTOO: Forever remember Key West, with permanent art or piercings from the Keys' first and oldest tattoo studio, or just get temporary body painting. 627 Duval Street, paradisetattoo.com.

27 GREENE STREET CIGAR FACTORY: Key West and cigars have a long history together. Here they'll sell you a case to take home, but first convince you to sample one with a craft beer, wine, or Cuban coffee. 540 & 614 Greene Street, greenstreetcigarcompany.com.

28 KEY WEST WINERY: Sample then take home premium tropical wines made from all fruit (no infusions) in a bright and airy space. 103 Simonton Street, thekeywestwinery.com.

29 BON VOYAGE: a great little souvenier shop, with some out-of-the ordinary and affordable Key West gifts. 614 Front Street.

SALT - SERVING ART & SPICE

Provisions: Key West

30 **SUGAR APPLE:** The largest health-food shop in town is dedicated to helping the health of others and the planet by pairing customers with the best products, recipes, and remedies for their well-being. Organic foods, homeopathic remedies, and a café and smoothie bar are just the beginning. Don't hesitate to ask for advice. 917 Simonton Street, sugarapplekeywest.com.

12 **DATE & THYME:** Stock up on organic and locally sourced produce and dry goods, alternative remedies, earth-friendly soaps, spices, and good vibrations. Then sip a smoothie with an organic breakfast or lunch on the sunny patio. 829 Fleming Street, dateandthyme.com.

31 & 32 **FAUSTO'S FOOD PALACE:** Key West's local and oldest-running grocer since 1926, Fausto's stocks a grand array of produce and dry goods both commonplace and gourmet, including local products. Stop by to stock the cupboards or just pick up a snack from the deli. Ask about home delivery. Two locations: 522 Fleming Street and 1105 White Street, faustos.com.

33 & 34 **PEPPERS OF KEY WEST:** Browse sauces, spices and rubs from just around the corner and across the world, or settle in at the tasting bar for a blazing tour. We always come in for a quick bottle, but leave with a bag full of treats and a few new recipes. 602 Greene Street and 500 Truman Ave., peppersofkeywest.com.

35 **EATON STREET SEAFOOD MARKET:** Really great, locally caught, fresh seafood, including Key West pink shrimp, yellowtail snapper, grouper, stone crab claws, and a lot more. Take it home and cook it up or have them make it into a sandwich for you. They'll give you a few good recipes, too. 801 Eaton Street, kwseafood.com.

36 **GLAZED DONUTS & RED BUOY COFFEE:** Donuts that are works of art, handcrafted and ready to be scarfed down... I mean savored along with some good coffee. 420 Eaton Street, glazeddonuts.com.

BIGGER STORES: New Town is where the box stores are. There are two Publix, a Winn-Dixie, Home Depot, Kmart, and Office Max.

GOOD FOOD CONSPIRACY: Get your organic on, from the health food market to the café and juice bar. Vegan, vegetarian and gluten-free options, an apothecary of herbs and remedies, and bulk spices. Mile marker 30.1, oceanside, Big Pine Key, goodfoodconspiracy.com.

SUMMERLAND WINE & SPIRITS: These guys stock an extensive and unusual selection of gourmet wine, craft beer, liquors and cigars, and will special order anything they don't happen to have in stock. Mile marker 24.8, oceanside, Summerland Key, keysliquors.com.

10

MURRAY'S MARKET: This gourmet neighborhood market stocks top-quality foodstuff plentiful enough for a boat picnic lunch or a gastronomic dinner masterpiece. Fresh steaks and other meats, produce, sprawling sub sandwiches, slaws, pastas, and even laundry soap. Mile marker 24.5, oceanside, Summerland Key, 305-745-3534.

KICKIN' BACK FOOD MART: Friendly pit stop for both on-the-go adventures and late-night sweet-tooth cravings. Canned goods, beer, wine, munchies, jerky, deli, kitty litter, and ice cream. Mile marker 21.3, oceanside, Cudjoe Key, 305-745-2528.

BAYPOINT MARKET: A tiny market with a big heart, Baypoint might not stock everything you want, but it should have everything you need: horseradish pickles, creamy milkshakes, black-cherry soda, sandwiches, Cheetos, french fries, and deli meat. Mile marker 15, oceanside, Saddlebunch Keys, 305-745-3882.

FIVE BROTHERS GROCERY TWO: This family-run market has some standard supplies, along with a few surprises. They also serve up delicious Cuban deli fare. Mile marker 27, gulfside, 305-872-0702.

WINN-DIXIE: Large supermarket, recently renovated. 251 Key Deer Boulevard, Big Pine Key, 305-872-4124, gulfside at the light.

"If I got Key West sized up right, they would receive War, Famine, Pestilence and Death without question – call them all by some fancy name, and then rope in the survivors and sell them good cigars and brandies at easy prices and horrible dinners at infamous rates."
— Mark Twain, 1867 visit.

11
Kids, Families, Dogs

Noble Selassie

IN THIS CHAPTER

Foresights, precautions, safety, laws
Free things to do for kids & dogs
Good attractions, giggles & learning for kids
Good walking & restaurants for tail waggers
Dog-friendly lodging
Kid and dog events
Wildlife checklist

Magic Potion: hermit crabs + O.J.
Results: giggles + imagination

When I was 7, my dad drove my mom and me through the frozen forests, from our cabin at 8,000 feet to an airplane bound for Florida. We had embarked on a magical journey hunting for shells, meeting hermit crabs, and exploring tidal pools by day, then playing Canasta with my grandparents after the sunset. We kept this family spring break ritual for many years, including after my brother came to be, expanding the trip to several weeks or more, despite grumbles and reprimands from school administrators who valued attendance over travel.

Around the same age, Steve's parents began a similar custom, which involved his mom and dad loading him and his sister up in a station wagon and driving south 1,000 miles, making sure to stop at the Florida welcome center just across the state line for free fresh-squeezed orange juice. Florida became a tradition he loved so much that when he became a father, he got an RV and drove down with his kids.

"You teach kids how to succeed when they successfully foil the educational system."
— Arlo Guthrie

For us both as children, Florida equaled a magical land. To this day, the embrace of the humid air, a smell of salt and stench of seaweed, crunchy grass under bare feet and blanketing sunshine all blend into a particular feeling — one that evokes strong memories of giggles, exploration, nature, and so many enshrined family memories.

Welcome to an enchanted land, families! May Florida cast its happiness spell upon you.

11

Dog side of chapter

Gruf, woof, aarff, boof, boof, murf

Translation: "Life is best measured in wags of a tail... and occasionally droplets of drool."

Bacon that needs to be eaten. Tennis balls that need retrieving. Wind in the nose through open car windows. Steak. Soft pillows. Did I already say bacon? If these are a few of your dog's favorite things, then you're in luck. We have all of that here.

In fact, Key West's official philosophy of "one human family" fairly well extends to humans' best friends as well. The live-and-let-live temperament of both people and canines around here makes it a pleasant place to visit with a dog. In fact, most restaurants with outside seating — which is most eateries in town — allow dogs.

On the downside, we are lacking one major comfort of home — squirrels. There are no squirrels to chase. But there are a lot of lizards, and four out of five dogs agree that they make an excellent entertainment substitute.

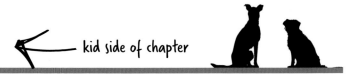

kid side of chapter

Kids - Foresight & Precautions

The Keys are a great place to ditch technology to go outside and play. Nearly every activity involves nature. Free and cheap ones abound, many of which are uniquely Keys experiences.

However, not all of Key West is kid-friendly all of the time. The town does have a reputation as an adult indulgence destination, where alcohol flows and inhibitions retreat. For example, at night Duval Street is not guaranteed to be G-rated. During Fantasy Fest most parents feel it is not suitable for children at any time of day. But other than those easily avoidable pitfalls, Key West is a family-oriented community, dedicated to teaching children about the wonders of their environment and giving them a safe island to call home.

Speaking of Duval, by day it is a swell place for kids, with lots of fun shopping, ice cream stores, and funky patio restaurants. Wandering there, or taking a trip to the movie theater is fun, but be warned, this chapter focuses on less-typical vacation experiences, which we hope will help make for a true trip of a lifetime, to be reminisced about around the dinner table for decades to come.

May the wings of the butterfly kiss the sun
And find your shoulder to light on,
To bring you luck, happiness and riches
Today, tomorrow and beyond.
                                        –Irish Blessing

Butterfly Conservatory

Dogs - Safety, Laws & Parks

LEGAL ORDINANCES

There is a leash law on all public property in Key West and Monroe County, though well-behaved dogs often get away unteathered without a lot of hullabaloo. The exceptions where dogs are permitted off-leash are the dog park, dog beach, and private property, under permission of the owner. State Parks allow leashed dogs in day-use areas, except for in buildings or on beaches and playgrounds. Of course, all poop must be picked up and disposed of properly. Dogs are not allowed on most beaches or the interior of restaurants.

37, 38 & 39 OFF-LEASH PLAY & BEACHES

The Higgs Beach Dog Park is a great social scene. There are two fenced areas here, one for all dogs and one for dogs under 25 pounds, each with a watering station, shade trees, and seating. This park is just on the other side of Atlantic Boulevard from Higgs Beach. The Vernon Avenue beach, also known as Dog Beach, is a tiny, rocky area, but it is better than nothing since it and Simonton Beach are the only two places dogs can romp on the sand in town, leashed or not. Dog Beach is by Louie's Backyard restaurant, a nice after-romp watering hole, which allows dogs in the bar until 5 p.m. Simonton Beach is on the north end, and is the only beach in Key West where you can enjoy a cocktail with a dog.

11

SAFETY

Whether to bring the pooch on vacation isn't just a matter of what you can and can't do with him, but whether he'll be okay with the heat. The intensity of the sun here can rapidly heat the inside of a car, even on a cooler day. Plan on it being too hot to leave a dog in a car, even for a few minutes, no matter what time of year you're visiting. Beyond cars, dogs used to northern climates sometimes have a difficult time adjusting to the temperature and humidity here, and can look pretty miserable wandering around with droopy heads and dangling tongues. Others seem to acclimatize just fine, however, and have a wonderful time chasing lizards, splashing in the water, and sleeping in the air conditioning.

Mighty Caleb

Wildlife Checklist

To learn more about these creatures, see nature chapter 15.

LIZARD: Little brown anoles are found on fences, trees and even the sides of houses. The green ones are native, and are more rare a find.

PELICAN: Brown pelicans rest on bridges and trees. They often glide with their wings just above the water and dive for fish.

CORMORANT: See these dark birds dive underwater for minutes at a time, then dry their wings on channel markers and bridges.

GIANT LAND CRAB: See them in the woods, where they burrow, and also sometimes along roads, sidewalks and seawalls.

GREAT WHITE HERON: 5 feet tall, they live only in the Keys and wear yellow legs. The ones with black legs are great egrets.

GYPSY CHICKEN: Key West's hens, roosters, and little chicks have roamed free for as long as anyone can remember.

IBIS: With a long curved bill, these birds like to be social and travel in flocks. The white ones are adults, the brown ones kids.

IGUANA: The dinosaur-looking reptiles have been on earth for millions of years. These vegetarians are friendly, as long as you are.

11

KEY DEER: There are only around 1,000 Key deer in the world, most of whom live on Big Pine and No Name Keys.

OSPREY: Look for these white-black hawks flying and fishing over water or perched in their huge nests on poles.

ROYAL TERN: These fellows and ladies kind of look like seagulls, but they wear bright-orange beaks and black-tufted crowns on their heads.

11

Free for All!

Many of Key West's most iconic attractions are free and outside, making them a perfect visit for those with two or four legs. In addition to the beaches and dog park, try a pose at the Southernmost Point, a sniff at the Mile Marker Zero sign and a stroll down Duval. Grab shade under the majestic courthouse kapok tree. Wander the historic Harbor Walk and the enticing neighborhood alleys of Old Town, with island architecture, lush gardens, and alluring fire hydrants. Explore the Key West Cemetery, where some of the gravestones are also known for their humor. Feed the giant tarpon on the Harbor Walk at 4 p.m. by A&B restaurant, or at Historic Charter Boat Row, at noon and 4. Humans like the Eco-Discovery Center and Turtle Museum, both of which are free, as are the Key West Wildlife Center, the Oldest House, the tropical gardens at West Martello Tower, Flagler Station, and the San Carlos Institute, which is a fascination of Cuban history. A quarter-mile walk through the Berg Nature Preserve on Atlantic Boulevard takes you past lizards, iguanas, crabs and birds to a lovely picnic beach. Playgrounds can be found at Higgs Beach and Bill Butler Park, while the expansive Bayview Park is a great place for some frisbee or kicking a ball around before celebrating the sunset at Mallory Square.

Are you a dolphin?

Nope.

Huh.

Kids only this side. Dogs & Kids →
over there

1, 2 & 3 THE BEACH

Keys beaches are peculiar because they slope gently, keeping water
shallow for a ways, which keeps waves tiny and undertow extinct.
This is great for safety, and also makes for fun running and splashing.
Smathers Beach is the biggest, offering greater choices for sand-castle
positioning and more distance to run in circles making airplane noises.
This social expanse is a also a good beach for teen kids wanting to
sunbathe or peek around at who's cute and worth trying to meet. Higgs
beach is smaller, but nice, with a space-themed playground and better
snorkeling. Fort Zachary Taylor has picnic tables, advanced snorkeling
and an historic fort to explore, but isn't as pleasant for young children,
as sharp coral pieces collect at the waterline. There are no lifeguards on
any Keys beaches, so relax and play at your own responsibility.

REEF SNORKELING, ECO-TOURS & SELF-PROPELLED BOATING
Who can't help but smile when a playful dolphin pops out of the
water or an ill-mannered parrotfish crunches on coral with his mouth
open? A multitude of tours delve into the water or stay just above,
from dolphin watching to kayaking and reef snorkeling. Paddle past
rays, seabirds, and near mangroves, plus learn about nature. For a
once-in-a-lifetime adventure, take the ferry to the Dry Tortugas. It's
an all-day trip, but the waters here are especially pristine and the land
filled with pirate history and a massive fort. The minimum age for
most snorkel excursions is 6.

ADVENTURE SPEED SPORTS
High-speed motorsports will thrust zazz into a day. Circle around on
a zippy jet ski tour, or rent your own. Usually children 4 and up can
ride as passengers and 16-plus solo. Most jet skis fit two, some three.
Parasailing, or riding a parachute pulled by a boat, is also a family
favorite here. Minimum age 6, but no swimming-skill requirements.

Smathers Beach

Attraction Highlights: Dogs & Kids

Note: Many pay attractions allow small dogs that can be carried, including the Hemingway Home and Shipwreck Museum. Here we focus on ones that welcome any size fur-bearing friend.

4 MALLORY SQUARE

Fire jugglers, acrobats and other buskers congregate a couple hours before sunset each night. If your kid's an attention hound, he might even get drafted to help. Elsewhere in the festivities, food, portrait artists, face painters and musicians add to the energy building up to the inevitable grand finale — watching the last rays of the sun disappear beyond the ocean. 400 Wall Street, mallorysquare.com.

5 NANCY FORRESTER'S SECRET GARDEN

Lush tropical forest covers Nancy's property, which is also home to dozens of rescued parrots. A lover of all animals and nature, she welcomes well-behaved dogs to join the humans in learning about the parrots every day at 10 a.m., followed by a healthy dose of laughing, singing, dancing, art-making, and music playing. Open 10 to 3 daily. 518 Elizabeth Street, nancyforrester.com.

6 & 7 AQUARIUMS & OCEAN EXHIBITS

There are two ways to get up-close with marine wildlife on the land. The Florida Keys Eco-Discovery Center fosters inquisitive minds with habitat displays, a live reef cam, a 2,500-gallon living reef tank, and a glorious book-gift shop (free, no dogs). The Key West Aquarium showcases marine life like jellyfish, sharks, and plenty of fish. Particularly adored by kids is the touch tank, where they can feel conchs, sea urchins, and horseshoe crabs. Entrance fee, leashed dogs are welcome in the aquarium. Eco-Discovery, 35 East Quay Road, (305) 809-4750, floridakeys.noaa.gov/eco_discovery. Aquarium, 1 Whitehead Street, (888) 544-5927, keywestaquarium.com.

Numbers by attraction name correspond to map on page 184.

For details on beaches see chapter 6. For eco/snorkel tours operators see chapter 8. For fishing see chapter 13.

Attraction Highlights: Kids

8 CONCH TOUR TRAIN

With its colorful caterpillar-esque trail of buggy cars, the Conch Train is even fun to just look at. Hop aboard for a 90-minute tour with Key West trivia, history and humor. Kids 12 and under ride free. 303 Front Street, (888) 916-8687, conchtourtrain.com.

FISHING

Bonding over a day of fishing with a child becomes memories that bring tears to the eyes of even the most gruff of fathers. Charter fishing choices are many, from calm backcountry fly-fishing to big offshore gamefish trolling. Choose a style that matches children's interests and comfort. Some captains are more adept with kids than others, so find one who not only likes tykes, but who encourages learning, patience, humor, and teaching conservation for upcoming generations. For fishing that is easier on the wallet, take your poles to bridges, shorelines, and piers. Kids under 16 do not need a shore license. For Florida residents, adult pier/shore fishing licenses are free.

9 BUTTERFLY CONSERVATORY

You don't have to be a little girl in a princess dress to find the magic here, but if you are, then this might be your favorite place in town. Relax among hundreds of butterflies, exotic birds, turtles, and flowering plants. Explore butterfly anatomy, life cycles and migration in the learning center. The educational-art gift store here is also great. 1316 Duval Street, keywestbutterfly.com, 305-296-2988.

GHOST TOURS: Once the sun sets, intrepid guides usher brave souls around Old Town's haunted buildings. Conch Ghost Tours, conchghosttours.com; Key West Ghost & Mysteries Tours, keywestghostandmysteriestour.com.

PIER FISHING WITH A PELICAN, BOW CHANNEL

Attraction Highlights: Dogs & Kids

10 BERG NATURE PRESERVE

Wind peacefully through mangroves, past butterflies, lizards, crabs, and frogs, to a quiet beach with shallow, safe water. This quarter-mile trail is largely unknown, making it a secret world of fascinating exploration, photography and picnics. Start at the south end of White Street at the pier, go left and look for a small sign by a gazebo.

GEOCACHING: Those who enjoy hunting the elusive geocache will find ample roaming opportunities throughout the Lower Keys. Bahia Honda, Fort Zachary Taylor, and the Key Deer Refuge all participate in state park geocache operations, plus local individuals are pretty active hiding stashes for seekers. If geocaching is passé now thanks to the Pokémons, we haven't gotten the memo. Whether those creatures exist down here remains unexplored, since they are far less interesting than spotting a dolphin or cormorant.

BLUE HOLE: A pond might not sound too interesting, especially if you're coming from Minnesota, but in a land where all of the rivers and most of the lakes are salty, this freshwater pond is a rare haven for wildlife. The Blue Hole isn't entirely fresh, however, which makes it even more curious. Saltwater seeps up through the limestone bedrock of this abandoned railroad quarry, while rain falls from above. The buoyancy of the rainwater keeps it on top, providing a habitat for alligators and other freshwater fish and reptiles, while the salt layer below allows tarpon and other salt-lovers to exist. A quick peek from the viewing platform is likely to reveal many pond turtles and an alligator just below your feet, but sit quietly awhile to hear the sounds of the forest and watch for rare birds and Key deer. A wheelchair-accessible trail winds through pine-rockland forest and wetlands. To get there, turn gulfside at the light at mile marker 30 on Big Pine Key onto Key Deer Blvd. Drive 3 miles and look for signs on the left.

Come forth into the light of things, let Nature be your teacher. – William Wordsworth.

Wisdom begins in wonder.
– Socrates

Attraction Highlights: Kids

11 SHERIFF'S OFFICE ANIMAL FARM: What began as a holding place for a few homeless ducks and chickens is now a park complete with Patagonian cavies, tortoises, goats, a sloth, peacocks, reptiles and many others rescued from abusive homes. It's conveniently located at the jail, where inmates care for the animals. Less conveniently, it's only open the second and fourth Sunday of the month from 1 to 3 p.m. It's free, and a great up-close experience. 5501 College Road, Stock Island, keysso.net, 305-293-7300.

MUSEUMS: On a rainy or sweltery day, explore inside. If you have an aspiring pirate, wander through the Mel Fisher Museum, to see treasures brought up from Spanish galleons. Climb the 88 steps of the Key West lighthouse for a nice vantage point. See art at the Customs House, and Cuban history at the San Carlos Institute. Try Ripley's Believe it or Not. A young naturalist will enjoy the Key West Turtle Museum or visiting the pile of six-toed cats at the Hemingway Home. For more museums and contact info see chapters 6 and 7.

12 FLAGLER STATION OVERSEAS RAILWAY HISTORIUM: Storytellers weave tales about what life was like in Key West with the arrival of Henry Flagler's railroad, its ambitious engineering and construction, and its tragic demise in the hurricane of 1935. Shoppers and kids also like the old-time-themed mercantile store. 901 Caroline Street, flaglerstation.net, 305-293-8716.

LLOYD'S TROPICAL BIKE TOURS: Ride through town alongside one of the Keys' most energetic and offbeat characters. Lloyd will explain architecture, pick you exotic fruit from the trees, make laughter and teach natural history, all with a little easy exercise. 305 304-4700, lloydstropicalbiketour.com.

8 KEY WEST SHIPWRECK MUSEUM: Actors tell tales of 1856 Key West during its wrecker heyday. Artifacts, films and other exhibits illuminate the stories of those who helped make it the richest town per capita in the country. The view from the tower is also a treat. 1 Whitehead Street, just next to Mallory Square, 305-292-8990, keywestshipwreck.com.

Attraction Highlights: Dogs & Kids

3 FORT ZACHARY TAYLOR: Explore the grounds of a Civil War fort and walk on hiking trails through the trees and by the ocean. The beach is only for humans, but the rest is open for sniffin'. 601 Howard England Way, take Southard to the western end. Small entrance fee, floridastateparks.org/park/Fort-Taylor, 305-295-0037.

13 OUTDOOR CINEMA: The Bayview Park Movie Series is free and family friendly. Movies are the first and third Friday of the month, October through May, Key West, kwoutdoormovies.com.

14 KEY WEST TROPICAL FOREST AND BOTANICAL GARDEN: Stroll through 11 acres of tropical forest and gardens, with secluded bridges, resting benches, butterflies, flowers, and many enticing wild smells. All they ask is to keep dogs leashed and to clean up after them. 5201 College Road, Stock Island, kwbgs.org, 305-296-1504.

15 LAZY DOG CHARTERS: Rent a kayak or SUP, put the pooch up front, and paddle through mangroves, bark at fish, watch birds, and enjoy smells. If you use your puppy-dog eyes, you might get invited on the doggie paddle to a secret sandbar where dogs can run to their heart's content. 5114 Overseas Highway, Stock Island, lazydog.com.

BOCA CHICA BEACH offers a very laid-back vibe with excellent primitive hiking along the water and through the mangroves. There is a leash law here, but more often than not dogs are well behaved and untethered. Please respect this local custom and act responsibly. This beach is not suitable for kids and childish adults, as some also come here to sunbathe in the buff. Turn oceanside at mile marker 11 in Big Coppitt, onto Boca Chica Road, and follow it to the end.

VETERAN'S MEMORIAL PARK is a small, quiet beach with shallow water wonderful for wading and playing, whether you have a tail or opposable thumbs. Oceanside at mile marker 40, on the south end of the Seven Mile Bridge. Further up the Keys, Sombrero and Coco Plum Beaches in Marathon and the secluded Anne's Beach at mile marker 73 also allow dogs on the sand and in the water.

BIG PINE BARK PARK: Splash into a pool to cool off, play with the community park toys, drink up from communal water bowls and play with new four-legged friends at the dog park. 30150 South Street, Big Pine Key. Next, stroll the No Name Bridge for wildlife watching, fishing, and socializing. Watson Blvd. at Bogie Drive.

Attraction Highlights: Kids

NATIONAL KEY DEER REFUGE VISITOR CENTER
Before journeying into the wild to find not-too-elusive
Key deer, visit the staff for tips and photos, as well as the Key Deer
Bookstore for a great collection of educational books and toys.
Dogs are also allowed on trails in the refuge, with a leash. As of this
printing, the center is in the Winn-Dixie shopping center at 179 Key
Deer Boulevard on Big Pine Key, but at some point they are moving
to a new location nearby at mile marker 30.6, Big Pine, 305-872-0774.

MINI GOLF AT BOONDOCKS: It's the southernmost, and the only
mini-golf course in the Keys, but the lack of competition didn't make
the course designers lazy. The 18 holes challenge with watery ponds,
suspension bridges, lush landscaping and cavemen. The course gets
even more challenging at night, after multiple trips to the "pro-
shop" bar, centrally located near several tee boxes. Mile marker 27.2,
gulfside, Ramrod Key, 305-872-4094, boondocksus.com.

A few good kids' events

GOOMBAY FESTIVAL: dancing, drums and exotic foods fill the air
in Bahama Village at this family-friendly street party, the weekend
before Fantasy Fest; fantasyfest.com.

INTERNATIONAL SAND ART COMPETITION: watch famous
sculptors play in the sand to see who can make the winning castle,
Casa Marina, near Thanksgiving; sandartkeywest.com.

CONCH-SHELL-BLOWING CONTEST: open to everyone, register
and buy your instrument at the door, beginning of March; oirf.org.

NATIONAL WILDLIFE REFUGES OUTDOOR FEST: Wildlife, hikes,
birding, paddles, photography, talks, March; favorfloridakeys.org.

KEY WEST FISHING TOURNAMENT: young anglers who make a
quality catch anytime from April to November are in the running for
prizes; keywestfishingtournament.com.

OCEAN FESTIVAL AND WATERFRONT CRAFT SHOW: support
Mote Marine's reef-saving efforts, paint with Wyland, enjoy food,
fishing classes, games, gifts, music, learning, and fun, April; mote.org.

EARTH DAY CELEBRATION AT BAHIA HONDA: a two-decade
tradition of live music, sand sculpturing, face painting, marine touch
tanks, environmental stations, and more; bahiahondapark.com.

Restaurant Highlights: Dogs

Key West has a high number of dog-friendly eateries, in part because most restaurants have some form of outdoor seating. There are too many to list here, but below are a few of the iconic ones.

16 **SCHOONER WHARF BAR:** Right on the waterfront, this casual eatery and bar is a local favorite for dogs and people. Plenty of shade and usually a water bowl or two out front. 202 William Street, schoonerwharf.com.

17 **PEPE'S CAFE:** Dogs are limited to the patio, but that's where the best people-watching is, and thus the greatest chances for maximizing ear scratches from strangers. 806 Caroline Street, pepeskeywest.com.

11

18 **BLUE HEAVEN:** As long as Rover can get along with the resident free-roaming chickens here, he'll appreciate the shady yard with cool bricks and sand to lie on. 729 Thomas Street, blueheavenkw.com.

19 **SALUTE! ON THE BEACH:** After frolicking through the dog park, bring the social scene across the street to this beachfront Caribbean-Italian hangout. 1000 Atlantic Boulevard, saluteonthebeach.com.

20 **B.O.'S FISH WAGON:** Grab a seat at this funky, simple seafood shack and share some conch fritters and fried fish. Cash only. 801 Caroline Street, 305-294-9272.

NO NAME PUB: A little-known secret is the back garden of this legendary pub, where humans and dogs come to share stories, food and spirits. 30813 Watson Blvd., Big Pine Key, 305-872-9115, nonamepub.com.

MANGROVE MAMAS: If Lucky likes live, nostalgic rock, then he'll love chilling on the patio of this colorful hangout bar and restaurant. mile marker 20, gulfside, Sugarloaf Key.

Lodging Highlights: Dogs

Dog-friendly lodging for all tastes abounds in Key West. There are luxury resorts for Fifi, private vacation houses for Bella, and cozy bed and breakfasts for Dusty. When you're booking a room, check into weight limits and fees, as policies are ever-changing, and book over the phone because not all rooms are designated for pets. Here are some places that go particularly out of their way to welcome dogs.

21 OLD TOWN MANOR: Just off Duval, this eco-boutique hotel is ideally situated to maximize exploration with easy return access for cool-down naps in the room. All breeds and sizes are welcome, and if you forgot your doggie bed, poop bags or water bowl, they'll deliver loaners to the room. There is a one-time fee of $50 for the first dog, $25 for additional. They may be left alone if crated. Crate rentals are $10. 305-292-2170, oldtownmanor.com, 511 Eaton Street.

22 BANANA BAY RESORT AND MARINA: Here the pooches are welcome, but the kids gotta stay behind. At the adult-only hotel, up to two dogs under 50 pounds are no additional fee. On the water, it's a nice place to make yourself at home, with barbecue grills, tennis courts, a freshwater pool with tiki bar, whirlpool, and a small sunning beach. To get to Old Town you will need a car or bicycle. 305-296-6925, bananabayresortkeywest.com, 2319 N. Roosevelt Boulevard.

23 CARIBBEAN HOUSE: Simple and affordable, the Caribbean House is completely pet friendly, allowing two dogs of any size to crash with their humans for no fee. Located in funky, festive Bahama Village, this 10-room, no-frills guesthouse is two blocks from the Hemingway House and Duval, and just three from the Green Parrot Bar. 305-296-0992, 226 Petronia Street, caribbeanhousekw.com.

24 FRANCES STREET BOTTLE INN: Dog rooms with a backyard, porch chairs and royal poinciana trees make this a serene tropical retreat for lazy days. The B&B is nestled in a quiet neighborhood, but just a few blocks from the bustling side of Old Town. Dogs of any size are welcome, with a one-time $50 fee. 305-294-8530, bottleinn. com, 535 Frances Street.

Lovely Peggy & Mikko

Lodging Highlights: Dogs

25 ROSE LANE VILLAS: In the heart of Old Town on a quiet lane, 6 one-to-three-bedroom villas, six-bedroom home, renovated, pool, all-size-dog friendly with a one-time $50 fee. roselanevillas.com, 522-524 Rose Lane, 305-292-2170.

26 STOCK ISLAND MARINA VILLAGE: The only marina in town with a green dog park, water bowls and bags, benches, and shade trees. There's also a new hotel and swimming pool here. 305-294-2288, 7005 Shrimp Road, Stock Island, stockislandmarina.com.

27 GATES HOTEL: Nice new hotel in New Town, includes welcome box of treats and toys, bed and water bowl. Dog-walking services available. $25 per night fee for small dogs, $50 for large, but max $100 total for the stay, can be left alone. 305-320-0930, 3824 N. Roosevelt Boulevard, gateshotelkeywest.com.

11

28 COURTNEY'S PLACE: Cute, friendly B&B and cottages in Old Town, dogs $15 per night, can be left in room. 305-294-3480, 720 Whitmarsh Lane, courtneysplacekeywest.com.

29 AMBROSIA: Boutique B&B in Old Town with suites, townhomes, and a cottage. $25 per pet per night, no size limit, can be left alone. 305-296-9838, 622 Fleming Street, ambrosiakeywest.com.

If you have a small dog, your options far exceed this list. Some include: Old Customs House, Margaritaville Resort, Douglas House, Palms Hotel, Casa Marina, Key Ambassador, Island City House, The Reach, Sheraton Suites, Doubletree Grand Key, and Bayside Inn.

Let sleeping dogs lie.

But only until it's time to play.

Sweet Sid

Boat Charters & Shopping: Dogs

We haven't personally tried all of these guys and gals out, but if they take dogs on board, then chances are they're good souls and sailors.

BIG PINE KAYAK ADVENTURES: Excellent eco-tours for people and pooches. Big Pine Key, 305-872-7474, keyskayaktours.com.

30 **WILD ABOUT DOLPHINS:** Snorkeling and eco-charters, Capt. Sheri's golden retriever will probably come along too. Stock Island, 305-294-5026, wildaboutdolphins.com.

31 **HINDU CHARTERS:** 1925 historic wooden sailboat, oldest in the Keys, family-owned, daily morning and sunset sails, plus custom charters. Key West Bight, 305-509-1771, sailschoonerhindu.com.

32 **NO WORRIES CHARTERS:** Capt. Paula's private charters for eco, fishing, or whatever you have in mind. 6-person max. Garrison Bight, 305-393-3402, noworriescharters.

33 **PREMIUM TIME:** 36-foot offshore trolling with cabin, also does Dry Tortugas. A&B Marina, 305-432-0046, fishmonstercharters.com.

34 **ISLAND TIME CHARTERS:** Private light-tackle, spearfishing, lobstering, scuba diving. Hurricane Hole Marina, Stock Island, 305-407-6036, islandtimecharterskeywest.com.

35 & 36 **DOG 30 & AMERICAN DOG OUTFITTERS:** These stores offer holistic foods, treats, toys and other essentials. Dog 30: 1025 White Street, 305-296-4848, facebook.com/dog30kw. American Dog, 1454 Kennedy Drive, 305-294-BARK, americandogkw.com.

Above: Miss Sophie
Right: Ty & Chopper in the backcountry

Dog Days of December

Cooler December temperatures are cause for outdoor celebration, and doggie events pile up this month.

PARADE OF PAWS kicks off the holiday season the second week of December. During this walk, fur-bearers parade their humans to benefit the Florida Keys SPCA, before congregating in the dog park for a holiday bazaar. Birds, cats, lizards, and other pets are represented in effigy with their photo on a paddle. fkspca.org/calendar-of-events.

SANTA comes to the historic waterfront the weekend before Christmas to get his picture taken with the dogs of Key West. Roosters, cats, and two-legged children are allowed on his lap as well, if they have been particularly nice this year. Benefits the Boys and Girls Club of Key West. keywestchristmas.org/Pet_Pictures_with_Santa.html.

11

Weiner-dogs take center-stage on New Year's Eve, during the annual **KEY WEST DACHSHUND WALK.** Honorary and wanna-be wieners of all breeds are also welcome, though the event does display an unusually high per-capita number of dachshunds for a town of 25,000 human residents. Ridiculous, and of course, hot-dog-themed costumes adorn many of the 200-plus dogs, who strut their stuff a grueling three whole blocks. Those who are too old or too lazy ride in strollers and wagons. The parade is accompanied by a police escort, a grand marshal, and a supply wagon of water and poop bags that also provides transport to any little legs who get too tired to complete the course. Spectators are encouraged, along with donations of dog and cat food for the local Community Pet Pantry. Google their page on facebook, the url is too long to fit here.

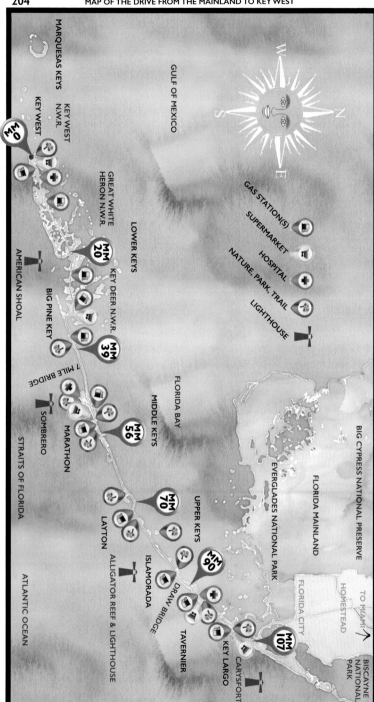

12

The Drive to Key West

Seven Mile Bridge

IN THIS CHAPTER

The Overseas Highway
Driving tips
Diversions & highlights

Betsy

Driving to an Alternate Reality

This drive is a little bit different than your typical commute to work or visit to your great aunt whom you haven't seen in two years. Imagine the hustle and bustle of the Florida mainland — high-speed traffic with cars racing, all intent to get somewhere before everyone else. You drive a little further, hang a left, and then suddenly all of that goes away as you find yourself in a tropical paradise.

Vistas like the Keys are typically reserved for remote islands with lofty airfares. The beauty here is that there's a road. To drive that road is not a chore, but is part of the adventure; as we are personally die-hard subscribers to the adage, "It is not about the destination, it is about the journey!"

Osprey overhead

12

Laughing Gull on the drive.

The free soul is rare, but you know it when you see it — basically because you feel good, very good, when you are near or with them.
— Charles Bukowski

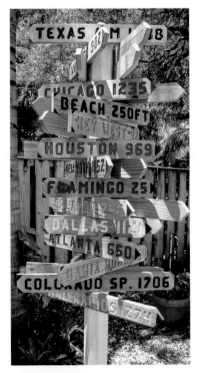

Directions in Key Largo

The Overseas Highway is the last gasp of U.S. Route 1, connecting Key West with the mainland. There are 42 bridges to cross along the way, ranging in length from 37 feet to 35,716 feet. Those who live along this ribbon of road use a peculiar vernacular of directions. When you hear someone say, "I'm going up the Keys," it means they're headed toward Miami; "down" the Keys is toward Key West. In addition, the use of street addresses is almost entirely replaced by reference to mile markers (MM).

Depending on who you ask, the Keys officially begin at MM 126, which is the start of the "18 Mile Stretch" of road between Florida City and Key Largo. Or they start at MM 113, the Monroe-Dade County Line. Or at MM 107, where the Jewfish Creek Bridge lands travelers into Key Largo proper. It's usually around there where, after a trip to the mainland, we roll down the windows to take in a deep breath of Keys air and celebrate being back.

The entire drive down the Keys may be completed in less than three hours, but it's not one that should be hurried. The drive itself is a transition into vacation mode, where the stresses of the outside world loosen with each mile. There are breathtaking sights and good food to be enjoyed along the way. Plus, the speed limit is 45 m.p.h. for much of the trip, and that's just the way it is, so embrace the new pace. With all of that in mind, you might want to allow yourself a bit more time to enjoy the ride.

12

The First Drivers: In December 1926 Claude Nolan became the first person to drive a car all the way from the mainland to Key West, then on July 18, 1927 J. Otto Kirchheiner became the first to drive the other way. It was a very time-consuming journey, crossing ocean cuts via ferry boats. The roadway would not be connected by bridges for another 11 years, until March 29, 1938.

Majestic Keys Overseas Highway

The Longest Bridge

The longest bridge in the Florida Keys, the Seven Mile Bridge connects Marathon (MM 47) with Ohio Key, (MM 40). It's a unique roadway that carries you above the sea, providing beautiful views of blue and green ocean, striking cloud formations, and magical sunsets. There have been many times I've driven across that bridge and looked out my window to find a wise and majestic pelican gliding on the air currents, nearly as fast as my car. It is not always this quaint however; as I recall quite a scene that unfolded on the Seven Mile Bridge some years ago in...

...1994...

12

A limo speeds over the Seven Mile Bridge. Inside, some bad guys hold a wife at gunpoint. Ahead, terrorists drive a truck with a nuclear bomb. The husband does what any loving spouse would — he commandeers a military chopper and calls in fighter jets.

The jets spray the truck with heavy rounds. It isn't fazed so they blow up the bridge ahead of it to stop the nuke from reaching the mainland. Kablam! Air-to-ground missiles hit the mark. The roadway explodes. The people of the Keys sigh. This is going to snarl traffic for a while. The truck driver slams on the brakes, barely stopping before the abyss. No, wait. Not quite in time. The front wheels slide over the edge. Suspenseful pause. The driver's eyes get wide with fear. It teeters, then plunges into the ocean. Miami is safe, but the wife isn't.

Her limo speeds toward the precipice. She knocks out the crazy-yet-exotically-beautiful lady holding her at gunpoint, then stands thorough the sunroof waving her arms frantically toward her husband in the helicopter. He bravely climbs onto the chopper's skids. When he's done flexing his biceps, he hangs onto the rails with his legs, upsidedown, to grab his wife's arms. He can't quite reach. The limo is nearing the hole in the bridge. Smoke and fire fill the air. The wife screams. Their fingers almost touch. The limo is just feet away. He reaches again. Just as the limo drives off of the blown-up bridge he grasps her wrist and pulls her to safety. Phew.

That incident really did snarl traffic for awhile, as the road had to be closed intermittently during the filming of that scene from *True Lies*. Luckily no one actually died, the bridge wasn't damaged and the nuke was only made of styrofoam. But the film, starring Jamie Lee Curtis and Arnold Schwarzenegger, was a global hit and one of many filmed on and near our majestic bridge.

Now that You're Down the Rabbit Hole... Welcome to Wonderland, Alice.

Highlights of the Drive

12

MM 126 TO 107 - THE STRETCH

The road from Florida City to Key Largo is called "the Stretch." It is scenic, but just a small preview of what's to come. For safety and environmental reasons, the north- and south-bound lanes are separated by concrete Jersey barriers. Their starkness is somewhat offset by the soothing "Belize Blue" color in which they were painted at the suggestion of marine artist Robert Wyland. It's just one lane in each direction, with several passing lanes and a 55 m.p.h. speed limit, though many people drive considerably faster through here.

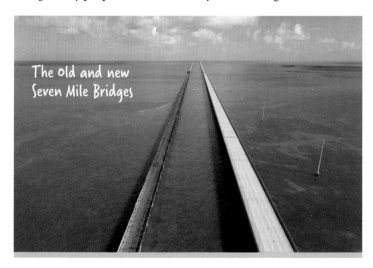

The Old and new Seven Mile Bridges

MM 107 TO 91 - KEY LARGO & TAVERNIER

The first town in the Keys is also one of the most famous, thanks to that Beach Boys' song and the Humphrey Bogart movie "Key Largo," plus its close proximity to the mainland. Scuba enthusiasts from around the world converge on Key Largo to dive on its numerous reefs and shipwrecks, as well as the oft-photographed underwater Christ of the Abyss statue. It's a long town, and the scenic side of it is not readily visible from the highway, so if you just drive straight through you'll mostly see an assortment of businesses. It's an excellent place to stop for anything you might have forgotten. If you have extra exploration time, Key Largo is home to great bits of nature, including John Pennekamp State Park, the first underwater park in the country. Once known as Rock Harbor, in 1952 the post office changed its name to Key Largo under pressure from local business wanting to exploit the success of the 1948 movie of the same name. Much of the drive is 45 m.p.h. here and traffic police are common.

NOTABLES: Humphrey Bogart Film Festival (Key Largo, October). Ride the movie boat African Queen, MM 99.7, oceanside. DePaula Jewelers for treasure coins and artifacts, MM 92, gulfside.

EDIBLES: Mrs. Mac's Kitchen, MM 93.3 and MM 99 (American).

DRINKABLES: Snook's Grand Tiki Bar, MM 99.5 gulfside.

PIT STOP: Key Largo Chamber of Commerce, MM 106, gulfside. Restrooms, info, friendly staff.

COOL OFF: Pennekamp Park, snorkeling from shore, diving, beaches. MM 102.6, oceanside, small entrance fee.

MM 91 TO 75 - ISLAMORADA (EYE-LA-MOR-AH-DAH)

Islamorada is a sport-fishing capital, with a high concentration of charter boats. It is one of the only places in the world where it is possible to catch sailfish and bonefish all in the same day. It is also home to good cuisine and adventure exploration. At MM 78 you can pull off on the oceanside for a view of Alligator Lighthouse and Indian Key, a small nearshore island with a ghost town and several historic markers. It's

"To those devoid of imagination a blank place on the map is a useless waste; to others, the most valuable part."
— Aldo Leopold

accessible via a short kayak paddle (rent at nearby Robbie's Marina). At Robbie's you can also feed baitfish to the huge, prehistoric-looking tarpon and shop at local art booths; just watch out for the pelicans who won't hesitate to steal fish from your hands! This is a great place for people of all ages to stretch their legs. Traffic can be congested here, especially from around MM 88 to 80, so drive with care. For most of this drive, you still can't see expansive scenic views from the highway, but that changes around MM 80.

NOTABLES: Rain Barrel artisan shopping and Betsy, the world's largest lobster, MM 86.7, gulfside; History of Diving Museum, MM 83, gulfside; Florida Keys History & Discovery Center, MM 82.1 oceanside (inside the Islander Resort), Robbie's Marina, MM 77.5.

EDIBLES: Sunshine Supermarket (Cuban deli), MM 91.9, oceanside; Craig's (American), MM 90, gulfside; M.E.A.T. (gastropub), MM 88, oceanside; Puerto Vallarta (Mexican), MM 86.7, oceanside; Midway Cafe, MM 80.5 oceanside; Lazy Days (seafood), MM 79.9 oceanside.

DRINKABLES: Lorelei (beach bar and restaurant), MM 82, gulfside.

PIT STOP: Islamorada Visitors Center, MM 87.1. Restrooms.

COOL OFF: Anne's Beach, MM 73.4, oceanside. Dogs okay!

12

♪ ...Come on pretty mama
Key Largo, Montego, baby why don't
we go...
— Beach Boys

♪ ...so long and thanks for all the fish.
So sad that it should come to this... ♪
— Douglas Adams

Christ of the Abyss, Key Largo

MM 75 TO 53 - THE COUNTRY

As your trek becomes a little less populated, the vistas become more expansive. At MM 64 you will find the Long Key Bridge, which is the second-longest bridge. There is parking at the base, where you can take a little walk onto three miles of the old bridge, which was recently resurfaced for recreation. This whole stretch is a pleasant drive through the country, but be forewarned, there are few services.

MM 53 TO 47 - MARATHON

Marathon is the major town between Key Largo and Key West, where you'll once again find supermarkets, a Kmart and Home Depot, as well as some good eateries and lodging. Marathon is also home to the last fast food chains before Key West. The small airport caters to private aviation, but there are rental cars available, in case your vehicle is misbehaving. If you turn left (oceanside) at the light at MM 50, in a little bit you'll get to Sombrero Beach, a very nice white-sand expanse with picnic tables, a playground, and clean restrooms. It is a beautiful place to take a small diversion and dip in the ocean. If you turn right (gulfside) at MM 50, you'll end up at Crane Point Museum & Nature Center, another fun visit. Just a little farther is the Turtle Hospital, the only licensed veterinary facility in the country dedicated to the treatment of sea turtles, which rehabilitates and often releases sick and injured ones. A tour here is highly recommended, especially if you have children. The traffic police are vigilant about speeding tickets. As you pass MM 47 your next landmark, the Seven Mile Bridge, carries you into the Lower Keys.

Directions: oceanside refers to the left side of the road when traveling toward Key West. gulfside and bayside refer to the right side when going that same direction.

Anne's Beach

NOTABLES: Crane Point Nature Center, MM 50, gulfside; Turtle Hospital, MM 48, gulfside; Pigeon Key, MM 47 (see more below).

EDIBLES: The Stuffed Pig (good breakfast), MM 49, gulfside; Castaways (seafood, sushi), 1406 Ocean View Ave. (near MM 48).

DRINKABLES: Sunset Grille & Raw Bar, MM 47.4, oceanside.

PIT STOP: Marathon Visitor Center, MM 53.4, gulfside. Restrooms.

COOL OFF: Sombrero Beach, MM 50, oceanside.

MM 40 TO 47 - SEVEN MILE BRIDGE

With the excitement of arriving at your destination buzzing around your mind, what a road-trip bonus it is to look out of your car with the Atlantic Ocean on one side and the Gulf of Mexico on the other, while feeling tropical air blow through the windows. Heading south over the Seven Mile Bridge always seems like a magical crossing to me. There is this long road rising above the glistening teal, green, and aqua water, which looks like it has no end. Sometimes you can't even distinguish where the water ends and the sky begins.

The bridge is 65 feet tall at its apex and, in fact, just a little shy of 7 miles, though it seems as though you are crossing a larger expanse. On the right you will see the Old Seven Mile Bridge. In the early 1900s the Flagler train lumbered along here, before the old Overseas Highway was built on top of those tracks. Also on your right is Pigeon Key, a small island that served as a work camp for the railroad builders. As many as 400 lived here in the early 1900s. Today there are several buildings still remaining and the island is a great place to visit and explore. At the time of this writing, access to Pigeon Key is limited to the ferry, which you can catch gulfside just on the Marathon side (1 Knights Key Blvd.), as repairs to the old bridge have, for now, shut down walking access.

12

Pigeon Key

If you happen to drive during the holidays, you might also see a Christmas tree lit up near the south end of the old bridge. There is no way to walk to that part of the bridge and it is quite high in the air, so it takes real determination by some festive folks to finagle the decorations up there. They remain anonymous cheer-givers, however, since it's illegal to be on that part of the old bridge. The authorities are no Scrooges, though, and don't ruin the holiday fun.

If you are in need of a short pit stop, at the far end of the bridge prepare to turn left just after the end into Veteran's Park, a small public area with restrooms and very shallow wading on a far outreaching beach. You can walk here quite a ways offshore without ever getting your thighs wet. The sand is nice, and it is a great spot to let the kids and dogs play in shallow water, or to cool yourself off after driving.

MM 40 TO MM 5 - THE LOWER KEYS

Welcome to the Lower Keys. You made it! Since this guidebook is about this area, more detailed information is found throughout the book, but here are a few highlights for the remainder of your drive to Key West. In general the Lower Keys have a rural feel, with scattered services. Most lodging here is camping or vacation rental homes. There are a few really great restaurants, but no fast food.

At MM 37 is Bahia Honda State Park, whose beaches are consistently rated as some of the best in the Keys. It's a nice place for a picnic or walk, and the park has a full-service snack bar and clean restrooms (small entry fee). Next up is Big Pine Key, home to a rare abundance of forests, mostly comprised of slash and scrub pine. It is also home to the once nearly extinct Key deer, a miniature version of a whitetail. At one time their population was as low as 30, but through major conservation efforts the current population is estimated somewhere between 600 and 1,000. As you drive through Big Pine, please be careful as the Key deer are quite oblivious to cars and tend to walk nonchalantly straight in front of them. Not only do you not want to kill one, you don't want to know the complications that running over an endangered species poses for a traffic ticket. To

Look for iguanas in trees.

protect them, the speed limits here are strictly enforced at 45 m.p.h. and drop to 35 at night. Big Pine Key is also home to a supermarket, gas stations, and two pharmacies.

After Big Pine, you are on the final push to Key West — a pleasant drive past quaint neighborhoods and views of the backcountry flats, shallows and salt ponds. You'll pass through Ramrod Key and Boondocks restaurant, home of the largest tiki hut in the Keys, MM 27. Next is Summerland Key, with two gas stations, a nice sandal and water-wear store, and Summerland Wine & Spirits, just past the Shell gas station on the left at MM 24.8. If you plan on having libations outside of a bar, this is the place to stock up prior to arriving in Key West. It has friendlier prices and the best selection in the Keys. Make sure to tell Steve the owner you read about him here.

You are now only 20 some miles from Key West, so continue to enjoy the ride and forget any urgency to get on "vacation." Congratulations, you're on it! Roll down the windows and let the wind carry any residual mainland anxieties away as the last miles roll by. Take in the views, you're sure to see pelicans, osprey, great white heron, cormorants, and other birds along this section. On a sunny day, look for iguanas grazing on the grassy shoulder of the highway.

12

NOTABLES: Blue Hole nature stop, turn right at the light in Big Pine onto Key Deer Blvd., go 3 miles and it's on the left.

EDIBLES: No Name Pub for pizza, history and funky ambiance, 30813 Watson Blvd., Big Pine Key. Baypoint Market for subs and ice cream shakes, MM 15, oceanside.

PIT STOP: National Key Deer Refuge Visitor Center, 179 Key Deer Boulevard (right at the light in Big Pine), in the Winn-Dixie center.

COOL-OFF: Bahia Honda State Park, MM 37, oceanside. Horseshoe swimming and snorkeling hole, mile marker 35, gulfside.

Key Deer
Big Pine Key

Driving Laws & Safety

On a straight, flat road with a mostly 45-m.p.h. speed limit and no ice or snow, there should be nearly zero traffic accidents. Unfortunately that's not the case. Combine slow speed limits and drivers gawking at the views, with impatient blockheads trying to pass illegally or irresponsibly, and head-on collisions become the primary cause of fatal traffic accidents here. The Overseas Highway is one of the most heavily patrolled stretches of road in the country, and police do not look kindly on reckless driving, speeding, and driving under the influence. So as you enjoy

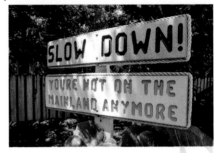

your drive through the Keys, forget the frustration of going slowly and just embrace the pace. There is no need to jeopardize lives by hurrying, and if you do you are sure to get some honks and "birds" from the locals. Conversely, if you see a line of cars behind you, pull over and enjoy the view for a moment, while they pass by.

A Military Watch

In the Lower Keys, near Cudjoe and MM 22, you might notice a big, white blimp on the gulfside. That's Fat Albert, a government project that monitors weather and drug traffic. It once had a sister blimp that broadcast the propaganda radio and TV Martí at Cuba, though Cuba has scrambled the signal since day one. As you approach Key West you may also see some fighter jets or other military aircraft. That's from the Naval Air Station on Boca Chica Key, and active base with a long presence here.

Fat Albert

13

Fishing

IN THIS CHAPTER

Types of Keys fishing
Types of game fish
Choosing the ideal charter
Subduing seasickness

Joy to the fishes in the deep blue sea

...thank you for food for you and me.

For food or sport, from 1 pound to 1,000 pounds, there's a fish out there for every style, taste and experience level of angler. From the peaceful shallow-water backcountry to the diverse coral reefs and onward into the deep, blue waters of the Atlantic and its Gulf Stream, it's no wonder fishing rules the Keys. This chapter includes a quick rundown of the most popular fish here and the types of fishing. For a complete set of regulations, including size, bag and season limits, be sure to also pick up a copy of Florida Fish & Wildlife Commission's (FWC) most current guide when obtaining your fishing license, which contains more comprehensive information. There's also a handy smartphone app for licencing and regulations, FishHunt Florida.

Types of Fishing

Backcountry

The backcountry, or "flats," are the shallow waters of the Florida Bay, on the north and west sides of the Keys, before the deeper waters of the Gulf of Mexico. It is a complex of sandy tidal flats, seagrass beds, sporadic coral heads, and channels meandering through uninhabited mangrove islands. Famous for its tarpon, bonefish and permit, it is also a great place to fish for shark, barracuda, mangrove snapper, redfish, and snook. Skilled anglers and fly-fishers covet this area. Here, the water is calmer than the ocean and the fishing boats smaller, which also makes it a nice destination for novices

13

Backcountry, a.k.a. Flats

and families who don't want to endure a rough ride. The downside is that many of these smaller boats don't have much if any shade, air conditioning, or toilet facilities. Wildlife viewing is particularly pleasant here, as the backcountry is also a national wildlife refuge, home to great white herons, royal terns, rays, and other majestic creatures. For those not familiar with the area, a guide is necessary not just for finding the best fishing holes, but because the waters are shallow, difficult to navigate, and environmentally sensitive, making it easy to run aground or even get full-out stranded as the tide drops.

Reef and Wreck

In the Lower Keys, the barrier reef lies around 5 to 7 miles offshore. In both the Atlantic and Gulf, patch reefs, coral structures and shipwrecks abound, all providing habitat and hunting grounds for a multitude of fish. Schools of snapper, permit, and amberjacks make for frequent catches, while coveted grouper create an especially memorable day. Other popular species out here include cobia, shark, barracuda, and kingfish. Always steer clear of yellow buoy balls, designating sensitive, no-take reef marine sanctuary zones. Guides are highly recommended in order to find the best crevices and underwater structures. Charters here might be on a very simple center-console type of craft up to a full-blown deepwater vessel complete with an air-conditioned salon and galley.

Offshore

On top, the water stretches as far as the eye can see, an endless, rolling carpet of blues, broken up only by an occasional circling bird or trolling fishing boat. Underneath, giant sea creatures emerge from the depths, chasing one another in a 450-million-year-old fight for survival. When "fish on!" is heard, the excitement builds. It could

13

Trolling, Offshore

be a mahi-mahi, tuna, or kingfish, perhaps a wahoo, sailfish, or swordfish — or maybe even the biggest prizes of all, a white or blue marlin. Deepwater charters run between 7 and a few dozen miles offshore, where bottom depths fall off quickly from the shallow reef to 600 and even 2,000 feet. Most offer traditional trolling with heavy tackle, but some use lighter tackle from center console crafts. While many days are calm, offshore fishing is prone to rougher seas, which may not be as enjoyable for a less-adventurous or novice angler.

Land and Kayak
Drive down the Keys, and you'll soon notice fishermen casting from bridges and piers, both day and night. Look a little further, and you might see someone quietly paddling around the mangroves and bays, sometimes reeling in fish almost as long as their kayaks. Both are excellent places to find tarpon, grouper and snapper, to name a few. Saltwater fishing licenses are required for these activities, though Florida residents may obtain a land-fishing permit for free. Not all bridges are open to fishing, so follow posted signs.

Spearfishing
For some, this is the most exciting, if not authentic form of fishing. The tradition of hunting fish with a sharpened stick goes back thousands of years. Today the sticks are more sophisticated, with elastic and pneumatic-power, but the one-on-one test of skill and ability remains unchanged. Many also spearfish for environmental reasons, like choosing which fish will go on the dinner table without harming other species or leaving tackle waste behind. Purists enjoy spearfishing while freediving, though many opt for snorkels and scuba tanks. Reefs and shipwrecks yield hogfish, snapper, jacks and grouper, but using a spear for some species and in some areas is prohibited, so review regulations before diving.

13

Spearfishing

Popular Fish Species

AMBER JACK
Good: year-round, inshore, reefs, wrecks, offshore.
Typical: 40 pounds, state record 142 pounds, Islamorada.
The largest jacks, called "reef donkeys," taste good, especially smoked.

BONEFISH - CATCH & RELEASE ONLY
Best: March through October, but found year-round, backcountry.
Typical: 3 to 10 pounds, state record 16 pounds 3 oz., Islamorada.
The "gray ghosts" of the flats, bonefish are stealthy, quick, and one of the Keys most beloved fish for traditional and fly-fishermen alike. They enjoy shallow water, lush grass flats, or sand, and can live up to 23 years.

COBIA
Best: November through April, backcountry, inshore, reef, offshore.
Typical: 30 pounds, state record 130 pounds 1 oz., Destin.
With a sleek, elongated body and head, sometimes they're mistaken for sharks, but can be ID'd by a dark strip running from gill to tail. Aliases: black kingfish, black salmon, ling.

DOLPHIN - A.K.A. MAHI-MAHI, DORADO
Best: April to September, offshore.
Typical: 20 to 50 pounds, state record 81 pounds, near Lantana. These beautiful, iridescent fish live only five years, so they grow fast, up to 20 pounds a year, feeding close to the surface in offshore waters. They are often found near floating objects, buoys, garbage debris, and sargassum weed clumps. They are menu favorite around the Keys.

13

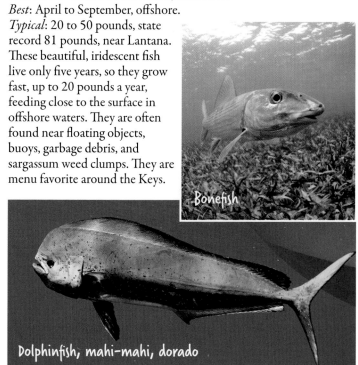

Bonefish

Dolphinfish, mahi-mahi, dorado

GROUPER (BLACK, RED, GAG) - LIMITED SEASON

Season: open May through December, reef, wreck.
Typical: varies, state record for a black 113 pounds 6 oz., Dry Tortugas.
There are many species; the most common catches are black, red, and gag. Most are protogynous hermaphrodites, starting as females then becoming males. Good to eat, but highly regulated. Do not take prohibited species: endangered Goliath, Nassau and Warsaw.

HOGFISH

Good: year-round, reef, wreck.
Typical: 1 to 5 pounds, state record 19 pounds 8 oz., Daytona Beach.
Easy to identify by their long snout and elongated dorsal streamers. Over sand they are light pink, while those in the grass deepen their shades to brown and gray. Their hog-like snouts root through sediment for bottom creatures, so they are difficult to catch on a line, but rather slow and fearless, making them an easier target for spearfishing.

Hogfish

LIONFISH

Good: year-round, reef, wreck.
Typical: 12 to 15 inches, state record 18.78 inches, Islamorada.
The invasive species may look beautiful with its red, brown and white zebra-like stripes and wispy spines, but it poses a significant ecological threat to the ecosystem. Do not release lionfish. Native to the Indo-Pacific, populations exploded here in the 2000s.
Their 18 venomous spines must be handled with ample caution, but once removed, lionfish are great for cooking and eating.

Lionfish

13

Goliath grouper are strictly no-take. They are endangered.

KINGFISH (KING MACKEREL)

Best: November through April, inshore, reef, wreck, offshore.
Typical: 20 to 40 pounds, state record 90 pounds, Key West.
Kingfish accelerate toward the surface to catch prey, jumping 15 feet or more in the air. They travel in large schools, and have streamlined bodies, tapered heads, and iridescent colors from black to bluish-green. Good-tasting, especially smoked in fish dip.

MARLIN, BLUE - CATCH & RELEASE ONLY
Best: March through October, offshore.
Typical: 150 to 600 pounds; state record 1,046 pounds, Panama City.
The star of Hemingway's fishing legacy, blue marlin are the ultimate manly big-game fish. It often takes hours to reel one in, while it dives deep, races out, and performs breathtaking acrobatics — an exhilarating and exhausting battle of willpower and strength for both man and fish. They feed mostly near the surface, where they slash through schools of fish with their spear-shaped upper jaw, stunning them, then gulping them down. One of the largest fish in the world, their trans-Atlantic migrations span hundreds of miles.

MULLET
Good: year-round, backcountry, inshore.
Typical: 1 to 3 pounds, 8 to 12 inches, can exceed 10 pounds.
Often used for bait fish, they are also good smoked. Mullet are a keystone species for marine health, feeding many larger fish as well as cleaning the water by eating algae and waste. Mullet swim in tight, shimmery schools, and often get teased on the playground because of their out-dated hairdos. They are usually caught with a cast net.

PERMIT - CATCH & RELEASE ONLY
Best: March to May, backcountry, reefs, wrecks.
Typical: 2 to 30 pounds, state record 56 pounds 2 oz., Ft. Lauderdale.
A Holy Grail of game fish, permit are especially coveted by fly-fishers. Their keen eyesight and intelligence make stalking them a battle of minds.

13

Permit

POMPANO, FLORIDA
Best: in winter, inshore, reef, wreck.
Typical: 1 to 2 pounds, state record 8 pounds, 4 ounces, Port St. Joe.
Anglers love the "edible permit" for their fight and taste. They school near piers, making them a favorite shore-fishing species. Distinguished from small permit by yellow (vs. orange or golden tint) on their throats, pelvic and anal fins, and lack of teeth on their tongues.

WHITE MARLIN

SAILFISH, ATLANTIC - CATCH & RELEASE
Best: November to May, offshore.
Typical: 50 pounds, 6 to 7 feet, state record 126 pounds, Big Pine Key.
A prized gamefish, sailfish cruise the deep waters near the Gulf Stream
and walls. They can burst to 60 miles an hour when pursuing prey.

SHARKS - CATCH & RELEASE ONLY
Good: year-round, backcountry, reef, offshore, 10 to 600 pounds.
Booking a shark-specific charter to test one's vigor against these
apex predators is increasingly popular. Backcountry channels are
home to spinners, bonnetheads, nurse, and lemons. Around the reefs
lurk bulls, blacktips, and hammerheads. Offshore, ocean-roaming
legends occasionally make an appearance, such as makos and great
whites. You can't keep the trophy, but "release mounts" are popular,
handcrafted from measurements and pictures of the catch.

SNAPPER, YELLOWTAIL
Good: year-round, reef, wreck, offshore. **Yellowtail**
Typical: 1 to 5 pounds, state record 10 pounds 3 oz., Naples.
Yellowtail is the most popular fish on local menus. Muttons and
mangroves (a.k.a. grays), are also coveted meals. Inquisitive and
smart, yellowtail don't display prominent teeth like other snappers.

SNOOK - LIMITED SEASON
Open: March, April, September, October, backcountry, inshore, reef.
Typical: 3 to 15 pounds, state record 44 pounds 3 oz., Ft. Myers.
Snook are distinctive with a prominent lateral
line, high, divided dorsal, and sloping forehead.
Opposite of grouper, they begin life as males
and some become females. Prized for a delicate
texture and flavor, they fall under stringent
regulations, and are prohibited from commercial harvest and sale.

SPINY LOBSTER (CARIBBEAN, CRAYFISH) - LIMITED SEASON
Open: August through March, plus mini-season near end of July.
Typical: 1 pound, Caribbean record 26 pounds.

Tarpon

Lobster live in protected reef crevices, sponge flats, and hard-bottom areas. Also called "bugs," a lack of claws is just one difference between these crustaceans and their northern cousins. They are a widely cherished meal, and fishing regulations are heartily enforced.

SWORDFISH

Best: May through August, October through January, offshore.
Typical: 40 to 50 pounds, state record 612 pounds, 12 oz., Key Largo.
By day swordfish hang at 2,000 feet near the continental shelf. At night they feed near the surface, which is when most people fish for them. Many enjoy eating them, as evidenced by worldwide overfishing.

TARPON (SILVER KING) - CATCH & RELEASE ONLY

Best: April through July, backcountry, inshore.
Typical: 40 to 150 pounds, state record 234 pounds, Key West.
These prehistoric giants are adored by fly-fishermen and light-tackle anglers for their spectacular fighting and aerobatics. They are most often fished for in estuaries, shallow flats, and backcountry mangroves. The annual migration creates an angling frenzy, so book a guide in advance.

TUNA, BLACKFIN

Best: August-November, offshore.
Typical: 2 to 20 pounds, state record 49 pounds, 8 oz., Key West.
Revered for their fighting skills and fillets, blackfin are smaller than yellowfin and bluefin, and are a favorite food of blue marlin.

WAHOO

Good: year-round, offshore.
Typical: 10 to 50 pounds, state record 139 pounds, Marathon.
A feisty member of the mackerel family, wahoo swim 50 miles an hour. They have streamlined bodies with a series of dark, vertical bars down their flanks. On the dinner table, they are touted for a delicate flavor.

Do not tell fish stories where the people know you... but particularly, don't tell them where they know the fish." — **Mark Twain**

I caught a tremendous fish
and held him beside the boat...

Then I saw that from his lower lip
... hung five old pieces of fish-line,
... with all their five big hooks
grown firmly in his mouth...
Like medals with their ribbons
frayed and wavering...

I stared and stared
and victory filled up
the little rented boat,

...until everything
was rainbow, rainbow, rainbow!
And I let the fish go.
— **Robert Frost**

13

Hooking a Guide

WHAT TO LOOK FOR IN A CHARTER CAPTAIN

Most guides are knowledgable, safe and will return you with ample fresh fish for dinner. But a perfect trip means finding a personality who fits your style. When you do, you'll end up with a relationship that lasts over many years, and fish. Here are a few considerations:

BOAT SIZE & AMENITIES: Backcountry vessels often have no head (restroom) or shade, but go to calmer waters. Reef fishing involves larger boats that may have shade, and usually a head. Deep-sea fishing is almost always on a liveaboard, with salons and air conditioning.

TACKLE: Backcountry is light tackle and fly-fishing. On reefs and wrecks, some guides use light tackle while others prefer heavy. Deep-sea most often involves trolling and heavy tackle. Confirm with your guide that he or she uses the type of tackle and style you enjoy.

GROUP SIZE: Shared or "party" charters are nice for affordability, especially for those just getting their feet wet in the sport. The downside to the lower price is the potential for a crowded boat, which means less fishing space and one-on-one attention from the guides.

CAPTAIN & CREW: For some, fishing is a social event. For others, it's a time for quiet reflection and focus. Finding a captain who fits your personality and ethics will make the day more pleasurable. If a choice must be made, choose personality and experience over a flashier boat.

WHAT TO BRING: Confirm if the charter provides tackle, ice, bait, and water. Also bring food, sunscreen, a hat, towel, polarized sunglasses, seasickness medication, a long-sleeved sun cover-up, a bandana or buff to protect your neck, and a camera or GoPro.

SAFETY & LICENSING: Most charters follow safety and legal requirements, but don't be shy to ask. If they are playing by the rules, they will be happy to provide proof. Laws are many, but the biggest are a licensed captain with a current first-aid card, insurance, life jackets, and a fishing license that covers guides and their clientele (that's you).

CHILDREN, LOVERS, PALS: Consider the needs of each member in the group. For kids, a guide adept at teaching can instill a life-long love of the ocean. For significant others and friends, ask them about seasickness, and if they are unsure, then consider a half day. It's no fun for anyone if one person is sick.

TIPPING: For captain and crew, it is customarily 15 to 20 percent of the charter cost, more for those who are particularly informative and engaging. Some mates are only paid on tips, and many captains do not own the boats, so tips are a vital source of each's income.

Many restaurants will cook your catch—blackened, baked or fried!

Licences & Regulations

If you are on a charter boat, you should not need a license, but elsewhere a saltwater fishing license is required. Purchase at bait-and-tackle shops, online, at 800-FISH-FLORIDA, or try the FWC's new FishHunt Florida app. Regulations are ever changing, include no-take and sanctuary zones, and a mandate for some fish to remain whole until ashore. For information visit myfwc.com. Remember, the laws aren't in place for anyone's inconvenience, but to ensure sustainable fishing for generations. As a steward of the sea, keep only what you will eat, and free the rest for another day.

Subduing Seasickness

No one is immune to seasickness, not even the most seasoned captain. Conversely, even those who seemed like hopeless cases have overcome it to enjoy careers on the water. Here are a few tricks to prepare, prevent, and when all else fails, deal with the misery.

13

ALCOHOL & FOOD: Most captains agree that the number-one cause of seasickness in the Keys is hangovers. Avoid drinking excessively the night before, as well as boozing on the water. Overly greasy, fatty and sugary foods eaten before and while on the boat can also nauseate. While at sea, try sticking to bland foods, like saltines, and don't overeat.

DRUGS: Dramamine and other over-the-counter drugs work for many when taken prior to leaving port. Some contain antihistamines, which can cause drowsiness, so look for non-drowsy formulas.

NATURAL REMEDIES: Ginger is a keen enemy of seasickness. Try chewing ginger gum, or drinking ginger tea or ginger ale. Homeopathic remedies Nux Vomica and Tabacum are nice alternatives to drugs, and can be found at most health-food stores. Wristbands that work with either magnetics or acupressure are most easily found online — some swear by them, others feel little effect.

TRIGGERS: Reading books or smartphones, looking through a camera lens, strong smells, and confined spaces are common triggers.

ACTIONS: When you feel it coming on, don't worry about it or you're bound to get it. At first signs, get your mind off of it by keeping busy. Staring at the horizon helps, as does the calming effects of fresh air.

SWITCH BOATS: If all else fails, next time try a different type of boat. Some people are more prone on a small craft, while others only get it on larger ones. Hull shapes have an effect as well. A sailboat and a catamaran each make entirely different motions while underway.

Fishing Events

JANUARY: Stock Island Village Marina King Mackerel Tournament, $375 entry fee per angler; fishska.com.

FEBRUARY: Cuda Bowl, Stock Island, backcountry and flats, open to all, $250 entry for one or $300 for two people; cudabowl.com.

MARCH: Merkin Permit Tournament, Stock Island, charity flats-and-fly-only catch-and-release, $1,000 entry fee; marchmerkin.com.

APRIL TO NOVEMBER: Key West Fishing Tournament: open to all, age groups, cash prizes, no charge; keywestfishingtournament.com.

MAY: Florida Keys Dolphin Championship, $500 per team entry fee; floridakeysdolphinchampionship.com.

MAY: Dolphin Masters Invitational, Key West, one day, open to all anglers, $750 entry per boat; keywestchamber.org.

JUNE: Big Pine & Lower Keys Dolphin Tournament: Sugarloaf KOA, $450 per boat entry donation; lowerkeyschamber.com.

JUNE: VFW Fishing Tournament, open to all, prizes, benefits needy veterans in Monroe County, $250 entry fee; vfwpost3911.org.

JUNE: Gator Club Dolphin Derby, Key West, open to all anglers, $150 entry fee; keywestchamber.org.

JULY: Del Brown Permit Tournament, Key West, open to fly-fishing, $1,200 per angler; facebook.com/keywestflyfishing.

JULY: Key West Marlin Tournament, presented by Bacardi Oakheart, in conjunction with Hemingway Days, $50,000 cash prizes, also dolphin, tuna, wahoo, and sailfish; keywestmarlin.com.

SEPTEMBER: Redbone SLAM Celebrity Tournament, Key West, bonefish, tarpon, permit; redbone.org.

13

14

History & Culture

Oil to Sea with No Seasickness Over the New Overseas Highway
on the Way to Key West Florida   168

Historic postcard

IN THIS CHAPTER

The Conch Republic
Native Americans, Spanish, British,
land scams, wreckers, the Feds,
sponging, cigars, Cubans, drugs,
lighthouses, hurricanes, sunken treasure,
& other history that shaped
today's culture of Key West

ABOVE IMAGE: STATE ARCHIVES OF FLORIDA.

History of the Conch Republic

Though typically a peaceful people, in 1982 the residents of the Keys started an uprising in response to tyranny. The U.S. Border Patrol had set up a permanent roadblock on the Overseas Highway, the only road passage in and out of the islands. The government believed it was doing the country a great service by searching every car leaving the Keys for illegal drugs and immigrants.

The people of the Keys, however, felt they were being unjustly quarantined from the rest of the country and that their livelihoods were being threatened by their sudden inability to transport marijuana, cocaine and Cubans to the mainland. Perhaps the 17-mile-long traffic jam that threatened the other financial life-blood of the Keys — tourism — had something to do with it as well.

Key West Mayor Dennis Wardlow and his attorney tried to resolve the matter peacefully by filing an injunction. To get to the hearing in Miami, though, they first had to outsmart the roadblock, so they piled into a private plane and flew to the court. But their ingenuity was in vain. The federal judge shot down the injunction. With this setback, the mayor now knew that rebellion was their only option.

As he left the courthouse, he stood atop the federal steps, his eyes and heart filled with fiery determination. He threw his fist up toward the sky and announced to the press that

Key West would secede from the United States of America!

The next day, it did. On April 23 in historic Mallory Square, Mayor Wardlow stood before an assembly of his citizens to read the declaration of secession, which thereby founded the Conch Republic as an independent nation. The rebellion began moments later as now Prime Minister Wardlow took up a loaf of stale Cuban bread and lightly whacked a person dressed up in a U.S. Navy uniform.

Smack.

The crowd went wild. Everyone was suddenly looking for their own loaf of stale bread and faux government official to whack with it.

Note: Slight creative license was taken here. We're not sure Wardlow threw his fist to the sky.

But after just one minute, before most of them could join in, the Prime Minister surrendered to the admiral in charge of the U.S. Navy base, who was an actual real admiral of the real U.S. Navy. Along with the surrender, he demanded $1 billion in foreign aid and war relief, with which to rebuild the Conch Republic after federal siege.

The rebellion kind of worked.

The U.S. government kind of listened to the people. They soon removed the roadblock, and the residents of the Keys were free. But oddly enough the $1 billion still has not arrived. Soon Conch Republic flags were raised and diplomatic passports issued and actually used for travel, being recognized by a handful of foreign countries with good senses of humor, including France, Sweden, Spain, Ireland, Russia, and most of the Caribbean. Visitors received visas, though you don't actually need a Conch visa to enter the Keys.

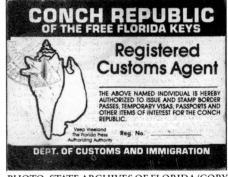

PHOTO: STATE ARCHIVES OF FLORIDA/CORY MCDONALD COLLECTION.

Through all of this, the U.S. government never challenged or even mentioned the secession. So if you thought the Conch Republic was a joke, it kind of was, but really maybe not. In 1994 the Monroe County Commissioners unanimously passed a resolution recognizing Wardlow's actions. That same year, Conch Republic officials were invited to the prestigious Summit of the Americas in Miami with Bill Clinton and other dignitaries. Today the Republic maintains a navy of roughly a dozen boats under the the leadership of historic tall ship Schooner Wolf, plus a small air force.

14

It's a good thing, as trouble still occasionally rears its head. At one point the U.S. Army tried to "overtake" Key West during a training exercise simulating the invasion of a foreign island. They failed to notify Conch officials, who mistook the exercise for an enemy attack and swiftly mobilized the island for war. Water cannons were fired from fireboats and invaders beaten with Cuban bread. Stale bread, of course. It was a quick victory. The Department of Defense issued an apology the next day, stating that they "in no way meant to challenge or impugn the sovereignty of the Conch Republic," and submitted to a surrender ceremony.

In another time of turmoil, a government budget freeze shut down the remote Dry Tortugas National Park. The Conch Republic raised private money to keep the park open for tourists and sent a flotilla of Conch Navy vessels to deliver the bounty. But upon their arrival they could find no one to accept the money nor reopen the park. They returned home unvictorious, but as fortune would have it, eventually the park did reopen when the U.S. government finally stopped squabbling and voted in a budget for the year.

So what does the Conch Republic stand for?

"The mitigation of world tension through the exercise of humor."

Or as stated by Secretary General Peter Anderson, the Republic is:

"A sovereign state of mind" seeking to bring more "humor, warmth and respect to a world in sore need of all three."

MOTTO:
WE SECEDED WHERE OTHERS FAILED.

Schooner Wolf of the Conch Republic Navy.

PHOTO: STATE ARCHIVES OF FLORIDA/DALE M. MCDONALD.

NOTE: FOR NATURAL HISTORY, SEE CHAPTER 15.

14

Spanish Galleon

ILLUS: STATE ARCHIVES FLORIDA
PHOTO: STATE ARCHIVES OF
FLORIDA/JOHN KUNKEL SMALL

Indian Mounds, Everglades, 1923

The Rest of the History of Key West

Just take a look around and you will still see the remains of days long passed, in the buildings, roadways, parks and paths. Lush and tropical, there is an enchanting sense that fills the air here, along with countless stories of prosperity and demise.

IN THE BEGINNING

There is solid evidence of humans living in the Keys as early as 1600 B.C., though there is a strong possibility we lived here much earlier. During the ice age of 10,000 years ago, the sea level was much lower and Florida's land mass twice the size of today. In fact, Mel Fisher found underwater tree stumps during his Spanish galleon salvage efforts, indicating a forest existed about 40 miles west of Key West. Sadly, this means artifacts of cultures living by the water would have been swept away by the ocean long ago. Still, Indian mound sites are found on a number of Keys. Only a few have been excavated, revealing kitchen middens (essentially piles of shells, broken pottery, and other castaways), though others are likely ceremonial and burial. None are known to contain gold or jewels, so no need to pillage.

THE SPANISH & THE BRITISH & THE SPANISH ARE COMING

Ponce de León was the first European to find the Keys. He laid eyes on them in May 1513 and pronounced them *Los Martires*, or the Martyrs, because from a distance the rocks appeared as suffering men. For the next few hundred years, there is no record of any European settlement here, though the histories of Westerners and the islands would continue to cross paths. The Keys bordered the trade route from Cuba and the New World to Europe, and as such travelers would occasionally stop here for fresh water, fish, turtles, and wood — or to salvage their ship when it wrecked in the shallow waters just offshore.

14

Written records concerning the native population of the Keys are scarce prior to 1821. We know through artifacts and scattered European sailing logs that aboriginal tribes inhabited the area, though it is less clear which ones, thanks in part to errors in translation and perception. Regardless, historians speculate that in 1492 between 100,000 and 350,000 Native Americans were living in what is now Florida. The Keys-dwellers were most likely mixed tribes, or sub-tribes developed by visitors who chose to stay, including the Calusa and Tequesta. If you are interested in learning more, read *Missions to the Calusa, Tacachale*, by John Hann, *Florida's first people*, by Robin C. Brown, and *Documentation of the Indians of the Florida Keys & Miami 1513-1765,* by Gail Swanson.

In 1763 Spain traded Florida to England, and by then the indigenous people, whoever they were, appear to be gone — either dead or refugees in Cuba. Around this time, the Creek Nation were also being forced from their lands in Georgia and the southeast, and migrating southward into Florida. At some point they started to be called the Seminole, who were in for their own tragic Florida history, but some of whom at least survived to keep their culture alive today.

When 1776 rolled around, the young and unorganized Florida didn't join the 13 colonies in the Revolutionary War, so British loyalists, or Tories, moved here. After the war, the 1783 Treaty of Versailles forced England to give Florida back to Spain, but granted her the Bahamas. Tories then relocated from Florida to the Bahamas. Forty years later their offspring would become some of the early residents of Key West, once Florida became part of the U.S. That happened in 1821 thanks to a clever treaty by then Secretary of State, John Quincy Adams.

KEY WEST IS BORN - WITH CONFUSION

The island of Key West was originally "owned" by Spaniard Juan Pablo Salas, who got it via a Spanish land grant. In 1822, one year after Florida became a U.S. territory, astute entrepreneur John Simonton purchased the island from Salas for $2,000, and that's when things began to get modern. Congress had to confirm the land grant before issuing a U.S. deed. As it turns out, in what was likely the first of a long-standing tradition of Florida real estate scams, Salas had also sold Key West to lawyer John Strong, who then resold it twice himself. Meanwhile Simonton brought on three partners: John Whitehead, John Fleming, and Pardon Greene (we mention them, as they have their own namesake streets in Old Town). It took six years of court battles and red tape to sort everything out, but when the dust settled Simonton and his partners emerged victorious on May 23, 1828.

By this time, Key West was small but established. It had already become the county seat, maintained a Naval presence to combat piracy, built a lighthouse, and was the most populated city in Florida. The 1830 census notes 517 residents, many from New England, and included 83 free blacks and 66 slaves. But it was in 1828 when the isolated town really began to boom, once it was declared a designated U.S. Port of Entry. Key West was an ideal location with a large, natural, deep-water port, a proximity to major shipping lanes, beautiful, abundant reefs, and now an immensely profitable industry...

14

WRECKING   /rek - ing/

The practice of taking valuables from a shipwreck which has foundered close to shore.

The reef along the Keys has always been a vital breadbasket for people living here. However, passing vessels often did not think it so delightful, especially when they found themselves in peril, run aground in shallow waters. Boats forced onto the shoals, either by poor navigation or storms, left their sailors and cargo at the mercy of those set up to help, or capitalize, on their misfortune.

Wrecking had been going on for years, but an 1825 act dictated all wrecked ships must be taken to a U.S. port of entry, and Key West was the only one in sight. Doctors, lawyers, insurance reps, politicians, and writers all flocked to the new tropical territory. Key West was a bustling economic center, and wrecking demanded a large support community of warehouses, shipyards, and auction houses. In just 20 years, by 1848 the town had more than 2,500 residents and 47 licensed wrecking vessels. Wrecking not only made Key West the largest city in Florida, but the most wealthy city per capita in the U.S.

There are stories that wreckers were practically pirates, and there is truth to that. Anywhere there are large profits to be made, a few scruples will dwindle. Some wreckers extinguished lights to encourage shipwrecks. Others charged ridiculously exorbitant salvage fees. But for the most part, the wreckers were tasked with the heroic, dangerous, and often monetarily thankless primary responsibility of saving the lives of those on a foundering ship.

FACING PAGE: COVER OF HARPER'S NEW MONTHLY MAGAZINE C. 1858/59. ENGRAVING OF A WRECKER IN FLORIDA KEYS.
LOWER LEFT: KEY WEST HISTORIC MEMORIAL SCULPTURE GARDEN "WRECKERS" WORK CREATED BY JAMES MASTIN.
LOWER RIGHT: PORTRAIT OF CONFEDERATE SOLDIER JOHN THOMAS LOWE, BORN 1830, A WRECKER IN KEY WEST. ALL CREDITS: STATE ARCHIVES OF FLORIDA.

14

SPONGING AND THE BAHAMIANS

Sponging soon added to Key West's economic boom, and as the sponge industry blossomed, so did Bahamian migration. Many of the immigrants were already proficient "hookers," as they were known. Key West soon solidified its monopoly on the U.S. market, which lasted for the next few decades. Eventually Greek settlers in Tarpon Springs and other Gulf Coast towns also grew dynasties, which would finally become uncontested in 1898 when the Spanish-American War caused the whole Key West fleet to flee and sell their cargo in Tarpon Springs. By then, Key West's waters were depleted. Sponging still is a wage-earner here, but nowhere close to the boom it once was.

THE FEDS: PART I

When the Civil War broke out, Florida was a Confederate state, but Key West remained Union, theoretically because of the large military presence already on the island and the ongoing construction of Fort Zachary Taylor. And who knows, perhaps the people then echoed the current resident philosophies of going against establishment, believing in equality for all, and generally not caring much about national politics. Whatever the reasons, the war had little negative effect. There were no battles. In fact, a Union captain took possession of the city one night while everyone slept. The war was an economic boon, with profits from ship seizures. Military construction also poured money, jobs, and infrastructure into town, including the two Martello Towers and Fort Jefferson out at Dry Tortugas.

14

RIGHT: SPONGER WITH WOOL SPONGES READY FOR THE EXCHANGE, KEY WEST, 1930.

BELOW: SAND KEY LIGHTHOUSE AND KEEPERS QUARTERS IN THE EARLY 1900S.

CREDITS: STATE ARCHIVES OF FLORIDA.

From the 1820s to '80s, eight Keys lighthouses were built on shoals in the open water, miles from land. Keepers lived in these feats of engineering, illuminating the lights each night. They led lives of danger, isolation, and incredible beauty. Hurricanes struck with no forewarning. It might be weeks between human interactions, and sometimes that was to heroically rescue passengers from a sinking vessel. This sort of extreme solitude could lead to mental derangements of all sorts. But on serene days, they wrote of seabirds nesting and sharks swimming by in crystal waters. Life eventually changed. In 1929 radios came, a generous Christmas gift from a Key West woman. Soon after, the keepers wrote of the wonders of listening to Sunday sermons and choirs, boxing matches, and presidential election results. Gradually the lighthouses became electrified, then fully automated, and the keepers moved ashore. But their towers still stand as beacons, fishing holes, and snorkeling meccas — photogenic sentinels to the stories of triumph and tragedy along the Keys reefs.

The first one completed was in Key West. Keeper Michael Mabrity set it alight for the first time in 1826, unwittingly starting a lighthouse dynasty for his family that would span the next 85 years. When Michael died of yellow fever in 1832, his wife Barbara took over, while also raising their six children. She weathered many hurricanes and was the only survivor from the lighthouse in the 1846 storm. She kept her post for 38 years until she was fired in 1864, because the feisty 82-year-old refused to keep her anti-Union sentiments to a reasonable roar. She passed away a few years later, but her daughter and granddaughter continued the family business, both in Key West and at other lighthouses in the Keys.

The Sand Key Lighthouse was a vital guardian of the main channel leading into Key West Harbor. In 1837 an unlikely keeper took the helm. Capt. Joshua Appleby's wife had died young, and he did his best to raise his young daughter. He worked as a fisherman and wrecker near Key West until he was arrested for intentionally running vessels aground to sell their cargo. He must have been innocent or had influential friends as it didn't take long before he was out of jail and was offered the keeper's job at Sand Key Lighthouse — switching from sinking ships to protecting them. In October 1846, while his daughter, her husband, and their 3-year-old son were visiting, tragedy struck. A hurricane rolled in that night, and by morning the 132-foot lighthouse had disappeared without a trace.

14

CIGAR TOWN USA & THE CUBANS

As you stroll down Duval today, you will see a few folks hand-rolling cigars. These are the remnants of the cigar boomtown, which exploded in the 1870s. When Cuba's Ten Year's War broke out in 1868, it forced thousands to flee in fear of violence and government tyranny. Many came to Key West, bringing culture, skill, and community vibrance. In 1874 Eduardo Hildago Gato became the first Cuban-born cigar factory owner on the island. Mr. Gato knew he had to attract the most skilled artisans, so he built 40 cottages and a community with parks, schools, and a baseball league to preserve Cuban culture.

Cigar making became the most lucrative industry on the island, and by 1885 there were more than 80 cigar factories employing thousands. It came at a good time for Key West. The wrecking industry was shrinking, thanks to lighthouses, better navigation and steamships. From 1895 to 1900 Key West averaged more than $2 million a year in cigar exports and remained the state's largest city, with more than 18,000 residents, only 6,000 fewer than today. More importantly, Key West became the cradle of Cuban independence, and a refuge for beloved revolutionary independence leader José Martí.

Unfortunately as the 19th century waned, so did cigars. Cigar magnate Vincent Martinez Ybor jumped ship, moving his business to Tampa. Eventually labor shortages in WWI and the rise of the cigarette led to the invention of the cigar-rolling machine. Hand rolling was old news and by 1931 all of the large cigar factories in Key West were closed. Today a few skilled people in town still keep traditions alive. If you are lucky enough to visit one of these shops, you will truly enjoy watching these artisans perform their craft.

14

LEFT: YBOR'S DAUGHTER JENNY ON HER WEDDING DAY, 1890. BELOW: MARTINEZ HAVANA CIGAR FACTORY, KEY WEST, 1900S. CREDITS: STATE ARCHIVES OF FLORIDA.

Martinez Havana Cigar Factory, Key West, Fla.

OTHER WAYS TO MAKE A BUCK

Fishing has sustained the livelihoods and bellies of people on this island since there have been people on the island. Early settlers from the Bahamas brought their conch fishing skills, plus worked diligently as salt makers, carpenters, seamstresses, farmers, and masons. The Bahamian influence on Key West is still clearly seen today in vibrant cooking, architecture, friendliness, and the tropical trees and plants they brought to the island for landscaping and fruit. Agriculture boomed a bit in the 1800s, as Key West processed and shipped Upper Keys' limes and pineapples. More morbid industries also took hold, but helped many earn livings, such as shark-skinning and the turtle kraals (holding pens) in Key West. Through the 1900s the kraals and turtle soup cannery employed many, but severely hurt turtle populations. It would take until the Endangered Species Act of 1971, to stop making soup on the historic seaport and start protecting our gentle friends.

THE SLAVE SHIPS

The practice of transporting people for sale was banned by Britain, the States, France, Portugal, and Spain by 1820, but that didn't stop the lucrative practice. Key West took in refugees from slave ships several times. The town's population was about 300 in 1827 when a British warship docked with 122 survivors from the slave ship *Guerrero*. Then in 1860 the U.S. Navy intercepted three illegal ships, including the *Wildfire*, bringing nearly 1,500 Africans to the town of now just 2,300 people. Each time the people of Key West did all they could to provide enough food and shelter, though sadly many were too sick to save after the transatlantic voyage. Some of the people they helped did eventually make it back to Africa, albeit to Liberia and not their homelands. Thank you, historian Gail Swanson, for discovering these stories, and bringing them to light through your diligent research and compassionate spirit.

14

PRINCESS MADIA, SURVIVOR OF THE WILDFIRE. DECK OF THE WILDFIRE, 1860, KEY WEST. CREDITS: STATE ARCHIVES OF FLORIDA.

WEATHER, FIRE & STUBBORN CONCHS

Life at the end of a small string of islands wasn't glamorous or easy. Heat, humidity, mosquitos, supplies lost at sea, tropical storms, disease, and fire all took their toll. Only 8 of 600 houses survived the 1846 hurricane. Still, from 1840 to 1850, Key West grew in population by 300 percent. The town had bouts of yellow fever in the 1800s. Fearing it was an airborne sickness, clothes of the deceased were burned and ships quarantined, until local doctor Joseph Yates Porter discovered it came from mosquitoes. He was the state's first public health officer and lived in the mansion at 429 Caroline Street for 80 years, being born and dying in the same room. Keeping with tradition, today the Porter House is home to two medicinal establishments, if one considers drinking to be medicinal.

DE-ISOLATING KEY WEST

There was a problem brewing, though. This beautiful tropical island that was almost technically in the continental United States was difficult to visit. The only way in or out was by boat, neither practical nor affordable. Enter Henry Morrison Flagler and his railroad, which would greatly aid in the growth and notoriety of Key West. The wealthy entrepreneur was determined to build a railroad to connect Key West to the mainland. In 1905 men and machinery began to arrive. Work camps were established and materials shuttled into the sparsely populated Keys. The work was hard, and the tropical climate did not make this monumental task any easier. The population of Miami at this time was a mere 5,000, or one-quarter of Key West's.

Amazingly, after only seven years, on January 22, 1912 the first train arrived in Key West, with a proud Henry Flagler on board. Sadly, or luckily, he died the next year after falling down a flight of stairs, never knowing that his lofty project was doomed to become one of the greatest Keys tragedies of all time.

But before its demise, the railroad was triumphant. It came at a good time. As the cigar, sponging, and wrecking industries withered, the railroad made it possible for tourism to begin digging in its claws in earnest. The '20s were quickly arriving, along with a great land boom in Florida. The railroad brought tourists in droves, and grand hotels like the Casa Marina and La Concha sprang up.

One has to wonder if tourism was at least partially fueled by prohibition. Rum was readily available from Cuba, and European and Canadian whiskeys from the Bahamas. Key West, being isolated and free-spirited, could get away with serving and selling more easily

14

than cities on the mainland. Regardless, rum-running was a relatively brief but very profitable activity for the brave-at-heart residents of the Keys and Key West, some of whom became very wealthy.

The fairy tale of the '20s was also short-lived, however. The 1930s found Key West in the Great Depression. Tourists vanished and by 1935 the population dropped to 13,118. Key West was suddenly the poorest city in Florida and declared bankruptcy. If things weren't already glum enough, the hurricane of 1935 struck on Labor Day. Winds were so strong that sand shredded the clothing off of people's bodies and cleared some islands completely of houses and vegetation. Forty miles of the grand railway were destroyed and almost 500 killed in the Middle and Lower Keys. That was about 25 percent of the Keys' population outside of Key West, and half of the casualties were WWI veterans working in government camps. Key West was again accessible only via water, or for the very fortunate, air travel on a newly established flight from Miami aboard Key West's own PanAm Airlines.

Newly elected President Franklin D. Roosevelt wasted no time in combatting the Depression, starting his New Deal public works projects, with programs including the Civilian Conservation Corps, Works Progress Administration, and Federal Art Project. In Key West this translated into building the Key West Aquarium, the sewer system, various art murals, and the construction of the Overseas Highway.

Key West's isolation was short-lived. The destroyed railway right-of-way and the bridges were converted to road beds and widened to allow two lanes of vehicle traffic. The Overseas Highway opened for car traffic in 1938, and now anyone — not just the wealthy — could drive from the mainland. The Keys, as the nation, were in recovery, but World War II would soon become a reality.

14

THE "RAMBLER" RETUNING FROM KEY WEST AFTER THE RAILROAD'S OPENING CEREMONY, JAN. 25, 1912. FLAGLER, HIS FIRST WIFE AND HER SISTER, 1850S. CREDITS: STATE ARCHIVES OF FLORIDA.

THE FEDS: PART 2

War is profitable, and Key West was imbued in boom times once again. In 1940 the Navy announced construction of a station at Trumbo Point. Expanding operations also included Boca Chica Naval Air Station. Now having around 15,000 active duty personnel to support the war effort, the Navy was in need of more fresh water. They paid to run an 18-inch pipeline all the way to Key West from the mainland, while widening the Overseas Highway. The result of the improved roadway was a name change to U.S. Route 1.

One of the military's lesser-known tasks was patrolling the waters of the Gulf and the Florida Straits for German U-boats. Needing all the manpower they could get, Roosevelt called for volunteer civilian patrols, deemed the Hooligan Navy. Author Ernest Hemingway was energized for the task. Orders were to call for backup if a Hooligan spotted a sub, but Hemingway was not inclined to be so passive. He loaded his trusty boat, *The Pilar*, with hand grenades and Thompson machine guns in order to launch an attack. Luckily for him he never saw one, or he surely would have been blown to bits. Unfortunately, the U-boat risk in the area was not unfounded. The first ship the Germans sank in the area was the freighter *Norlindo*, on May 4, 1942, northwest of Key West. U-boats continued to sink at least 100 more ships along the Gulf. One of those, the tanker *Gulfstate*, torpedoed off of Marathon in 1943, poses an environmental threat today.

SHRIMP

Tourism was on the decline after WWII, but in 1949 fishermen struck "pink gold" with a new commercial variety of shrimp. Key West pinks as they are called today, are large, flavorful, and very pink. The industry escalated and Key West was back in boom times. The shrimp boat fleet was around 500 strong. In 1953 the pre-tradition of today's Mallory Square was started as the citizens petitioned for public use of the pier for fishing. The petitioners prevailed, and today people still enjoy gathering there at the end of every day to celebrate the sunset. Today pinks are still part of the economy, but to a lesser degree.

RIGHT: KEY WEST SHRIMPERS, 1962.
FACING: HEMINGWAY ABOARD HIS BOAT *THE PILAR*, 1935. STATE ARCHIVES OF FLORIDA.

14

Tourism rose through the 1960s, as well as the hippie culture, which embraced the laid-back, island, live-and-let-live lifestyle. Marijuana was becoming more popular, not just in Key West but across the nation. We all know that a higher demand requires a greater supply. As the mid-'70s ushered in the end of the Vietnam war, the marijuana boom found its way to the ever-opportunistic entrepreneurs of the Keys. The islands' remote location and the relatively low presence of law enforcement, laced with a few bouts of corruption, helped the Keys become a huge import hub for drugs.

The largest supply came from South and Central America. Some suppliers enlisted Cuba for their import trade. Being only 90 miles from Key West, it made the perfect stop on the way into the country. Marijuana and eventually cocaine came to the Keys via boat and plane, and were then transported to the mainland for distribution.

Yet again, a segment of people in the Keys made exceedingly huge amounts of money in a relatively short amount of time — some of them through diligently working to establish and maintain import routes, and others just by chance. Smugglers used radio scanners and radar to keep track of law enforcement, and if a bust looked imminent, they would hastily dump their cargo into the sea. Large bales of marijuana and smaller ones of cocaine, known as "square grouper," were a common item to find washed ashore. There were times where tons were found awash on various beaches and caught in the mangroves. Many who found it, even if they weren't smugglers themselves, couldn't resist trading it off for a large stack of cash.

Drug-running eventually abated. Today a square grouper catch is rare, but still once in a while someone snags one in the mangroves; or some hard worker from the boatyard shows up with a new pickup

14

truck. If you should be so lucky, the proper procedure is to notify the Coast Guard. It is not recommended to consume any square grouper. While it could be fresh, it might be 40 years old or poisonous.

TREASURE, TROUBLES & TRIBULATIONS

The '70s and '80s marked an era of creative influx into town, with the likes of Jimmy Buffett, Hunter S. Thompson and others reinventing the Keys under their influences. The first Fantasy Fest took stage in 1979. But arguably the biggest shaper was a boy from Indiana who had read Robert Louis Stevenson's *Treasure Island*. Mel Fisher didn't just dream of finding treasure, he pursued it with tenacity. He worked alongside Kip Wagner, salvaging the 1715 fleet off of Florida's east coast in the '60s. By 1970 Mel set off to find his own fortune, searching for the lost 1622 fleet. It would take 16 years but on July 20, 1985 his crew found the "mother lode," of the *Nuestra Señora de Atocha*, a shipwreck that has since given up nearly a half-billion dollars in silver, emeralds, and other artifacts. Mel has since gone to the great galleon in the sky, but his fascination with treasure continues to live on through his museum, underwater salvage operations and everlasting spirit around town. It's a good story, and one that's readily available in many books.

The '70s and '80s also saw an influx of refugees escaping Cuba and Haiti, seeking asylum from poverty and political violence. The apex of this was the Mariel Boatlift in 1980. Over the course of six months Key Westers and others made humanitarian boat runs to help 125,000 Cuban refugees cross the perilous straits. Some ended up being criminals released by Castro, but most were reportedly decent folks.

With the '90s came a greater awareness of environmental protection and in 1990 the waters surrounding the Keys became the Florida Keys National Marine Sanctuary. Overseen by the National Oceanic and Atmospheric Administration (NOAA), many saw it as a federal attack on their livelihoods and right to locally legislate fishing, industry, and recreation. To this day, some of our friends are still angry at NOAA. On the other hand, the Keys are a unique landscape that doesn't just belong to the people along this 127 miles of road, but to the whole world and every creature on it. The fate of the barrier reef here is vital not only to the health of the world's oceans, but to the planet. It's an uphill battle, with pollution, warming waters, and rising sea levels, but in the quarter-century since its designation, there have at least been a few success stories.

"Today's the Day!" – Mel Fisher

CREDIT: STATE ARCHIVES OF FLORIDA.

14

MORE HURRICANES

Hurricanes continue to brush the Keys often, but in modern times are rarely cataclysmic, thanks to better forecast models, warning systems, building codes, and infrastructure. Still, in recent times, Key West felt the brunt of George in 1998 and its 105-mile-per-hour winds that wiped out Houseboat Row. The last storm of significance to wander through the Lower Keys was Wilma in 2005. The winds and rain were not significantly strong; however two storm surges spiked up to 8 feet, leaving widespread damage.

INTO THE NEW MILLENNIUM

Today the Keys are a tourism economy. Commercial fishing is still significant, but sport fishing, scuba diving, lounging, and celebrating are what lure more than three million visitors each year. With tourism comes many benefits, and a few downsides. Affordable housing is one of the largest issues. That and the fact that some projections put the Keys partly underwater in 50 years. But in the meantime, most seem to believe there's no reason to throw in the towel — only a reason to toss it down on the sand, and then lie peacefully on top of it.

TODAY'S MELTING POT

With its background of wreckers, cigar makers, rum-runners, Caribbean cultures, hippies, tourists, drug smugglers, hurricanes, and the military, it's easy to see how Key West became the eclectic and culturally diverse community it is today. It's a town with its fair share of shadiness and foul play, and we try not to sweep that under the rug. Knowing the uglier sides of history and what we are capable of — both good and bad — is the best way to learn from our human errs. Refreshingly, the vast majority strive to keep a welcoming community to all who want to be part of our slightly dysfunctional family. Art and nature are abundant, and an active part of life here. Some come in evening gowns, jackets and ties, while many seldom even know where their shoes are. Most importantly, our residents and visitors alike seem to have a universal understanding: We are one human family.

14

Key West declared "One Human Family" as its official philosophy in 2000, in part due to the 2000 presidential election. City leaders were dismayed by us-vs.-them sentiments "presented to us daily in the media, entertainment and news." Declaring the motto was a way to encourage the goodness of humanity, and the need to actively care about one another — to promote tolerance over discrimination, love over fear, and the right of every person to feel safe and accepted, regardless of religion, skin color, sexual orientation or nationality.

Well, history tends to roll in circles sometimes, and in December of 2016 the city commissioners did it again. In response to the dismal hatred spawned by the presidential race that year, Key West voted to reaffirm One Human Family. At least several thousand people seemed to agree, displaying banners and stickers, along with smiles and kinsmanship, during the historic Women's March in January. If you like the motto, get your town to adopt it, too. We don't mind sharing!

ONE HUMAN FAMILY PROCLAMATION

PROCLAMATION

Unanimously adopted by the City Commission on October 17, 2000

Whereas, Key West is an enlightened island community that is passionate about all living together as caring, sharing neighbors; and that each of us are dedicated to making our home as close to "paradise" as we can; and

Whereas, we truly believe that all other people are our equals during our short lives here on Earth; and

Whereas, we are dismayed to see misleading "us versus them" viewpoints presented to us daily in the media, entertainment, and news; and Whereas, we want to proclaim that the truth, as we see it, is that there is no "them," there is just "us," all of us, together as ONE HUMAN FAMILY, now and forever; and

Whereas, we want to share our unique perspective and simple (but true) words of home "ONE HUMAN FAMILY" with our global neighbors, so others can find inspiration to grow beyond the artificial limitations of racism, nationalism, sexism, classism, monotheism, prejudice, homophobia (and every other illusion used to try to separate us from all being equal); and

Whereas, we acknowledge that the genie of human equality is now out of the bottle, and that tyranny and oppression of any sort can never again be tolerated anywhere in the world, by anyone.
Now, therefore, I Jimmy Weekly, Mayor of the City of Key West, do hereby declare that as of today, October 17th, 2000, ONE HUMAN

FAMILY is now the official philosophy of our beloved City of Key West, and that we will freely share our official philosophy with all other fellow humans; each of us striving to be a shining example of that simple motto in our daily lives, from this day forward.

14

15
Nature & Wildlife

Pelicans, Cudjoe Key

IN THIS CHAPTER

Mammals, birds, reptiles,
plants, bugs, fish, ocean critters,
habitats, poop, geology,
where to see it all, plus
the environment and
the future

Gentle and curious Key deer graze next to prehistoric-looking green iguanas. Five-foot lanky great herons stand still for hours, waiting patiently for a meal. Rays glide gracefully across tidal flats as turtles meander through beds of seagrass. Here, wildlife is intertwined with daily life, where nature puts on a spectacular array for anyone curious enough to observe. Here is a refuge for many endangered species.

Above the water, the Keys are home to more than 250 species of local and migratory birds, 40 kinds of reptiles and even several mammals found nowhere else on earth. It is a delicate and unusual ecosystem unlike any other in the United States, with mangrove forests, salt ponds, tropical hardwood hammocks, and shallow tidal flats all working together to house one of the most biologically productive ecosystems in the world.

Below the water lies the world's third-largest barrier reef, second only to Australia and Belize. Reef biodiversity rivals that of the rainforests. Countless fish live and migrate through here. Others use the safety of mangrove-root forests for nurseries. Manatees, dolphins, sharks, lobsters and conchs are just a few who call this alluring universe home.

Mammals

KEY DEER: Key deer are the smallest in the whitetail family, growing up to 3 feet tall and around 85 pounds. They are an endangered species found only in the Keys. There are between 600 and 1,000 around today, mostly on Big Pine and No Name Keys. Visit the Key

Deer National Wildlife Refuge Visitor Center on Big Pine Key for advice on daily sightings. With a little patience, you are sure to spot one walking through a neighborhood, or grazing amongst grasses and trees. Though Key deer are very docile and friendly, petting and feeding them is strictly prohibited. It introduces dangerous elements into their diet and makes them accustomed to humans and roadways. It may also be uncomfortable for you, if you happen to meet the verbal wrath of a protective local.

Key Deer, Big Pine Key

15

LOWER KEYS MARSH RABBIT: The Keys are also home to the smallest marsh rabbit. They are just 15 inches long, endemic to the Keys, and also endangered. They are good swimmers and received their Latin name *Sylvilagus palustris hefneri* in honor of playboy bunny creator Hugh Hefner and his generous research funding to ensure their well being. They can be spotted early morning in grassy wetlands and salt marshes near the Blue Hole.

OTHER MAMMALS: The Keys don't have many land mammals, but you might catch a few familiar faces, like raccoons, possum, and mice.

If you see an injured animal call FWC at (305) 470-6863.

Birds

BROWN PELICAN

Sometimes these comically elegant birds will fly silently by, gracefully gliding millimeters above the water. Then a squadron will zoom overhead in a tight fighter-plane formation, before breaking rank and diving head-first from 65 feet in the air. As they dive, they twist their heads to the left to protect their trachea and esophagus from impact. As they hit the water, they open their beak to scoop up 2.6 gallons of water, and with luck, a number of stunned fish. Once back on the surface, they empty the water and swallow the fish. In the 1960s and '70s pelicans were nearly extinct. DDT made their eggshells thinner, causing a great problem for the hefty birds who stand on their eggs to incubate them. Today they are back, especially in the winter, as they come here to escape the cold. See them on fishing piers looking for handouts and perched in mangrove outcroppings.

Brown pelicans prepare to land on American Shoal lighthouse. The one with a brown head is a juvenile, the white head an adult.

15

OSPREY: These fish-hawks are excellent anglers, averaging a catch every 12 minutes, while sometimes diving underwater. They live for 20 years and mate for life, returning to the same nest every year. Some migrate 160,000 miles over a lifetime, while others simply live in the Keys. Their pole-nests are easy to spot around the Keys. Look for one on the Perky Bat Tower on Lower Sugarloaf, another at mile marker 24.9 on Summerland, and another on the north end of Big Pine. Osprey are a great success story, as they were also on the brink of extinction from DDT, but now thrive around the continent.

GREAT WHITE HERON
In the mornings and evenings, these exceptionally large and graceful birds dot

Osprey with chicks

the horizons of tidal flats and mangrove shallows. The largest of all herons, they stand more than five feet tall, with seven-foot wingspans. Unlike their cousins, the far-migrating great blue herons, the whites don't venture much further than their own backyard. They look a little like great egrets, but they are in fact their own unique selves, distinguished by their larger size and yellow legs (egrets have black). Great white heron seem to only keep company with their own kind. John Audubon brought a few home with him in the 1830s, and noted that the white herons attacked and killed some of the blue herons. They later killed his friend's ducks, chickens and cat, then began chasing his children. It is hard to blame the herons for being grumpy about being kidnapped, though. Around 1900, great white herons were nearly wiped out when their feathers became coveted hat decorations, partly thanks to Audubon's beautiful depictions of them, which brought them national recognition. Now they live peacefully in their own refuge — the Great White Heron National Wildlife Refuge in the Lower Keys backcountry.

15

Royal Tern

Great White Heron

ROYAL TERN: The tern's orange bill and black-crested headband give it away from a seagull. See them resting on channel markers and docks. They can live 30 years. There are several kinds of tern here, and at one time all were threatened by humans eating their eggs, then by DDT. Today royal terns have made a stellar comeback.

Cormorant

DOUBLE-CRESTED CORMORANT
See them atop power lines, channel markers and bridges, striking triumphant poses to dry their wings. They are expert divers and can stay submerged for 15 minutes while hooking fish. Their feathers are not waterproof, which gives them speed underwater, but requires frequent drying.

Female Frigate

MAGNIFICENT FRIGATEBIRD
Besides having a really fun name, this grand water bird comes with a long-forked tail and a seven-foot wingspan. The males sport a bright-red throat pouch for the ladies. Excellent pilots, they sometimes stay in the air for more than a week, but they cannot fly wet, so they catch meals on the surface or coerce smaller birds into dropping theirs. See them high above water and roosting in mangroves.

WHITE-CROWNED PIGEON: These Caribbean locals look similar to traditional pigeons, but are dark with a white cap. They come only as far north as Florida and are threatened here from hunting and habitat loss. An excellent flyer, they cover dozens of miles a day in search of their favorite fruit, berries from the poisonwood tree.

WHITE IBIS: Endearingly goofy in both stature and swagger, these gregarious wading birds tend to travel in social flocks, grazing for small creatures in grassy lawns and parking lots. They sport a long, curving bill. Youth come in brown and grown-ups in white. In Egyptian lore they represent great wisdom as the totem of Thoth, the god of knowledge.

Male Frigate

15

Roseate Spoonbill

Ibis... or ibises... or ibii

REDDISH EGRET: The rarest of Florida herons, these are a spectacle to observe, putting on a theatrical display of leaping and twirling while catching a meal. Little is known about their lives, but if you're lucky and spot one, she'll likely be feeding in calm shallows like salt ponds.

LAUGHING GULLS: A chattery bunch, these seagulls are familiar to many, but here they are more polite than those who live on crowded coastlines. They might take a human handout down here, but they are plenty content plucking a catch out of a pelican's mouth, picking a berry, or snatching up their own fish. They live 22 years.

TURKEY VULTURES: One of the largest raptors, turkey vultures fly in wobbly circles riding thermals, searching for decomposing animals. Despite their commonness, we know little about them. ID them by their bald head and "finger" feathers. See them circling over land, hanging out near dumpsters, and otherwise cleaning up the Keys.

Turkey Vulture

ROOSTERS & HENS: Key West is known for wild "gypsy" chickens, which first came here with settlers in the 1800s. They proliferated again in the 1950s, with an influx of Cuban refugees. Nearly every chicken here is wild and free-roaming, and the roosters sport notably colorful feathers.

Help Protect the Birds

Stress harms birds, especially when they are scared from their nests, exposing their eggs and young to predators and the elements. To ensure their survival, please birdwatch from a distance. If it looks like they are getting ready to take off, then that is a sure sign of being too close. Injured birds should be reported to FWC at (888) 404-3822.

Brown Booby

"The more clearly we can focus our attention on the wonders and realities of the universe about us, the less taste we shall have for destruction." Rachel Carson

Reddish Egret

15

GREEN IGUANA: Their mere presence scares unsuspecting tourists, but these docile vegetarians are harmless, unless cornered. Youth come in bright green, changing to gray and black as they mature. The orange ones are impressing the ladies. They can grow to seven feet and live 20 years, but most are smaller and younger. Iguanas have been around for 140 million years, and probably first arrived here as stowaways on European ships. They really took off this century, as people released their pets. Today, they are considered invasive, and make growing a garden a challenge, but are quite fun to watch. See them basking in the sun on grassy roadsides, seawalls, and tree branches.

Cuban Brown Anole

Giant Day Gecko

AMERICAN ALLIGATOR & CROCODILE: The Keys and Everglades are the only places on Earth where crocodiles and alligators coexist. Crocs like salt water and have two long teeth visible when their mouths are closed. Alligators need fresh water, which is why there are only a handful here. A small gator can be spotted at the Blue Hole on Big Pine Key. Crocodiles are elusive, sometimes seen in closed canals or beaches. They are dangerous but rare and shy away from humans.

ANOLES (GREEN & CUBAN BROWN): These little, energetic lizards are all over, on fences, walls, trees, and wherever else they please. They can live eight years and eat plenty of insects and spiders. They are particularly voracious cockroach munchers. Greens are native, while browns came in the late 1800s. If you see a chubbier lizard with a spiral tail, that's the northern curlytail, a native of the Bahamas.

GECKOS (REEF & GIANT DAY): The native two-inch reef geckos come in brown and tan. The bright-green day geckos are bigger. Famous as the insurance mascot, giant days are new here, probably introduced by people who decided to liberate them from their terrariums. Both are found in neighborhoods, on exterior walls, and trees.

SNAKES: Many kinds of snakes live here. Most are nice, but four are venomous: the Eastern diamondback, pygmy rattlesnake, Eastern coral snake and cottonmouth. All are rare, but to be safe, refrain from pestering any snake.

Green Iguana

15

Insects & Crawlies

BUTTERFLIES: More than 50 kinds of butterflies live here, including two rare ones. Bartram's Hairstreak is found only on Big Pine Key and in the Everglades. The Miami blue is one of the scarcest insects in North America, with only one known population in the world in an undisclosed location in the Key West National Wildlife Refuge.

CRAWLERS: The Keys giant, or Haitian centipede, grows to 6 inches and likely rafted over from Cuba during the Pleistocene Epoch. Their venom is poisonous and painful. Scorpions sting, too. Both are nocturnal, enjoying dark hideouts during the day, under leaf piles, palm fronds and rocks. At night, scorpions glow under a UV light.

PALMETTO BUGS: The joke is that "palmetto bug" is just a fancy name for a cockroach. While palmetto bugs are a large species of roach, they prefer outdoors to houses. The Keys have several species of house cockroach too, but with luck you won't meet any of them.

SPIDERS: Just like us, spiders love tropical vegetation and climate, so many have settled here over the millennia. Fortunately, the only ones venomous to a human's health are the elusive brown recluse and black widow. More common sights are the small, round, red-black-white spiny-backed orb spiders, who love it amongst the flower blossoms and often build expansive webs between trees and handrails. The spectacular golden silk orb weaver, or "banana spider," is about two inches long, five if you include the legs, and shows off a brilliant decoration of yellows and blacks, sometimes with reds and greens. They are the oldest surviving genus of spider, with fossil remnants dating to 165 million years ago. All orbs spin giant webs across pathways and in trees. Though they won't hurt you, it is very shocking to run into one of these webs and meet the owner. If you come across any spider, remember they are the good guys, controlling insect populations and being a food for many other animals. Many cultures, dating at least as far back as the Egyptians, consider it horrible luck to kill a spider, but a healthy one can bring good fortune, health and creativity.

Bartram's
Hairstreak

PHOTO BY HOLLY SALVATO, COURTESY U.S. FISH & WILDLIFE SERVICE.

ANTS: There are 94 known species of ant here, and all of them lead exceedingly interesting lives. The most helpful to know about are sugar ants and fire ants. Sugar ants are amiable little buggers with a sweet tooth. If you leave food out, you may come back to a long trail of tiny ants carting it off, piece by piece. They don't bite and disperse when the sweets are gone. Fire ants are tiny, bright-red fellows with nasty tempers. If a nest gets disturbed, they won't hesitate to latch on and bite a lot, causing swelling, horrible itching, and burning. Most can be treated with ice packs, antihistamines, and a few shots of tequila.

MOSQUITOS & NO-SEE-UMS: Mosquitos have always plagued the Keys, however today we have one of the most comprehensive mosquito control departments in the world, with more than 100 employees, pesticide foggers, spray trucks, four helicopters, and two airplanes. We don't love the pesticide part (though they claim it isn't harmful to humans), but the Keys would be uninhabitable without it. Even with that vigilance, mosquitos are a pain. In town, you might not see them, but out in the mangroves they can get thick. They are most prevalent around dawn and dusk, as are no-see-ums, the tiny black specs also known as "flying teeth." The best prevention is lightweight, long clothing and repellents. Once you're bitten, if you can resist scratching for a few minutes, the bites normally go away without much fuss.

KEYLIMEPIE WASP: In 2016 a Cuban scientist discovered a new species of wasp. The parasitic *Keylimepie peckorum* wasp is only a tenth of an inch long. He gave it its name to draw attention to conservation of the delicate ecosystem of the Keys. The only problem is, he didn't find it here, but rather in a drawer in a research facility where it had been stored for 30 years. Now he has set out to try to find one in the wild, with the hopes that it is not yet extinct.

GLOWING CLICK BEETLES: If you see a firefly whose lights don't brighten and dim, then it's really a glowing click beetle, a.k.a. fire beetle. These slim beetles have the brightest bioluminescence of any insect in the world. They also make a snapping motion and loud click, which allows them to quickly bounce upward to escape predators or flip themselves back to their feet. They are considered a happy beetle of good fortune.

15

Golden Silk Orb Weaver

Sea Life & Ocean Creatures

WEST INDIAN MANATEE: These gentle, elephant relatives grow to 10 feet and 1,200 pounds. See them in harbors, residential canals, and seagrass beds, munching on 150 pounds of aquatic plants per day. They can hold their breath for 20 minutes and live 60 years. Boat propellers helped make them endangered, but today they are doing better, though still threatened.

DOLPHINS: Dolphins present each other with "gifts" of seaweed and underwater trinkets while playing and courting. Try this game out on your beau or belle while on a snorkel. It works pretty well. Bottlenose and others play throughout the Keys, but are easiest to see on tours (see chapter 8). These nine-foot cuties often surf boat wakes, too. If you see some, avoid sharp turns and slow down gradually to prevent injuries.

SEA TURTLES: Before T-rex roamed the earth and plants grew their first flowers, green sea turtles swam the oceans. For more than 200 million years they persevered, withstanding global mass extinctions and ice ages. It's yet to be seen if they can survive humans, but for the moment at least, five of the worlds' seven species of sea turtle reside in the Keys. The gentle green and loggerhead are the most common, but still threatened. They grow to 500 and 350 pounds respectively. The 12-foot, 2,000-pound leatherback and the 150-pound hawksbill are both critically endangered. The little 100-pound Kemp's Ridley is the rarest sea turtle in the world. Sea turtles can live 100 years. See them underwater and on top, as they surface for air and warmth. Never approach a turtle on a beach as it is likely nesting. For a guaranteed sighting, go to our beloved Sea Turtle Hospital in Marathon.

Spotted Eagle Ray

Diadema Urchin

15

RAYS: Watching rays fly gracefully through the water is breathtaking, and luckily a common sight both on reefs and in the backcountry. The most prolific are roughtail stingrays, brownish with wings up to 7 feet. They are skittish, and often the only part you'll see is the poof of sand they leave on their exodus. Spotted eagle rays make grand leaps from the water, especially near dusk. Many others live or travel through here, including an occasional giant manta, which can reach nearly 30 feet and 4,000 pounds.

HORSESHOE CRABS: Horseshoe crabs predate sea turtles by 200 million years. They aren't crabs, but are actually related to arachnids. Their eggs are vital food for migratory shorebirds, though they also get credit for saving the lives of millions of humans. Their blood contains copper and a coagulant triggered by bacteria, which helps test vaccines for harmful bacteria. They can be elusive, but the best bet for seeing them is in shallow, muddy or grassy water around mangrove shorelines.

CARIBBEAN REEF OCTOPUS: Octopuses are astoundingly intelligent and curious, and our nomadic Caribbean reef octopuses would probably be the smartest of all, if they lived more than a few months. They aren't easy to spot, rapidly changing colors from blues and greens to crimsons and browns. They also change body texture and can disguise themselves as floating algae and even coconuts. They love crustaceans and steal from stone crab fishermen. A Keys local said one grabbed his lobster tickle stick, "as if to say, leave some for me."

URCHINS: If you lay a careless foot on an urchin, you will curse it with sailor words you didn't even know you knew. But these spiny critters are the grand keepers of the reef — the keystone herbivore maintaining the delicate balance between coral and algae. Without them, the reef dies, as we learned in 1983 when a disease killed more than 90 percent of the billions of long-spined Diadema throughout the Caribbean in just 12 months. After that, the staghorn and

"The happiness of the bee and the dolphin is to exist. For man it is to know that and to wonder at it." — Jacques-Yves Cousteau

Caribbean Reef Octopus, hiding, kind of.

15

elkhorn corals began a rapid decline from which they have yet to recover. There are many urchin species, and they won't hurt you unless you run into them. Look for them on underwater rock outcroppings.

JELLYFISH: In their world, jellyfish float tranquilly along ocean currents eating zooplankton and getting gobbled up by turtles. In our world, they leave behind painful rashes and welts. Moon jellyfish have short tentacles, a clover pattern of organs, and are common around reefs in the fall. Their sting makes an itchy, irritating, but usually mild rash that can be prevented by wearing a long-sleeved rashguard. Cassiopeas, or upside-down jellies, are brown, green and gray, found near mangroves, where they rest upside-down resembling plants. Their sting is so mild most humans don't notice. Portuguese man-of-war are not technically jellyfish, but they'll ruin a vacation. Watch for small blue-purple gas-filled balloon-looking pouches floating on the surface, which trail long tentacles below. Contact causes extremely painful welts and can put people into shock. Comb jellies, or sea gooseberries, look like a swarm of tiny, nearly transparent jellyfish, but since they capture prey with sticky glue, they don't sting.

SEA ANEMONE: Resembling carnivorous flowers, these colorful predators attach to coral, then ensnare passing prey with stinging tentacles. They retract when they sense danger, like you getting too close. In the Keys and elsewhere, their populations have been greatly reduced by illegal collection for sale for home aquariums.

SPONGES: Some sponges hide baby lobster, others look like Spanish jars from a shipwreck. The fact that you can look through clear water to see them is because of... well, them. A gallon-sized sponge filters a swimming-pool's worth of water every day. There are more than 70 varieties of these primitive animals here, feeding on plankton and microbes. On the reef, the giant barrel sponges, or "redwoods of the reef," can live

Young spider crab

15

Anemone on tidal flat

Vase sponge

more than 2,000 years. Researchers are finding that some can treat cancer. Touching them can also create skin irritation, but we know you wouldn't ever touch anything on a reef anyway.

CORAL: Though they look docile, these animals lead lives of drama, launching vicious attacks on neighbors and devouring zooplankton. They also lead lives of beauty, with delicate polyps swaying gently in the currents, playing host to creatures great and small. Each year around the fall full moon they synchronize spawning across the Caribbean. On a single night they release clouds of eggs and sperm into the water. Together they build vast communities with millions of polyps working in a cooperative that supports nearly all ocean life at some point. Florida's reefs are made up of more than 80 species of corals, which take calcium from seawater and mix it with carbon dioxide to construct elaborate limestone skeletons. Meanwhile zooxanthellae, a microscopic algae that lives on the coral, provides oxygen, nutrients and protection, plus gives coral its stunning colors. In return the algae receives nutrients, and the two live in symbiosis.

SARGASSUM: These floating clumps of brown seaweed look unassuming, but look closely to see a community of tiny fish and other beasts living underneath. Sargassum is a leafy network of branches and balls, which are filled mostly with oxygen for buoyancy. It floats on the Gulf Stream for months providing a home for many life forms.

QUEEN CONCH: Conchs move slowly through seagrass and sandy areas. Because they live 40 years, their spiraled shells are often covered in algae and barnacles,

Hard and soft corals

Moon jelly

Foureye Butterflyfish

15

making them appear uninhabited. If you find one underwater, don't touch it. Chances are someone's living in it, and even if they are not, conchs are endangered, protected, and it is illegal to possess a shell.

GIANT LAND CRAB (BLUE LAND CRAB): Sporting one absurdly pronounced claw, these big crabs look both fearsome and goofy as they scurry through parking lots and across roads. They live in burrows in the mangroves and enjoy leaves, fruit, berries, and insects. They only go to the ocean to mate, and live 13 years.

Fish

SHORE FISH: While walking along a dock or swimming at the beach, there are a few fish you're almost guaranteed to see: the slender Atlantic needlefish, yellow-and-black striped sergeant majors, colorful parrotfish, and yellowtail snappers.

needlefish

GREAT BARRACUDA: At six feet with teeth protruding sloppily over the edges of their lips, they are a little intimidating when they follow you. But they are rarely threats. Rather, they are bold and inquisitive members of the underwater community, and an exhilarating sight to behold. A particularly fast fish, they can swim up to 27 miles an hour.

GOLIATH GROUPER: Legends are born from these underwater giants who grow eight feet long, weigh 800 pounds, and may live up to 100 years. They lurk in reef caves, ambushing meals by sucking them into their expansive mouths. For around 300 years, up until 2001, they were called jewfish, until the Committee on Names of Fishes voted to change it. Some were appreciative of ditching the name that most likely had offensive origins, though as one Rabbi astutely commented, "I tell you, in the universe of things that need to change, the name of a big grouper is low on the list." Seeing one on the reef is a treat, partly because they are endangered,

Parrotfish, yellowtail snapper, sergeant major

15

but mostly because swimming with them feels like floating with the grandmother of the ocean. They sometimes come to the surface to check out dive boats at Looe Key. See photo pages 144 and 222.

LIONFISH: Strikingly beautiful, this invasive species poses a large ecological threat to the Keys and Caribbean. Legends abound as to how they got here from their home turf in the Indo-Pacific, but what is known is that their numbers went from zero to explosive in the 2000s. Take caution of their 18 venomous (but not deadly) spines. If you catch one, biologists the world over ask you to please not release it.

STRIPED MULLET: When you see a patch of milky, clouded water in otherwise blue-green surroundings, you probably have mullet. They swim in tight schools eating algae and detritus off the seafloor. They are a most important ecological fish here because of that bottom cleaning, as well as being a favorite meal for many gamefish. They have excellent vision and jump frequently, sometimes to avoid predators, but also some believe as a form of self-expression.

SHARKS: Dozens of species live here, ranging from little bonnetheads to occasional great whites. Though Florida leads the country in shark attacks, there are virtually none in the Keys' warmer waters that don't involve spearfishing or provocation. In the backcountry, find young sharks from one to four feet along tidal sandbars and channels. At the reef, see docile nurse sharks and the more foreboding reefs and bulls.

TARPON: With huge, shimmery scales these prehistoric fish swim in the backcountry and often congregate near docks, where they get easy meals from fishermen cleaning their catches. Their fins stick out of the water on occasion, leading a novice eye to believe it's a shark. Typically they weigh 40 to 100 pounds and grow three to six feet, though they can be eight feet and 800, pounds and live more than 50 years. See them around the seaport in Key West.

Barracuda & bull sharks at Looe Key

15

Plants

POISONWOOD & MANCHINEEL: Both create a horrible rash. Poisonwood is common along many trails, lurking in forms from an unassuming bush to a 60-foot tree. Look for black spots on the leaves, which have a yellow rim and look droopy. If you touch one, washing with soap won't work. The sap is not water soluble. We've heard WD-40 helps, or wiping with the bark of a gumbo limbo tree, often found nearby. Keep the rash from sunlight as it's phototoxic. Poisonwood plays an important role supporting butterflies with nectar and white-crowned pigeons with fruit. Manchineel are very rare, but if you see a tree painted with an X on it, don't touch it or stand under it, especially if it's raining. If you do, seek medical help immediately. The Spanish called it *arbol de la muerte,* or tree of death. The Carib tribes dipped their poison arrows in the sap, which is supposedly what did in Ponce de León. Poisonwood is said to be a hundred times more potent than poison ivy, and manchineel a thousand.

GUMBO-LIMBO: The wood of this sturdy Keys native is easy to carve, making it a favorite for old-time carousel horses. It grows fast and even grows from cut limbs. Its thin, red, flaky bark is one of its most distinguishable characteristics, which makes for the worn-out joke that it's called a "tourist tree" because it's always red and peeling. In folk medicine it treats gout, high blood pressure, gum disease, stings, bites, measles, poisonwood, backaches, and inflammation. You'll see them all over town, and enjoy their shade on a sunny day.

PALM TREES: There are more than a dozen kinds of palms here, many native to Florida. Ironically, the most iconic one, the coconut palm, is not. It appears they first came to the

15

Gumbo limbo
limb with giant
day gecko.

Poisonwood.
Do not touch.

Caribbean with the Europeans, a theory that holds plausibility since native cultures use the Portuguese name. Whatever the origin, they are ingrained in Key West culture and cooking, and you are bound to see more than a few.

KAPOK TREE: The sacred trees of the Mayan are wondrous sights, for when you die, your soul climbs a Kapok whose branches reach all the way to the heavens. In Key West there are four Kapok trees so spectacular they just might be straight from Mayan mythology. Curl up inside their giant, ribbon-like root buttresses and stare up at their sturdy branches that seem to reach out for a mile. One is in front of the courthouse on Whitehead Street near Fleming, the other three are on the corner of Truman and White. They only blossom every five or ten years, with large, stinky flowers that open in the evening to attract bats. During WWII, life jackets, called Mae Wests, were stuffed with the lightweight, waterproof fiber from the Kapok's seed pods.

ROYAL POINCIANA: Every April, May and June the umbrella-like canopies of the royal poincianas light up with brilliant red and scarlet flowers. This member of the bean tree family makes for a perfect pal under which to spread a blanket for a shady afternoon picnic. There is a particularly old and graceful one in the front yard of Saint Mary Star of the Sea school on Truman between Windsor and Simonton.

SEA GRAPE: You're sure to see these along beaches, shorelines and landscaping. They are easy to spot with large, round, playful leaves. They bear bunches of small, green grapes that turn purplish-red when ripe. If you can beat the birds to them, they are edible straight off the vine, sour with a dry aftertaste. Picking grapes is illegal on public land, however just fine on private property with permission.

FRUIT TREES: Because the Lower Keys have never frozen, at least in recorded modern history, fruit trees do well. Walk around town, and you'll see a bounty of edibles: bananas, Key limes, mangos, sugar apples, pineapples, sapodilla, avocado, tamarind, and many more.

Sea grape

15

Royal poinciana

Habitats & Ecosystems

PINE ROCKLAND: Canopies of slash pines rise above the ground cover, providing for lush plant diversity. Underneath a freshwater lens supports fauna and flora. An endangered community globally, in Florida it mostly survives on Big Pine Key and in the Everglades.

TROPICAL HARDWOOD HAMMOCK: Wander these for gumbo limbo and Jamaican dogwood, plentiful berries and those who eat them. They sit high enough to avoid saltwater intrusion and likely got their name from the Native American word "hammock," or shady place.

FRESHWATER WETLANDS: With no rivers, small oases are vital to those who need unsalted water, like Key deer, alligator and raccoons. Limestone supports ponds and wetlands, where sawgrass, ferns and buttonwood thrive. Most prevalent on Big Pine and the Lower Keys.

INLAND SALT PONDS: These high-salinity waters entice wading birds with good fishing. The ponds can cover several acres, occurring inland of mangroves. The largest are on Boca Grande and Barracouta Keys.

BEACH RIDGE HAMMOCKS: High sand berms from storm surges make the narrow line between beach and hardwood hammocks, giving root to hearty trees who can grow in this gravelly, salty substrate. Due to their fragility, most are closed to the public.

SHALLOW WATERS: The backcountry encompasses shallow waters north and west of the highway. Mud flats, tidal sandbars and seagrass beds act as nursery to hundreds of marine animals, making them essential fishing holes for wading birds, sharks, rays, and sea turtles.

Shallow offshore reef

Tropical hardwood hammock

SEAGRASS: On first glance, the seagrass beds aren't as magnificent to stare at as the colorful reef, but give it a few minutes and you might be enthralled for hours with all of the little creatures — 40,000 fish and 50 million small invertebrates per acre. The seven species of seagrass here oxygenate water, stabilize ocean bottom, and keep water clear. It harbors food for manatees, turtles, urchins and conchs, and protects a slew of fish and crustaceans. Be careful with boat motors. A small prop scar can take a decade to heal, if it does at all, and fines start around $1,000 per damaged linear foot.

REEF: Reefs are home and nursery to a quarter of all marine life, but take up only about .02 percent of the total area of the ocean. In the Keys they support 45 species of stony coral, 500 types of fish, 1,700 kinds of mollusks, and countless other organisms — not to mention the diving and fishing industries that keep many of us employed. There are four types of reef here: hardbottom, patch, shallow offshore (barrier), and deep offshore. Reefs also protect coastlines from storms.

MANGROVES: The most prolific plants here, mangroves are striking pillars of the community, separating land from sea and acting as nursemaid to nearly all local marine life and birds. Their seeds float until they find a place to root. The new plants cause dirt and sand to settle, eventually forming an island where other plants and animals can exist. They thrive in salt water by salt-resistant waxes and sweating out salt through their leaves. Of the three species of mangrove — red, black, and white — the reds line most of the Keys' shores. A stilt-like root system prevents erosion, buffers waves, and slows runoff to keep water clear. Enjoy the mangroves, and remember they are protected.

Lone mangrove... tomorrow's land.

Seagrass bed

The mangrove's complex of roots

15

Wildlife by Season

Even though much of our wildlife lives here year round, there are times when certain species shine.

JANUARY & FEBRUARY: Just as humans flock to the Keys to escape the snow, so do birds. Look for: pelicans, blue-winged teal, roseate spoonbills, bald eagles, osprey, piping plovers, broad-winged hawks.

MARCH & APRIL: Spring is teeming with life — on land, underwater, and in the sky. As the north warms, flocks of birds make pit stops on their homeward migrations, providing epic birdwatching. It's also a good time to see those who call the Keys home all winter: reddish egrets, black-necked stilts, Cuban yellow warblers, sea turtles (they start nesting in April), and Bartram's Hairstreak Butterflies.

MAY & JUNE: The tiny, spotted Key deer fawns take their first wobbly steps around now. As summer sets in, some birds return from their winter hideouts, like the mangrove cuckoos. Rains increase, stirring tree snails, and tarpon move from the ocean to the flats. Look for: sea turtles, frigatebirds, woodpeckers, cardinals, and gray kingbirds. See nesting green herons at the Blue Hole on Big Pine Key.

JULY & AUGUST: Baby sea turtles begin emerging from their sandy nests. Key deer fawns are still lanky, and the bucks begin to show off their velvety, growing antlers. Fruits from seagrapes, poisonwood and others keep birds busy, while evening frogs serenade all who will listen. Look for: white-crowned pigeons, southern leopard frogs, narrow-mounted toads, and swallow-tailed kites.

SEPTEMBER & OCTOBER: At the peak of fall migration, the Keys are a perfect stop for birds headed south. Some stay just a few hours, while others settle in for the winter. Key deer bucks sharpen their antlers and begin the rut. Look for: Peregrine falcons, gnatcatchers, Sawgrass skipper butterflies, songbirds, and wading birds.

NOVEMBER & DECEMBER: Just as the year started, so it ends with new faces settling in for winter, enjoying the Keys breezes, cooler nights, and good fishing. Look for: American kestrels, belted kingfishers, turkey vultures, Swainson's hawks, pelicans, ospreys.

15

The tiny Key Moose has yet to be discovered. To date there are no reports of sightings, nor even reports of people who believe in its existence.

Parrotfish, Poop & Playas

Float with your ears under the water near a reef and you'll tune into a whole symphony created by the comings and goings of creatures, especially the ill-mannered parrotfish, who loudly chew their food with mouths open, letting bits fall from their beak-like teeth all over the ocean floor. What they lack in table etiquette, this keystone reef species makes up for in every other way. These stunningly colorful gluttons are the reason there are sandy beaches in the Caribbean. They spend nearly every waking moment eating algae off of the reef, while their sturdy teeth chew off bits of skeletal coral too. Eventually, it comes out the other end as sand. One parrotfish can poop a couple hundred pounds of sand a year, and together they can leave behind as much as a ton per acre of reef. Some estimate they created 85 percent of sand on the reef and beaches here. More importantly, they clean the reefs, preventing a furry overload of algae. Parrotfish and some other reef fish also hide out in self-made mucus cocoons when they sleep, probably to protect against parasites and other predators.

"one should pay attention to even the smallest crawling creature for these too may have a valuable lesson to teach us." Black Elk

Stoplight Parrotfish

Below: A piece of seaweed on top of parrotfish poop conceals a young fish... we didn't even know he was there until we looked at the photo later.

15

Geology

Just to set foot on the Keys is to walk with ancestors. The land here is made from limestone, the bodies of ancient coral polyps, those little animals who grow forests of branching horns, monuments in the shapes of brains, and cities of delicate stars. With each step, we tread on the fossilized skeletons of mellow clams, valiant crabs, and microscopic plankton and algae — the backbones of life on earth.

Many millions of years ago, marine sediments began accumulating in the deep ocean, and by 125,000 years ago they'd piled up high enough to put the Keys only slightly underwater, just enough for reef life to flourish. It must have been a spectacle, as dense and biologically productive as any rainforest. The reef ran from Big Pine Key north. South was reef too, and then became a complex of sandbars, shoals and channels, perhaps not unlike some of our backcountry today.

Through no fault of its own, this blossoming civilization came to an end 100,000 years ago. It was about that time that humans and dogs started working together, and the first homo sapiens chose to explore outside of Africa. Around then an ice age surge also happened, which commandeered enough of the ocean's waters to drop sea level 300 feet. The reef was exposed, died, and began to fossilize.

Florida Bay was land, from the Keys to the Everglades. It probably supported forests, savanna and wetlands, roamed by mammoths, mastodons, and giant sloths. People might have lived here, too, but we will probably never know, because 11,700 years ago the ice age ended and the poles began to relinquish their ice. Slowly the ocean rose.

Fossilized brain coral

Living brain coral

15

In 2002 treasure hunter Mel Fisher stumbled upon a rare piece of evidence from this time — an underwater forest of prehistoric pine dating to 8,400 years ago. But by 6,000 years ago nearly all of the land had disappeared, along with the evidence of what and who might have called it home. However, the coral polyps rejoiced in shallow water, and began rebuilding into the reefs we know today.

The Keys are the very last high points of a sunken land. Cars whiz down the Overseas Highway, going somewhere of vast importance, indifferent to the millions of generations of life just inches under the tires. But proof of that life is easy to find. Examine the crushed rock in our driveways or exposed caprock, and fossils are everywhere. The Keys are literally just one giant fossil bed. Walking on the beach, ponder for a moment the empires that rose and fell, the immeasurable number of beings with complex interactions, biologies and social systems that, during their lives, helped to support all life in the ocean and on earth. All of those beings that are now ground up into fine particles, all of their stories contained, literally, in a grain of sand.

Tidal sandbar

To see a world in a grain of sand
And a heaven in a wild flower,
Hold infinity in the palm of your hand,
and eternity in an hour.
— William Blake, circa 1803

Global Warming

The Keys are a poster child for climate change. Average projections predict a rise of 3 to 7 inches by 2020, and 2 feet by 2060. With the land only three to eight feet above water, these shifts will alter many habitats. On land, fresh water havens become salty and houses are flooded both from tides and water seeping up through the limestone. Rising sea temperatures are already causing bleaching in reefs, as corals expel their colorful, symbiotic algae. Warmer waters enable diseases and invasive species to spread, while higher carbon dioxide levels lead to ocean acidification (higher acidity means less carbonate is available for corals and shellfish, weakening their structures and stunting their growth). Florida's state government has yet to acknowledge global warming, but in 2010 our county joined with several others in south Florida to plan for the changes. Let's hope the world's scientists are wrong on this one. Only time will tell what the future holds.

15

Small Steps for Big Improvements

The fun of telling the tales of Keys' creatures can be counteracted by sadness. The survival prospects of many beings here is bleak. Perhaps someday we'll come together to leave this planet better for future generations, but until that day comes, if you visit the Keys, make it a point to see the reef. Even if you don't love water, muster up the courage to snorkel, so you may experience it while it is here. And if you feel inclined to help, try these:

- Ditch plastic bottles for reusable water containers.
- Free yourself from disposable plastic bags. Get canvas.
- Use reef-safe sunscreen everywhere, not just by the ocean.
- Resist jewelry made from coral and sea life, often illegally harvested.
- Don't buy tropical fish, many are captured illegally.
- Eat sustainable seafood. Seafoodwatch.org has an up-to-date guide.
- Never touch coral or animals, as it can stunt growth or kill them.
- Use non-toxic household cleaners and garden products.
- Walk more, drive less.
- Eat less meat and buy as much locally sourced food as possible.
- Choose products with minimal or no packaging. Buy in bulk.

GET INVOLVED: The Keys' Coral Restoration Foundation works tirelessly to grow and transplant coral onto degraded reefs. To get involved, adopt a coral online or volunteer dive with them in person, coralrestoration.org. The Turtle Hospital is the first and foremost of its kind, rehabilitating and releasing sick and injured turtles. You may see their ambulance zipping down the highway saving lives. Adopt a turtle and follow its progress, turtlehospital.org.

Flying Fish

"For us of the minority, the opportunity to see geese is more important than television, and the chance to find a pasque-flower is a right as inalienable as free speech." Aldo Leopold

16
Resources

Banana Tree, Cudjoe Key

IN THIS CHAPTER

Conch Pocket Translator
Transportation contacts info for bikes, cabs & more
Newspapers, radio stations, websites
Emergency numbers
Temperature & distance conversions
About the authors
The end.

Conch Pocket Translator
Glossary & Pronunciation Guide

AFT: direction, toward the back of the boat.

BACKCOUNTRY: the shallow waters of the gulfside, with mangrove islands, channels and tidal flats, popular for fishing and kayaking. Also called the flats.

BAHIA HONDA: a state park near mile marker 37, known for its scenic beaches and difficult pronunciation. Conchs say Bay-ah or Bee-ya, which is also how the recording on the interpretive exhibit says it. Most others use the typical Spanish sounding of Bah-hee-ah.

BAYSIDE: see gulfside.

BIGHT: a bend or recess in a shoreline that makes a bay and/or harbor.

BLIMP: see Fat Albert.

BLOWING: describes the wind speed for boating conditions. "It's blowing," usually means high winds and rough seas. "It's blowing 4" or "8" or "25," refers to the specific wind speed. Blowing 4 is a nice, calm day on the ocean.

BONE ISLAND: Key West. See also Cayo Hueso.

BUBBA, BUBBA SYSTEM: in the friendly definition, Bubbas are long-time members of the community who look out for one another. In another definition, the Bubba system is a deeply rooted network of developers, landowners and politicians who bend rules to ensure their mutual continued financial success — or, more simply, politics.

BUCCI: Cuban coffee served in a small cup like espresso, very strong, usually with sugar. Also called Cuban crack.

BUG: Spiny lobster, rock lobster, Caribbean lobster, Florida lobster. Some call fishing for lobster bug hunting. Also what the DEA plants in people's houses for surveillance. Also an insect, with six legs.

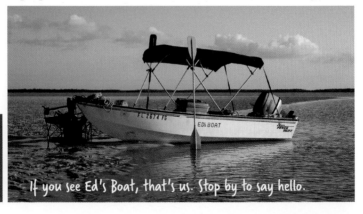

If you see Ed's Boat, that's us. Stop by to say hello.

BUOYS: Floating balls used to designate something underwater or an area above it. Cantaloupe-size styrofoam balls designate the location of lobster and crab traps in the water before they are retired into art and patio decorations. Buoy season on the water runs from August when lobster season opens, through mid-May, when stone crab season closes.

CAFÉ CON LECHE: Cuban coffee like a latte, using a strong bucci shot(s), steamed milk, and often sugar. When you order, they will ask you how many sugars you want. One is light, three are quite sweet.

CAST NET: a mesh net with weights around the edge, which is thrown into the water to catch bait fish.

CAY: see key.

Finish each day and be done with it. You have done what you could... Tomorrow is a new day. You shall begin it serenely and with too high a spirit to be encumbered with your old nonsense.
— Ralph Waldo Emerson

CAYO HUESO: Key West. The original name given to the island by the Spanish, translates to Bone Key. The name was given either because of the seven-year apple trees found here, which the Spanish called hueso elsewhere, or because of human remains (bones) found here. Eventually it became Key West, either because of its geographical location on the west end of the island chain, or because of a mistaken translation of hueso for ouest (Spanish for west).

CENTER CONSOLE: A boat with the steering wheel and throttle controls located in the center of the boat, used mostly for fishing due to the unencumbered deck and overhead space for casting lines.

CHICKEE: Seminole word for house, another name for a tiki hut.

COCKROACH: see palmetto bug.

COLD AIR: to locals, anything below 73 degrees (23C).

COLD WATER: to locals, anything below 80 degrees (26C).

CONCH: a person born in Key West. Also a shelled sea animal and popular food.

CONCH CRUISER: a hand-painted car, truck or bicycle, often decorated with shells, flowers, shark effigies, and other artistic creations. Usually they never leave the Keys, like the people who created them.

CONCH REPUBLIC: an unofficial micronation created when Key West seceded from the Untied States in 1982. "A sovereign state of mind seeking to bring more humor, warmth and respect to a world in sore need of all three."

CORTADITO: a bucci with a little milk, a small cafe con leche.

CRAWDAD: spiny lobster.

16

CUBA LIBRE: rum and Coke, traditionally with lime. It translates to "free Cuba," a toast given by U.S. Army Captain Russell in 1900 while celebrating the U.S. victory over Spain there, which happened to lead to the first importation of Coca-Cola into the country. "Por Cuba libre," may the day be not too far off again, for freedom.

CUBAN REFUGEE RAFT: many brave souls have attempted to cross the 90 miles of ocean from Cuba in makeshift boats. The ones that can be found tucked in mangroves and abandoned on secluded beaches likely were the successful ones, and their journeys and makeshift vessels are quite a feat to ponder.

CUDJOE KEY: pronounced *Kuhd-Joe*. The Key from around mile marker 20 to 23. To the authors, it's simply called "home."

DINGHY: a small boat, with or without a motor, used by those living on the hook (docked offshore) as transportation to and from shore.

DIRECTIONS: the Keys don't really use traditional directions. Up is north and east, toward the mainland. Down is south and west toward Key West. Gulfside is the side of the road the Gulf of Mexico is on, which is on your right or starboard going down and left or port going up. Oceanside is the Atlantic on your left going down and right going up. Bayside is the same as gulfside, which is also where the backcountry flats are. With only one road, it's totally simple, but if you want further clarification, see north, south, east, west, up and down in this glossary.

DOLPHIN: Most often here it means dolphinfish, a.k.a. mahi-mahi or dorado. When it's on a menu, that is definitely what it means. Sometimes it means dolphin mammal, like Flipper. Those are not eaten here. But they do live here.

DOUBLOON: A gold treasure coin, worth many times more than its silver counterparts, pieces of eight and reales.

DOWN: south. See also directions.

DRAW, DRAFT: the amount the hull of a boat and/or propeller sticks underwater. The less draw, the shallower of water the boat can travel in without grounding. Skiffs draw around a foot, while sailboats can draw four feet or more. Also good terms for after boating, as in a bartender can draw you a good draft beer once you're back on land.

DUVAL CRAWL: bar-hopping down Duval Street, or after too much bar-hopping, the only way to get back to the hotel.

EAST: up. See also directions.

FAT ALBERT: A giant, white blimp tethered to Cudjoe Key. The Air Force erected it in 1980 to monitor Cuba and the Florida Straights. There were once two, and the other one broadcast the U.S. propaganda TV and Radio Marti, though the signal was scrambled in Cuba and no one ever heard it there during all the decades that it aired.

16

FISHER: Lots of people are fishermen and women here, but with a capital F it usually stands for Mel Fisher and his family, who found a sunken Spanish galleon in 1985 with nearly half a billion in treasure on board. Mel has passed on to the great treasure ship in the sky, but the legacy of the King of the Conch Republic lives on through a museum and in the imagination of thousands of kids who dream of finding their own treasure chest buried by swash-buckling, sword-fighting buccaneers of old.

FLATS: see backcountry.

FORE: direction, toward the front of the boat. If yelled, then consider ducking, as in rare cases it might mean a golf ball or other projectile is coming at you.

FOUR LANE: The final stretch of highway leading to Key West where the speed limit increases to 55 m.p.h. and there are finally two lanes in each direction for passing. It's also a favorite speed-trap for police.

FRESHWATER CONCH: an honorary citizen of Key West, or someone who has lived here seven years.

FWC: Florida Fish and Wildlife Conservation Commission, the law enforcement agency that manages wildlife resources, safety and violations. To report poaching or injured animals, call their 24-hour hotline 888-404-3922.

When we contemplate the whole globe as one great dewdrop, striped and dotted with continents and islands, flying through space with other stars all singing and shining together as one, the whole universe appears as an infinite storm of beauty. — John Muir

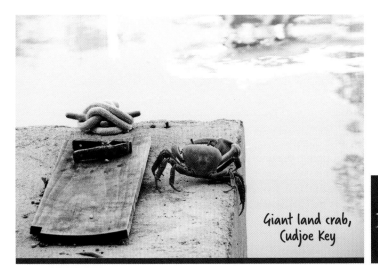

Giant land crab,
Cudjoe Key

16

GALLEONS: Spanish treasure fleets brought their New World wealth to Spain aboard galleons. Some fleets were ill-fated. A hurricane sank the 1622 fleet west of Key West. In the mid 1980s Mel Fisher and crew found two of those galleons: the *Nuestra Señora de Atocha* and the *Santa Margarita*. In 1733 a hurricane sank another fleet, which Art McKee would find in 1938. He soon opened a treasure museum in Islamorada, which was the first of its kind in the world.

GALLEY: a boat's kitchen.

GLASS: this could either mean the wind is down and the seas are so calm and flat that they look like glass, or it could be referring to fiberglass on a boat. Or a glass for tequila. The pressing question is whether it's half empty or half full. Whichever it is, if it's not all the way full, it might be time for a refill.

GREEN FLASH: an optical phenomenon at the moment of sunset, where green rays emanate from the sun dipping below the horizon. It is not a myth, though atmospheric conditions often prevent seeing it.

GROUPER: a large, regal fish. Goliath grouper can grow to 800 pounds (455 kg) and over 8 feet (2 meters) and are a critically endangered species, though some divers and snorkelers are lucky enough to spot them. Other non-endangered species of grouper are a favorite local menu item.

GULFSIDE: the side of the Keys toward the Gulf of Mexico. See also "bayside" and "directions."

GUNNEL: The top edge of the sides of a boat.

GWECKO W. PHLOCKER: A tie-died, witty and happy-go-lucky local radio personality for 104.9 the X Key West. Find him broadcasting live along with his untamed coiffure from events around town. Also known as Reverend Gwecko and the Soundman from Hell.

GYPSY CHICKEN: a free-roaming Key West chicken, beloved by many and bemoaned by some, especially when they crow at 3 a.m. They were brought here in the 1800s for eggs and food, then later for cock-fighting sport. Once that became illegal, their lives have been mostly peaceful ever since.

HEAD: a boat's toilet.

HOGFISH: A reef fish that's a must-try for eating. A restaurant on Stock Island that's popular for serving it.

HOOK: anchor or anchorage (see "on the hook"). A fishing hook. Also a movie about not wanting to grow up. We approve.

16

To live is the rarest thing in the world. Most people exist, that is all.
— Oscar Wilde

HOOKER: A term used in several distinct applications. 1: a fisherman. 2: a prostitute. 3: the king of boogie, as in John Lee. 4. what happened to Capt. Kirk, as in TJ. Misuse or misinterpretation of this word could either end with hysterical laughter or an awkward evening, but either way it will be expensive. For example, if you go to the seaport and say you're looking for a hooker, you might end up on a fishing boat, such as the High Class Hooker, and spend the day catching deep-sea sportfish with Capt. Gene. If you ask the same question on Duval Street, you might end up with an expensive lady date, or a man dressed like a lady, but chances are neither will be high class.

HOWARD LIVINGSTON: Along with his Mile Marker 24 Band, Howard plays happy island music around the Keys and beyond. If you were hoping to catch that cheeseburger-eating, margarita-drinking sailor, you'll likely love Howard, our more permanent local music maker.

IGUANA: fascinating, prehistoric-looking, big vegetarian lizards, usually green, brown, black or orange. They're not aggressive, just don't handle their bacteria-laden poop before eating.

ISLAMORADA: The Keys roughly between Tavernier and Craig Key, translates to "Village of Islands" and/or "purple isle." Great fishing, but hard pronunciation. Spanish speakers want to say *eesla-moraah-dah*. Locals say *eye-lah-mor-ah-dah*.

KEY: A small island. Probably adapted by the Spanish from the indigenous Hispaniola words *cayo* and *cayuelo* (very small island). The English used *cay* or *kay*, and it is likely that varying pronunciations morphed into the word *Key*. Keys are also good for starting cars, opening locked doors, and interpreting secret codes.

Green iguana, Sugarloaf Key

ROARING DREAMS TAKE PLACE IN A PERFECTLY SILENT MIND.
- JACK KEROUAC

16

KEY LIME: A citrus fruit more sour and aromatic than typical Persian limes. They are the key ingredient in Key West-born Key lime pie, though most of the limes are now grown on the mainland and Central America since hurricanes wiped out the Keys lime farms a while back.

KEYS BREEZE: The warm, light, soothing wind that gently blows all of your stresses, angers, and inhibitions away. Many attribute it as the primary reason they visited the Keys and never left.

KEYS DISEASE: In the negative sense, it is someone who is unable to resist the temptations of living in a vacation mecca, who parties too hard and ends up burnt out, homeless or otherwise dysfunctional in society. In the positive sense, it is a focus on simplifying life so as to be able to enjoy each day to its fullest, which includes shedding material possessions and finding a way to earn a living that is compatible with one's beliefs. Either way, once you have contracted it, going back to an office job on the mainland is no longer a possibility.

LIVEABOARD: a motorboat, sailboat or houseboat that serves as one's primary residence. Typically these are docked at a marina or "on the hook," though sometimes they are dry-docked on land. It's sometimes a free and romantic existence, but not without its inconveniences. Some liveaboards are able to motor and sail, while others are simply floating quarters.

LOBSTER: A crustacean. The Caribbean spiny lobster is served widely in Keys restaurants. It has no claws, unlike its northern cousins. Also called bugs and crawdads. Lobster also refers to a sunburnt tourist.

MAILBOXES: the large aluminum tubes on the back of modern treasure-salvage boats. They are used to deflect prop-wash onto the seafloor to blow away sediment and uncover loot. Also called blowers.

MAINLAND: noun: geographically, anything north of Key Largo. adjective: a state of mind that is usually associated with overly aggressive drivers, people who take themselves too seriously, those who don't respect the environment, or depressed souls who watch TV news and discuss national politics.

MIAMI: aaahhhh!

MID TOWN: a designation for an area of Key West between New Town and Old Town. We surmise land brokers originally fabricated this shoulder neighborhood in order to inflate prices, as the only maps we can find designating "Mid Town" are courtesy of real estate offices.

MM: Short for mile marker, the unit for distance measurement on the Overseas Highway. Green road signs display each mile, starting with MM 107 in Key Largo and ending at MM 0 in Key West. Addresses along the Overseas Highway mostly correspond with mile markers. For example, 82990 Overseas Highway is at MM 82.99, or basically right by the MM 83 sign. This address system falls apart in Marathon and then again in the Saddlebunch Keys, but is otherwise reliable.

16

MOJITO: Alcoholic drink containing ample Key lime juice, muddled mint, sugar, white rum, soda water, and ice. Only order one from a reputable bar when the bartender is slow, as they take patience to make correctly and require fresh ingredients, not mixes. Cuban origin.

MOORING BALLS: a floating ball attached to a permanent structure on the seabed, which boats can tie off to in harbors and around reefs.

MULLET: a fish that is good smoked and often used for bait. Essential for the ecosystem, they are food for most sportfish and keep the water clean by feeding on algae and other bottom decay. As they eat off of the bottom, they sometimes create temporary milky clouds in the water. Also a hairstyle that is short in the front and long in the back, or as Joe Dirt described "business in the front and party in the back." Rocked by Rod Stewart and Chuck Norris, among others.

NAUI: A scuba diving certification association, short for National Association of Underwater Instructors.

NEW TOWN: The section of Key West that roughly corresponds to the area east and north of 1st Street and Palm Ave., which includes all of the big box stores.

NO TAKE ZONE: an area of particular environmental sensitivity, often around popular diving sites, where no fishing or lobstering may be done. The zones are denoted by a perimeter of 30-inch yellow buoys, as well as on most nautical charts.

NOAA: The National Oceanic and Atmospheric Administration, which oversees the Florida Keys National Marine Sanctuary that encompasses all of the waters surrounding the Keys.

NORTH: up. See also directions.

OCEANSIDE: Anything south or east of the Overseas Highway.

OLD TOWN: The section of Key West that roughly corresponds to the area south and west of 1st Street and Palm Ave., which includes the historic districts, seaport, and Duval Street.

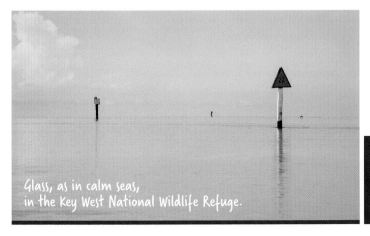

Glass, as in calm seas,
in the Key West National Wildlife Refuge.

16

ON THE HARD: When your boat is out of the water and stuck on land for a while, usually so the bottom can be painted or repairs made.

ON THE HOOK: A boat that is anchored or moored offshore. Many people live on the hook in the Keys. It's a simple existence, welcomed by those souls strong or stubborn enough to brave daily dinghy rides to shore and a general lack of air conditioning, refrigeration, and on-board showers. The trade-off is lower rent or none at all. On the hook can also refer to a fish that has taken the bait, or a lady or dude at the bar who appears to be willing to go home to consummate the first date with you.

OVERSEAS HIGHWAY: The roadway between mainland Florida and Key West. The last 126 miles of the 2,369-mile highway U.S. Route 1.

PADI: A scuba diving certification association, short for Professional Association of Diving Instructors.

PALMETTO BUG: it is a kind of large cockroach, but one that prefers the woods. American and German cockroaches are usually the house nuisances, but in Florida they are all called palmetto bugs.

PARROTHEADS: Jimmy Buffett fans, though we're not sure if the king of island music actually approves of their practices, which can include simultaneously wearing several patterns of Hawaiian shirt, fake flower leis, plastic parrot beaks and sombreros with squeaky cheeseburgers, flamingos and sharks hanging from them. Then again, in the words of Jimmy, "if we couldn't laugh we would all go insane."

PIECES OF EIGHT: the largest denomination of ancient Spanish silver coin. Called reales de a ocho in Spanish, and worth eight reales.

PINKS: Key West pink shrimp are wild-caught in the Keys. They are characterized by a mild, sweet flavor and their pink color when raw.

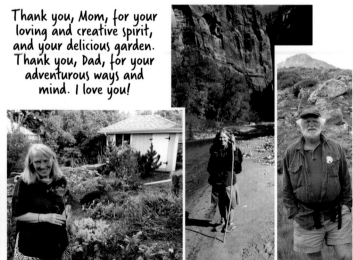

Thank you, Mom, for your loving and creative spirit, and your delicious garden. Thank you, Dad, for your adventurous ways and mind. I love you!

16

Only 3 percent of the total Gulf of Mexico harvest are pinks, though in the Keys we enjoy the fortune of having them on most menus.

PLANKTON: Microscopic organisms that make up the most basic elements of the marine food chain, and can include the eggs and larvae of many crustaceans, fish and other animals. There are many types, such as zoo- and proto- styles. These tiny things are the basis of which all life on our planet depends.

PORT: Left side of the boat when facing forward (opposite starboard). A harbor where boats can dock. A town on a harbor or a river. Wine from the Douro Valley in Portugal. An opening for loading. What the printer plugs into on the computer.

REAL: pronounced ree-ahl. A Spanish denomination of currency, and a popular piece of coin jewelry in the Keys.

ROCK (THE): What some people call Key West, especially in reference to those who never make it "off the Rock," to the mainland or even as far as over the 300-foot bridge to Stock Island.

RUM: the unofficial drink of the Caribbean and the Keys, made from fermented and distilled sugarcane. It comes in dark and light, depending on the type of aging, and is the backdrop for many a sea tail of pirates, rum-runners, adventurers, and other ne'er-do-wells.

RUM-RUNNER: a concoction of rum and any number of juices and liqueurs, including pineapple, orange, blackberry, banana, and grenadine. It was probably invented at the Holiday Isle (now Postcard Inn) Tiki Bar at MM 84 in the 1950s, though sadly the historic and iconic bar is now closed indefinitely. Rum-runners smuggled rum from Bimini to Florida during the alcohol prohibition of the 1920s and early '30s. They were a surly, adventurous, dangerous, and beloved group, depending on which history you prefer.

SARGASSUM: Sounds like a made-up word, but is actually floating brown seaweed that harbors life for many small creatures. Large patches of it are good places to fish for dolphinfish.

SCUBA, SNORKEL, SNUBA: Scuba divers strap an air tank on their back and dive underwater. They must be PADI or NAUI certified. Snuba divers jump in the water with a hose that delivers fresh air from above, and requires no certification. Snorkelers float on the surface of the water and breathe through a tube, also no certification.

SELFIE-STICK: though not native to the Keys, it has become an invasive species here. Urban Dictionary defines one as: "A gizmo for those in constant need of attention and self affirmation... a way to annoy all the normal people around you." Urban Dictionary gives it a second meaning, too: "Slang for one's johnson." Either way, it might be best to minimize its appearance while in public.

SKIFF: a small boat with a partially flat bottom, popular in the Keys for its shallow draft, which makes the backcountry more accessible.

16

SNAPPER: A popular sport and culinary fish, coming in species including yellowtail, mangrove, mutton, and red. Also what the Jets and the Sharks do in the heat of a *West Side Story* music-dance-off.

SNOOK: Another popular sport and culinary fish.

SNOWBIRDS: Part-time residents, usually of retirement age, who flee from the cold each winter and land in the Keys. Also actual birds who perform the same migration pattern.

SOUTH: down. See also directions.

SOUTHERNMOST POINT: the Southernmost publicly accessible point of the continental U.S., marked by a cement buoy and a line of tourists waiting to take pictures; southernmostpointwebcam.com.

SPANISH MAIN: Spain's New World empire from the 1500s through 1700s. Their plundering of the Caribbean, South and Central America gave them coffers for European dominance, which eventually benefitted all of Europe and led to Western colonization of the United States. In return, the native inhabitants received all of the European diseases, slavery, death, and general destruction and elimination of their cultures and society.

SQUARE GROUPER: an abandoned bale of weed, cocaine or cash found floating in the ocean or tangled in the mangroves, which allows the finder to unexpectedly retire. Also a good restaurant at MM 22.5.

STARBOARD: the right side of a boat when facing forward. Also a marine-grade plastic used in constructing some parts of a boat.

STOCK ISLAND: the island directly north of Key West, home to a few good restaurants, marinas, and the commercial fishing and lobster yards. It has a reputation for being a little rough-and-tumble, but is generally safe during daylight hours.

STRETCH (THE): The 18 miles between the mainland and Key Largo, which is contained within claustrophobic cement barriers painted happy blue to mitigate road-rage from those who want to speed but cannot because much of it is a single lane in each direction. Despite having some scenic value, driving it is often perceived as a bit of a long, dull chore on the drive north, yet as an exciting threshold to cross on the way south.

SUP: Acronym for standup paddleboarding, or stand-up paddle boarding, or stand up paddle-boarding. Besides being a sport that has been particularly skilled in evading a standard spelling, it's a fast-growing form of healthy recreation that draws an abundance of fit bodies in bikinis and board shorts. Imagine surfing, but without waves, using a big paddle to push yourself along. Also a greeting, from the shortening of the phrase, "What's up."

TICKLE STICK: a pole used to coax lobster from their rocky hideouts.

TIKI HUT: a thatched-roof structure, usually with open walls, containing a bar, restaurant, or hangout spot. While they give a nod to Polynesian culture, their origins in south Florida come from the Native American tribes who developed the building technique in the 1800s while being chased into the Everglades by American troops. Today those tribes build most of the tikis in the Keys.

TORTUGAS: The furthest southwest island-reefs in the Keys, located 68 nautical miles past Key West. Accessible only by boat or seaplane, they include Dry Tortugas National Park and Fort Jefferson National Monument. Tortugas is Spanish for turtles, which were plentiful there when Ponce de León first landed.

TREASURE HUNTER: one of many men and a few women who seek sunken cargo from the lost Spanish Main treasure fleets. They often can be identified by the Spanish coins they wear around their necks. The bigger the coin, the bigger the... well the more the coin is worth.

UNFINISHED HIGHWAY TO HAVANA: the pier on the end of White Street in Key West, which kind of appears to be the beginning of a bridge to Cuba. In 2016 the pier was renamed after philanthropist and developer Edward B. Knight, but most people missed or ignored the memo and still call it the White Street Pier.

UP: north. See also directions.

UP NORTH: if you are in Key West, this term might just mean Stock Island or Key Largo. Otherwise it means anywhere with winter.

WEST: down. See also directions.

WET FOOT, DRY FOOT: A long-standing policy whereas any Cuban who made it to American soil was considered a refugee who could pursue legal residency after a year, plus receive health and other benefits in the meantime. The policy was terminated in early 2017.

WINTER: what we see at Christmas when we visit family up north.

YOLO: just like the selfie-stick, this invasive species has been difficult to eradicate. The abbreviation for "you only live once" is best summed

up by the Urban Dictionary as, "one of the most annoying abbreviations ever." It's also a brand of high-end paddleboard.

Thanks Mom and Dad, for... well, everything!

Love you guys!

16

Transportation

See pages 17 to 21 for more transportation information.

BICYCLE RENTALS
Island Bicycles: 305-292-9707, 929 Truman, islandbicycle.com
We Cycle: 305-292-3335, two locations, wecyclekw.com
Eaton Bikes: 305-294-8188, 830 Eaton, eatonbikes.com
Big Pine Bicycle Center: 305-872-0130, bigpinebikes.com

TAXIS
Five 6's, 305-296-6666: keywesttaxi.com, bike racks, hybrids
Five 6's Maxi Taxi, 305-294-2222: larger vans, group transportation
Key Lime Taxi, 305-292-0496: keylimetaxi.com, airport van
Friendly Cab Company: 305-292-1111
Big Pine Taxi, 305-872-2662: serving Big Pine and the Lower Keys
CRT, app-based, town taxi, airport: 786-831-0156 marathoncrt.com
Ubers are currently not allowed in Key West.

AIR TRAVEL
Key West International Airport (EYW): 305-809-5200, eyw.com
American Airlines: 800-433-7300, aa.com
Delta Airlines: 800-221-1212, delta.com
Silver Airways: 801-401-9100, silverairways.com
United Airlines: 800-864-8331, united.com

GROUND TRAVEL
Keys Shuttle: www.keysshuttle.com, 888-765-9997
Greyhound: greyhound.com, 800-231-2222, 305-296-9072
Go Buses: gobuses.com. 855-888-7160
Key West Bus Transit: cityofkeywest-fl.gov, 305-809-3803
Key West Express Ferry: www.seakeywestexpress.com, 888-539-2628

CAR RENTALS IN KEY WEST
Alamo: 888-826-6893, 2516 N. Roosevelt Blvd., alamo.com
Avis: 305-296-8744, Key West Airport, avis.com
Budget: 305-294-8868, Key West Airport, budget.com
Dollar: 305-296-9921, Key West Airport, dollar.com
Enterprise: 305-292-0220, 2516 N. Roosevelt Blvd., enterprise.com
Hertz: 305-294-1039, Key West Airport, hertz.com
National: 888-826-6890, 2516 N. Roosevelt Blvd., nationalcar.com
Thrifty: 877-283-0898, 3495 S. Roosevelt Blvd., thrifty.com
Key West Jeep Adventures: 305-901-3777, keywestjeep.com

SCOOTER & ELECTRIC CAR RENTALS
Sunshine Scooters: 305-294-9990, sunshinescootersinc.com
Conch Electric Cars: 305-294-0995, conchelectriccars.com
Adventure Rentals: 305-293-8883, keywest-scooter.com
Pirate Scooter Rentals: 305-295-0000, piratescooterrentals.com

Media

NEWSPAPERS

Key West Citizen: (daily, print), keysnews.com
Keys Weekly: (weekly, print), keysweekly.com
Keynoter: (semi-weekly, print), flkeysnews.com
The Blue Paper: (investigative reporting, online), thebluepaper.com
Konk Life: (weekly, print, community newspaper), konknet.com

RADIO STATIONS

104.9 the X Key West: rock, alternative, local, thexkeywest.com
Pirate Radio: 96.7 & 101.7, rock, indie, local, pirateradiokeywest.com
Island 106.9 WIIS: new, independent, local, island106.9.com
U.S. 1 Radio 104.1: classic rock and comfort hits, us1radio.com
Conch Country 98.7 WAIL 99.5: country, rock, conchcountry.com
National Public Radio, WLRN Miami, 91.5: news and more, wlrn.org

TOURIST WEBSITES & BLOGS

allaboutfloridakeys.com: the newest Keys tourism site, which we are particularly fond of for many reasons, not just because they graciously hired us to write content for them and have been very supportive of the book you're currently reading. Thanks, guys, gals!
visit fla-keys.com: official site of Keys Tourist Development Council

TV STATIONS: Depending on your lodging, there should be a full range of TV stations, including a few local ones. Many here don't watch TV, though. Imagine a life free of commercials and TV news. It is staggering how much switching it off increases the joy of living.

TRANSLATORS: visitor emergency assistance program with multilingual operator, 800-771-KEYS (5397).

The Lower Keys &
Key West from space

NASA/METI/AIST/Japan Space Systems, U.S./Japan ASTER Science Team

16

Random Services You Might Need

MARINE CANVAS & UPHOLSTERY: For boat canvas, cushions, dodgers, Biminis, T-tops, yacht interiors and the like, Oceanside Canvas is by far the most professional and reasonable around. They provide impeccable work, and above-and-beyond customer service. They can get you out of a jam by taking care of the unexpected repair in time for you to sail or motor into the sunset! Oceansidecanvas.net, 305-896-6612, mobile service from Key West to Big Pine Key.

MARINE ELECTRONICS: For marine electronics specialists, vessel management services, electrical audits and such, call Adam at Advantage Marine for a high level of professional service, attention to detail, and dedication. Factory authorized and trained. More than 15 years in the field in Key West. Mobile services from Big Pine Key to Key West. 305-731-9747, marinersadvantage@yahoo.com.

RV PARTS & SERVICE: Spindrift RV maintains a small parts store for RVs, and they also do mobile service. Mile marker 22.8, oceanside, Cudjoe Key, 305-745-3131.

CHIROPRACTOR: Dr. Barrett runs his business Keys style — simple and relaxed. He's a one-man show, without a staff, so he doesn't follow a pack-'em-in attitude. Instead, he gives each patient ample time and attention. He's a true Keys personality with a hearty laugh, bushy beard and decades of experience. Mile marker 30.3, oceanside, Big Pine Key, 305-393-9469, paulbarrettchiropractic.com.

CAR REPAIR: Vince and his staff at Precision Auto Repair & Tire Center have never let us nor our friends down. He provides trustworthy and affordable service for all kinds of cars, including our Subarus, which are a bit exotic around these parts. Mile marker 17, gulfside, Sugarloaf Key, 305-745-3366.

DENTISTRY: Dr. Charles "Fred" Troxel is a really nice dentist. In fact, even those who despise a trip to the dentist as much as we do, look forward to a visit. His office is laid back, with large windows and a caring staff. He also repairs sea turtles' shells for the turtle hospital. Restorative & Esthetic Dentistry of the Keys, Big Pine Key, 305-872-2366, keysmiles.com.

16

Travel is fatal to narrow-mindedness. — Mark Twain

About the Authors

We are a couple of goofy kids cleverly disguised as 40-something adults. We're also hopeless romantics. Good eaters. Seasoned sea captains, as long as it's our 15-foot skiff. Intrepid explorers, unless there are big spiders involved. Expert laughers.... and total failures at taking ourselves seriously.

But life wasn't always so.

Back when we lived in the real world, Steve ran a large awning company, working 80 hours a week in south Jersey. Karuna, the daughter of Buddhist hippies, spent her life bouncing around Colorado and the West, scraping by with freelance writing, TV and filmmaking gigs. Eventually for both, the days began to seem hectic, superficial and unfulfilling. Disillusioned, we each made our way to the "end of the road" in the Keys, hoping to find a greater meaning.

The Keys have a knack for proving that everything happens for a reason. After some years of solo soul searching and lessons learned the hard way, the islands finally brought us together. A life with a true companion, in a peaceful place. We are thankful every day.

Our unofficial motto is "be nice." Imagine a world where everyone tried that — to one another, to all creatures, to the water, the land and the earth. It's a long shot, a worthy goal. Please feel free to share it.

This is our first travel guide of many. Look for more Quixotic books soon, and feel free to let us know what you think, and share your stories; editorial@quixotictravelguides.com. Learn more at wanderingdogcreations.com and quixotictravelguides.com.

Camping in the Rockies.   Exploring abandoned places.

16

Emergencies

Emergency: 911
Florida Marine Patrol: 800-324-5367, *FMP
US Coast Guard: 305-292-8856
Police, Fire, Rescue: 911
Police non-emergency Key West: 305-809-1111
Police non-emergency Monroe County: 305-289-2351
Lower Keys Medical Center Hospital: 305-294-5531
Poison Control: 800-222-1222
Florida Fish & Wildlife (violations, injured wildlife): 888-404-3922
FWC Law Enforcement: 305-289-2320
Hurricane Information: at your lodging or fla-keys.com, 800-771-5397

Quick Reference

°F	°C
61	16
70	21
80	28
90	32
100	38

Mi	Km
.62	1
5	8
25	40
75	121
100	161

approximate conversions

KEYS ZIP CODES

Key West	33040
Stock Island	33040
Big Coppitt	33040
Saddlebunch	33040
Sugarloaf	33042
Cudjoe	33042
Summerland	33042
Ramrod	33042
Big Pine	33043

KEYS AREA CODE: 305
COUNTRY CODE: +1

Thank you businesses, who donated toward printing costs:

5 Brothers Grocery, Big Pine Kayak Adventures,
Oceanside Canvas, Salt, Big Pine Key Boat Rental,
Cudjoe Gardens Marina, Honest Eco,
Parawest Parasailing, Southernmost Resort Wear & Gifts,
Summerland Wine & Spirits, and the Jolly II Rover.

(Note: these folks helped out with donations after the editorial content was independently decided and created, meaning they didn't get in because they gave money, they are just nice people who believe in us and this book.)

16